On No! Not That!

The Life of John D. Bennett, Inventor and Artillery Captain

By John DeVilbiss Bennett

Contents

Maps

Illustrations

Foreword

I live by the philosophy that I am in the Lord's hands and nothing is going to happen to me until the Lord is ready. He is my Lord and Savior, and I pray that He would guide me in all that I do.

John DeVilbiss Bennett

Chapter 1
Oh No! Not That!
Dedicated to my wonderful wife of 64½ years who said,
"Oh no! Not that!"

What do old men do when they are too old to do what they used to do?

They sit around and dream about what they used to do, or they can decide to write their memories while they can still remember about what they did while the memory part still works.

As my dear sister-in-law Delma said, "Hurry with your story because I am getting old and may not be around to read it."

This story has to be about what happened yesterday because what happened today is out of the question. That part of the mind, even after taking B12 for your memory, just doesn't work anymore, so if you want to remember what you are doing right now, you have to ask your wife, she tells you everything anyway.

People wonder what it is that others will remember you for. Presidents do a lot of that. If you live long enough people probably were not around when you did it so you can tell them anything and they won't know the difference.

When you get in trouble is when one of those old codgers comes around that was there when you did what it was that you were going to be remembered for and he remembers, and you can't lay the blame on him for whatever it was that you were going to be remembered for. Poor cat. That is bad so you have to do the best that you can with your stories and don't put down anything that you can't wiggle out of. Best to blame it on someone who is no longer around to defend himself.

Never give exact dates or places or who was there that might have been party to the crime. Just say something like it was a bunch of cousins there when Grandma's cat got electrocuted or just how long the prayer meeting went on after the cat's fur came straight out, or who found Grandma's cat dead out in the yard the next day out under the big old water tank in the yard. Do the best that you can, and that is what I am going to try to do so all my nieces and cousins and our granddogs will be exposed.

I guess really if one is going to try to understand the operations of my mind and my rambling, then you should know what caused it all, and therefore I shall give you a little background on my heritage. It is really very good, but it did get a little diluted by the time it came to me. How else can you expect a descendent of Lady Godiva to be?

After all, I don't like cucumbers because Dad said they weren't fit for horse food. My mother wouldn't even let me whip my little sister when I thought she needed it.

Like father, like son. What you see is what you get.

2

Chapter 2
The Gentler Side of the Ancestors
From Diebelbesin to DeVilbiss

We will start with Johan Diebelbesin, born about 1683 in Germany. He was the father of several kids, one of which was Casper C. Devilbiss, born in 1721, in Alsace-Lorraine, France. Casper likewise had several children, one of which was George Devilbiss, Sr., who was born in 1747 in Frederick, Maryland. Now Casper came over to the new world on a boat called *Britannia*. The property acquired had the title from the King of England, not the colonies. According to my cousin George DeVilbiss (not the one mentioned above), we can't call ourselves the Sons of the Revolution because the Casper Devilbisses were Tories. He was a slave owner.

The first George Devilbiss, who was born in 1747, married into the Ogle family. It is their genealogy that was traced back to Lady Godiva. The first Ogles came to America in 1665. George Devilbiss was the father of Alexander. They were all devout Methodists.

George had several children, but I will tell you about only two. One's name was John. By referring to John's will, you will see that he was left only one dollar, with no reason given. Information from reliable sources reveals that both of his wives were Catholic, which is the reason for his being disinherited. One of their children turned out to be a Jesuit Priest and the other was involved with the beginning of Cornell University.

The other son that I will tell you about was named Alexander. He didn't believe in slavery, so he freed his slave. He moved to Ohio, and founded the town of Alexandria in the spring of 1830, and there founded the first council type of government. He was a devoutly religious man, and was a class leader in the Methodist Episcopal Church.

There are so many Caspers, Johns, Georges, and Alexanders, that it is almost impossible to keep them straight. Anyway, after the Alexander that founded the town, there was sort of a split in the way the family developed. One side you might say was the scientist or medical side. They invented such things as the Toledo scales (like you see in the meat market), paint sprayers, atomizer-type perfume sprayers that were sold to the French perfume industry, and the drill that was used for drilling through the skull for brain surgery. They built large supply factories all over the north and eastern parts of the Unites States and were known as The DeVilbiss Company.

J. W. DeVilbiss.

The other part of the family was religious to the core. John Wesley DeVilbiss, Sr., son of Alexander, became a Methodist missionary. He sailed down the Mississippi River on the way to the Republic of Texas to work as a circuit rider. At New Orleans his plans to sail to Texas by ship were changed because the Mexican navy had been blockading Galveston. So he sailed up the Mississippi River to the intersection of the Red River, up the Red River to Alexandria, and traveled cross-country to Nacogdoches, Texas.

Early in his preaching career someone mispronounced his name, putting the accent on the second syllable instead of the first. He liked it, and changed his name, capitalizing the "V". Many of his relatives changed their name after he did. Taking the Devil out of his name seems like a good thing for a preacher.

4

He preached the first Protestant sermon (1844) and taught the first formal education in San Antonio. This is documented in the Texas history books[1]. He preached with a Bible in his hand and a pistol on the pulpit. He was a circuit rider, and traveled his circuit on horseback at a time when travel was quite dangerous. He nearly lost his life more than once fording flooded rivers. In his book he records stopping on his way to bury travelers who drowned crossing flooded streams or who froze to death in northers. During most of his forty years of preaching his area was on the frontier, and it was subject to Indian raids.

As a preacher his pay was meager, and he often supplemented his income by teaching school, making saddles, or surveying. Sometimes he was paid in chickens. The church reassigned preachers every year, sometimes to the circuit they were already in, but frequently to a new circuit.

In 1845 he married Talitha Ann Menefee and built a log cabin for them in Seguin. In 1846 Sequin was resurveyed and he lost his house because it was on the wrong lot. Later that year his wife gave birth to a daughter who died, and two months later she also died.

That same year he moved to his new assignment in San Antonio. He purchased a lot and erected a bell to call the people to church. He lost the lot because of a bad title, but his bell that still hangs on the side of the little church at La Villita. The Mexicans called him "The little priest who owns the bell." The next year he went together with a Presbyterian minister to build a church, using his benches, building materials and bell and the Presbyterian's lot and adobe building.

Where the old red courthouse still stands, the people used to hold cock fights. The Texas Rangers were always there. Someone told the Rangers that Grampa had said something bad about them so they

---

1 H. A. Graves, *Life of Rev. J. W. DeVilbiss [Reminiscences and Events in the Ministerial Life of Rev. John Wesley DeVilbiss (Deceased)],* (Galveston: W. A. Shaw & Co, Stationers and Printers, 1886)

were about to throw him in the river. Grampa said, "Now, wait a minute. If you think I said something bad about the Rangers, come to church Sunday and listen for yourself." Needless to say they did and he converted a bunch of them, and from then on he had Ranger protection. He did much traveling around his circuit in the presence, if possible, of the Texas Rangers, and always the presence of God.

In 1847 he married Martha Lucinda Kerr, a member of his church in San Antonio. From 1856 to 1859 he was in charge of the German District. He learned to speak German, and founded many German-speaking churches all over south and central Texas. During the first three years a trip around his German-speaking circuit was over 1000 miles long, all on horseback. From 1866 to 1870 he was the agent for the American Bible Society. We know a statistic for part of that time: in 10-1/2 months he traveled over 3500 miles delivering bibles and preaching. In 1875-76 he was the agent for Southwestern University, a Methodist school in Georgetown.

Methodist historical marker number one is at one of the churches he founded at Oak Island, Texas. We great grandkids like to refer to it as our Methodist Mecca. Twice a year we still go to the church at Oak Island to worship and attend a barbecue picnic, where we can visit with old friends and kinfolks. He also founded the Travis Park Methodist Church in San Antonio. There is a stained glass picture of him in one of the windows.

Chapter 3
John Wesley DeVilbiss, Jr.

John Wesley DeVilbiss, Jr. was my grandfather, the son of the circuit rider. His wife was Sophronia Applewhite, and they had ten children. There was Daisey, who died when she was two, Mary (Auntie Riggan), Uncle Ike, Uncle Mibe, Uncle Everett, Martha (my mother), Aunt Ledell Cude, Aunt Dime (Helon Youngblood), Aunt Bess Ward. They had a son whose name was Robert, who

Marvin (standing, left), John, Mary, Ike, Sophronia, and Robert (in Sophronia's lap)

7

died at an early age. He was riding horseback, standing up on the back of the horse, and he jumped off the horse in the horse lot and stuck a mesquite thorn in his foot. He took lockjaw from that and died. I believe that is all of the children they had. I'll tell you a little about each one of them.

Ike

The state of New Mexico was allowing people to come out and homestead. Uncle Ike went out and homesteaded some land in the Animas Valley of New Mexico, which is very close to Lordsburg, in the southwest corner of the state. It was to me the most God-forsaken place in the world. You'd drive your car down the road and the dust would come up and hit the windshield and go sliding down the glass. It was terrible. But that country, the Animas Valley, is between mountains all the way around, and that dirt was just fill dirt, you might say, that's washed off the mountains. All you had to do was to have one joint of pipe and you could have a water well. You could have a windmill and not use but one joint of pipe because the water was close to the surface. And back in those days they created water districts, and if you happened to have a piece of land that had the rights to the water why you had good land, but if you had land that didn't have rights to the water, even though the water was within sixteen feet of the surface you couldn't have a water well. Oh it was terrible. Anyway, he raised his family out there.

Marvin (Mibe)

Uncle Mibe in his younger days spent time in Mexico and South America. I can remember when I was a little kid that he got sick, he got worms or some such thing, and Mother she took care of him. He came and lived with us on the farm, and I remember that while he was down there recuperating from this ailment that he had, he built several Mexican houses there

Martha and Mibe

8

on the farm for Dad. I can also remember that we were little old kids and the house down there had kind of a runway through it. You could start in the living room and go through the bathroom and kinda cut through one of the bedrooms and go around and back up through the hall and back in the living room. And I remember when we were little old kids we'd be running around there naked and he'd be sitting there with a fly swatter, and every time we'd go by he'd swat us on the butt with that fly swatter. We all thought an awful lot of him when we were growing up. He finally married and moved off down towards McGregor, down close to Taft.

Everett

Then we had another uncle who was named Uncle Everett. Now when Everett was a young guy back in the early days he got a job in a store in Encinal. He met a lady down there, and her name was

May. She was quite a bit older than he was, I think she might have been 20 or 30 years older. Uncle Everett wasn't but 19. Everybody was shook up when Uncle Everett married Aunt May.

Everett's Son

Uncle Everett and Aunt May had several kids, but I want to tell you about one in particular. His name was George Everett. George was an electronics genius. He really was a genius when it came to electricity. Back in the early days he built some radios. One of them he had there in the store in Taft,

Ike, Marvin, Robert, and Everett

Texas. He had met a girl who lived in Sinton, and that was 20 miles away. Those two would court each other over the radio. It would be time for George to talk to his girlfriend, and Uncle Everett would holler out in the store, "Everybody come on, George is going to talk on his radio." So he'd call up and talk to his girlfriend, who he eventually married. He was such an early pioneer in the ham radio business that his code number was the number "5", which meant that he was about the fifth person in the United States to have an amateur radio license. They used to have a house there in Taft that had a breakfast nook, and he took that nook over, and that was his radio station. He used to have wires all over the house. During the war George taught radar. He went to Canada and learned to use radar because the Canadians were ahead of us. So he learned about radar and then he taught radar in the Navy. He did all kind of things. George was really a genius.

You know I told you that George Everett was in the Navy, an electronics expert, and he became deaf as a poker. Before he retired from the Navy he was in Bermuda. He worked at a naval research station in Bermuda that was out there for the purpose of trying to learn about ocean sounds. They wanted to be able to tell if a whale went by or a submarine went by. He did a lot of research on that. George stayed out there until he retired. After he retired he went right back to the same job, the same place, doing the same thing as a civilian employee. They lived out there for years studying the sounds that whales make. He did all of this research on sound, yet he was pretty durn deaf. He was a smart man. In later time, being as George was so deaf, he did a lot of experimenting on trying to see how people who were hard of hearing could hear television. He did experimenting by putting a wire that went all the way around his yard. He hooked the wire to the speakers on his television. Whenever the television made a sound it put an inductive field in that wire, and anywhere you were in the field of that wire you could pick up the sound with your hearing aids. One of the things he did was to start wiring up churches. He put a wire all the way around a church on the inside. Anywhere you were inside that loop you could hear perfectly because you could pick it up with your hearing aids. He taught me how to do that. I wired up our church in Marble Falls and had it fixed up. We even had some Sunday school rooms wired up where you could hear what was going on.

Martha and Mary

Mary (Auntie)

Then there was Auntie Riggan. She was the oldest of the girls. She married a man by the name of Jim Riggan who had a grocery store there in Pearsall. It was sorta in competition with the Kemper's store. He was a very peculiar person. We kids were scared to death of him 'cause when he went in to take his nap, boy, there couldn't be any noise around the household while he was sleeping. Poor old Auntie took pretty good care of him.

Auntie's Son

Now Auntie had a son named Maury Riggan. Maury helped his daddy run that store. And he married Fay Howell, who was my Uncle Roy Howell's daughter by his first wife. I always loved Maury. Maury was an electrician, he was an electronics man, oh he just did everything. He had a whole cellar full of *Popular Mechanics* magazines. When I was going to college I didn't have the money to go to school, I believe it was my third year. Daddy said he just did not have enough money to let me go to school. So Maury and his mother got together and they lent me the money to go to school. I never will forget it. I wrote down the debt in my Bible. And you know we finally paid that debt off after we got married, paid him off so much a month after I got married. I remember one time I was so broke at school and I just had to have some money, and I wrote Maury and said, "Maury, I'm so broke could you possibly send me five dollars?" And he sent me five dollars, and I thought I was rich. You see, back when I went to school my entire four years of college education cost two thousand dollars. Five hundred dollars a year got me though college. Course I had a job in the M. E. (mechanical engineering) shop, so that helped out. Times sure were hard.

Maury had a farm east of Pearsall and one year Maury decided what he needed to do was to get me to come out there and live with him and Fay on the farm and run his peanut thrasher for him that summer. I did that and that helped pay off some of the money that Maury lent me. I worked out there all one summer. He had a pretty good-looking Mexican gal who used to help keep house. When Maury and Fay would be gone to town me and that Mexican gal would turn on the phonograph and dance, while we were supposed to be working. Oh me! I even stayed in town with Maury some of the time. And you know, he would even lend me his big old Hudson to go on a date. He sure was good to me, he and Auntie were. I really loved Maury Riggan.

Maury had the most fantastic radio and phonograph I'd ever seen in my life. You know it even had wires that went from the radio to a control panel that you could have by your chair, and from your chair you could turn the radio on and tune it and everything. It was all done through wires, it wasn't like the modern day things that are radio controlled, it was wire controlled. But that was some radio, I'll tell you.

Maury had a dairy out on his farm out of town. He had a great big barn. They had an upstairs to it. I remember that they used to have barn dances upstairs in that barn. I think that was kinda going on while I was overseas. I think that all of the cousins, and Wynona, they would go out there and they'd all square dance in the top of that barn of Maury's. They had a lot of fun doing that.

Ledell
Aunt Ledell was married to Roy Cude, and he worked in the oil fields. He fell out of the derrick one time and it

Martha and Ledell

12

killed him. After she became a widow, she didn't have any money. Her daughter Mary Frances married Megas Smith, who was a lawyer, and they used to live down in McAllen. He became a state senator, and then a district judge. And Megas was one of these people who was deathly allergic to dust. Dust messed him up bad. He and Aunt Ledell would have a lot of fights about the dust in those days, and that's when Ledell would get mad and she'd come back up to the farm and live with Mother and Dad.

Ledell's Daughters

There are two cousins I need to tell you about, and they were Aunt Ledell's two daughters. One was named Mary Francis and the other was named Helon. The younger daughter, Helon, married a man from Jacksonville, Florida who was in the undertaking business. She kinda moved off and we never did hear from her or have much to do with Helon. Mary Francis was just a few months older than I was. She was my pride and joy of the whole bunch. She was smart! She was in my class at school. I can remember in my English class we had this school teacher named Ollie Hawkins, and the English classroom was way at the far end of the hall. And we'd go in there in the English room and we'd hear clippity clop, clippity clop. That was Ollie Hawkins come tearing down that hall stomping her feet, and gosh the closer she got to the classroom the farther under our desks we scrunched 'cause we were all scared to death of Ollie Hawkins. She made us read "Tale of Two Cities" and Shakespeare and a whole bunch of stories, and you know what, I was too busy piddling around when I was a kid, I didn't have time to read them damn stories. So I never did read one of those stories. But we had to give a report on them, and all I ever knew about those stories was what Mary Francis told me. She read the stories and she knew them real good, and she lectured me on the stories, and with what she told me on the stories I was able to pass, just barely, but I was able to pass my English work. Oh, boy, that was some time.

Helon (Dime)

Aunt Dime's husband, Earnest Youngblood, was a bee man. He was in the honey business. He had hundreds of hives of bees, and he was really good at it. I remember that Uncle Earnest had a bipolar problem, and in fact they claim that he went crazy for a while, and they had to lock him up. But there was some lady that was a chiropractor, and she finally got him cured. She gave him some chiropractic treatments and got him out of it. Aunt Dime was famous for making hand-pulled taffy. Every year she used over a thousand pounds of sugar to make it. Course I'm not telling you about all of these kids that are in the family. There's too many of them.

Bess

Aunt Bess married Monroe Ward and had two sons, Hubert and Bobby. Later she ran a restaurant called the Rock House in Pearsall for several years. After that she had a rooming house for college students in Kingsville.

Martha (Mother)

There is another thing that I need to talk about and that's my mother. My mother was a saint if there ever was one. She not only raised all of her brothers and sisters, and was a mother to them after her mother died, she took care of Dad, who was crippled. She took care of all of her brothers and sisters when they were in trouble. She was the person who took food to everybody in Frio County when they got sick. She just took care of them like nobody's business. She was a wonderful, wonderful woman. Everybody loved Martha Bennett. And you know what, she had a daughter (Betsy) who followed in

her own footsteps. She was a saint. She took care of everybody. She worked with the colored Baptist church for years and years on their program where they feed the people who are handicapped or in need of food or don't have the money to buy the food. She took cookies to everybody on all occasions; she was just a saint.

Grampa's wife, Sophronia, developed tuberculosis, and when she died, why Grandpa took all of the furniture out of the room that she died in and had a big bonfire and

Sophronia

burned it all up. Mother had to raise that whole bunch of kids. Auntie Riggan had married and moved away and Mother was in charge. She raised all of that bunch of kids. And even in later life she was taking care of them. Mother lived down on the farm, and while we were there Uncle Mibe came to live with us and Aunt Ledell came to live with us and Aunt Bess came to live with us. Aunt Ledell didn't have any money after her husband was killed. Aunt Bess, why she was married to a drunk; Uncle Monroe, he was a perpetual drunk. Aunt Bess had to leave him, and she came down to live at the house. So Mother had Aunt Bess, Aunt Ledell, and Uncle Mibe, seems like she was the refuge for all of the people that were in trouble. She even took care of Hubert, Aunt Bess's son. Hubert got diarrhea when he drank cow's milk and became constipated when he drank goat's milk. So he alternated between goat's milk and cow's milk. Whenever they came to visit they came with a goat on the running board, tied to the side of the car.

Mother sat on the third row in the Methodist Church in Pearsall with her sisters Mary and Helon, and if they were in town, with Ledell and Bess. It was called "DeVilbiss Row." A parlor in the church is named the "DeVilbiss Room" after the sisters.

Grampa's Telephone

Now Grampa DeVilbiss was a pretty energetic man. I know that back in the early days he lived in Derby. He built a cotton gin in Derby. They had a pretty good water well at the cotton gin because they had to have pretty good water for the boilers that ran the steam engine for the gin.

Grampa DeVilbiss

And I can also remember that Grampa installed a telephone wire from Pearsall to Derby, and that was extended on out to the Roberts Ranch and they had a telephone there. The telephone even went down to my mother's house, down on the farm. So Grandma Bennett had a telephone and Mother had a telephone

and Uncle Harry had a telephone at his house, all of them were on a party line. Aunt Maude always answered the telephone and listened in on every word that you said. And I can remember the telephone number that Aunt Ledell had in Pearsall. It was 81W. Whenever that one wire telephone line broke down and one of the poles would fall down, or something, I'd have to get on my horse, go ride the telephone line and fix it. I had to keep that thing up. Service never was very good on the telephone line because there were too many people on it. And boy, I'll tell you what, the phone would ring and

Bess (left), Helon, Ledell, Martha, Everett, Mibe, and Mary at family picnic in 1945

everyone would pick up the receiver and listen in on the conversation. We used to get so mad at Aunt Maude's bunch because they were always listening in.

Now later on sometime, I don't know when it was, Grampa built a bunch of houses in Pearsall. And all of those houses had a peculiar design to them. They had

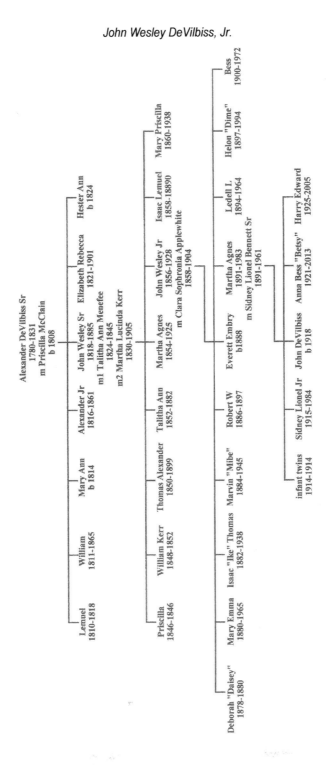

DeVilbiss Family Tree

porches on the front and all of them had square columns to hold up the roof. And I remember that there was a skirt around those houses, and the skirt didn't go straight down, they kinda flared out at the bottom, and lacked maybe six inches getting to the ground. You could tell Grampa's houses anytime you rode around Pearsall. There must have been at least half a dozen of them that were still standing when I was growing up.

There is one more thing that I'd like to say about Grampa DeVilbiss. When he died he had the prettiest little knife. Wasn't over about three inches long, had pearl handles on it, two blades, and it had engraved on the handle "John Wesley DeVilbiss". Being as my name was John DeVilbiss, they saved that knife and gave it to me. And I was so proud of it. But naturally I lost it somewhere and I never did find it again. I sure did grieve over loosing that knife. 'Cause it was so nice and such a good memory of Grampa. In the later years Grampa lived with Aunt Ledell in a house that he built in Pearsall. Grampa and Aunt Ledell and Mary Francis and Helon took care of Grampa until he died.

Grampa DeVilbiss

18

Chapter 4
New Kid on the Block

My daddy's side of the family didn't get to America for over 200 years after my mother's side.

My grandfather's father was William Bennett, Sr. He was born in England in the year 1807. William married Elizabeth Doxey. They had 10 kids, and the one that I was most interested in was John Bennett. He was born April 2, 1848, and always said that he had just missed being born a fool.

Now John had a brother who was in Cape Town, South Africa. At the age of 14 years John went to South Africa to be with his brother Abraham and his wife. While John was in South Africa, their father was killed in a roundhouse accident in Derby, England. John must have gotten a pretty good education in the line of engineering. We have no records of what education he might have gotten but you will notice in reading the log that he kept on board the ship *Bessie Grenfield* while sailing from Africa to Boston he keep referring to his "studding" [studying].

John sailed to America on the *Bessie Grenfield* on March 20, 1869, turning 21 while he was enroute. John arrived in the US of A May 15, 1869. He kept a most interesting and informative log of the trip. His sister Polly transcribed a copy of his log and even included two poems which we believe she may have written. A copy of the log is included. John Wayne Bennett transcribed Polly's copy of the log, drew the map and route that the *Bessie Grenfield* probably took.

My Brother John's log on board the
Bessie Grenfield

Bound from Cape Town to Boston U S America
March 20 [18]69

Here I am at last after 2 months wandering up & down Cape Town and am glad to find that everything is settled now & that I am going. Had not been on board an hour when Lt. Finney came of[f] to say that Mr. Moltens had at last found a situation for me at Beaufort; not a first rate one but still a commencement; but I was mortified to think that only yesterday I signed and paid £5 so that it was impossible to leave. Mr. Finny said it was all for the best & gave £1 to increase my small stock of money, truly such kindness have I received since I left my brother, that it has astonished me, nor can I ever forget it. Captain came on board about 6 oclock but weather (fog) prevented us heaving the anchor, though he seemed anxious to do so for I heard after, he had a bet with another Captain who left 2 hours before

Sunday March 21   Last night it rained hard (capital thing for the farmers) and annoyed me much by coming through the roof & dripping upon my bed, I may say that my first lessons in cooking commenced today, also first symptoms of sea sickness which are unpleasant. Won't sail today being Sunday. I am told from religious scruples of the captain's though the wind is likewise not fair, Captain & crew seem a very fair & respectable set, scarcely any swearing or anything of that description going on—very glad—

March 22nd Lifted anchor this morning at about 9 oclock and being scarcely any wind we make very little progress though the ship rolls tremendously from the swell rolling into the bay. Made hearty breakfast, sickness disappear'd, how long it will last I don't know. Having shipped as cook & steward I find my hours are from 4 unto 8 pm—long time.

March 23rd The breeze we have had since we got outside the bay still with us & we are bowling on at a very fine speed, May success

& fine weather attend us. The Schooner presents a beautiful appearance to the eye being under all her canvas except strinsails [probably studding sails]. I did not think so small a thing could carry so much. We are steering for St. Helena, & be there probably in a few days. Asked the Captain if he would tell how much the ship ran in 24 hours in fact the days reckoning & he very kindly said he would today we are about 250 miles from the Cape having made the last 24 hours 180 miles. I hope I shall thus be enabled to find the length of the passage. saw the stormy petrel or Mother Carry's chicken today—very well all day & in good spirits.

March 24th The ship is in the two strinsails & going about 8 knots, the sailors think they will make a quick passage from the vessel being so light, though she is as full as crew would press her, her cargo chiefly sheepskins, we pump this ship night and morning of the bilge water till the pump "sucks" as the sailors call it then we know the vessel's safe. The days reckoning 270 miles.

March 25th This morning the breeze is not so strong, but am thankful to say there is a breeze. & as one of the sailors justly said it is better to have a week fair wind than a strong headwind. The vessel I think will not make such a good run as yesterday. I occasionally help pump the ship of bilge water, to pull on the ropes or anything like that. any little odd job, for instance this morning I oiled the handrail[,] roused the ship, the Captain. like him better every day I am with him. I think he see's my position & tries to make me comfortable, though it seems to me he might do more for having agreed that I should pay £5 for my food—not for my passage. I am fed no better than the common sailors, certainly I don't do as much work—but they all give him the character of meanness he has what sailors call soft "tack" is soft bread for himself but takes good care I have none. What trivial thing to speak of, but of such things are logs made of, such things one takes notice of on a long monotonous voyage. The days run 160 miles. About 6 pm it came on to blow with rain a fair wind too so we very likely make a good run for tomorrow.

March 26th The Captain still very kind to me, i.e, he allows me plenty of time scarcely anything to do, so I have commenced with my French again & I sincerely hope nothing will again interfere to stop my progress, for it is about 2 months since I saw anything of it, my short hand that I commenced to study in England, nearly 6 years & attempted again 2 years ago seems to be quashed[.] I got so far that I could go no farther without some one reading to me but that person was not to be found. The vessel today is under reefed foresail. The wind blowing strong (fair) and still going at a good rate[.] Hope to see St. Helena in 3 days more. I wonder how Mary Alice is progressing with her French & how my mother (the good old soul) is getting on, she little thinks her youngest boy is where he is, on the wide ocean, when she thinks he is in the Cape. I've not written home for some time now (& the next time will be when I am settled in America) but somehow I've not cared to write since my Father's death (I hope he is in Heaven & that I shall meet him there) not that I have thought the less of home for I think I have thought more. Probably I have added more to my mother's grief by not writing, but I heard Mr. Merchant say once if you cannot send good news do not send any. & it has been that that kept me from writing. for the last year I have been unsettled & did [not] wish them at home to know it, now I've taken the step & trust in Providence for the future. After over 4 years residence in the Cape, it is strange I leave it with about the same money I brought into it, true I've more experience. Captain says the last day's run was 200 miles, but I don't think there is much dependence to be placed on the statement, for he & the mate frequently do not agree in their reckoning's.

March 27th I am thankful to say that the breeze is still with us. though it causes the vessel to roll as anyone may see from the writing, the clouds & overhead and probably there will be rain, it rolls so much we are obliged to put strips of wood to keep things on the table, but occasionally we have a cup of hot coffee spilled over our legs, which is not nice, the days run 270 miles as I suspected a very fair days run.

Sunday March 28th Another Sunday has come round, but it seems very little like a Sunday to me, how different it was five short years ago when I had the priviledge of attending so many places of worship, aye, I often look back to that time & compare it to this one, for if I remember right, I have not heard a sermon, with the exception of last Sunday week for 2 years, & I really think the impressions I received when at Derby will never wholly be effaced, still it is difficult to keep close to God the way I have been situated, many deep and greivious sins have I committed since I left England & I still though rejoice in the efficacy of Christ's blood, yet conscience, will lash you & make you suffer for them truly you are punished, if not in the world to come, in this, for though you have the belief & knowledge that you are saved, still conscience will not be still & we must be punished—we read it in the Word—if I have time today I shall read one of Spurgeon's sermons, for I have them still whereever I go they & my Bible (the Weslyans gave me) goes with me. today the cook has a bad hand so there is more work for me to do. How fortunate we are for the breeze is still with us & we are nearing St. Helena rapidly if what the Captain says is correct, strange I so doubt him, why I do so I cannot say, I read this one of Spurgeon's sermons "Cheer for the fainthearted" & hope I have received benefit from it, the days run is the smallest since we left Table Bay, viz 170 miles.

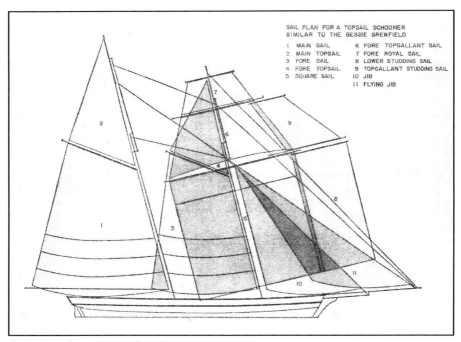

Sail plan for a topsail schooner

March 29th Very little wind this morning & though every sail which can be of any use is brought into requisition I still think we shall make a poor run, 1 oclock just as I expected the run is only 140 miles, but we must think ourselves lucky if we do that every day and have no calms, may have a fornight [sic] of it on the line, the days run 140 miles.

March 30 7 pm, Not till now have I had time to write anything with the exception of midday & that I devoted to French, been on my feet the whole of the day, boiling & perspiring in the galley, & now I feel so dirty, I would like to have a bath but fresh water is scarce[.] if I have one it must be salt water drawn over the ship side, you cannot get water to wash your clothes in, I dont think I ever felt so miserable & filthy, but must put up with it, the breeze springs up or rather is a little stronger toward night & go ahead nicely then. My position here is a peculiar one, when I am at work the Captain is Captain & I am cook but when everything is done for the day then he treats me as an equal chatting & talking for hours, he is a young man about 23 the owner of the vessel went to sea when he was 9. I cannot see even what I am writing now it is so dark. The days run 150 miles.

March 31st Not anything extraordinary has happened today nothing but the usual monotinous routine of sea life cooking on my part. Tonight I am going to wash a pair of trousers. a pair I have spoilt on board with that wretched cooking I am sick and tired of it everything I touch (not being able to keep my hands clean all day for it is only at night when I can manage to get them what I shall call clean from grease) seems to be so dirty & greasy, & then having to get coal from below in the forecastle among tar and every imaginable dirtiness nothing but filthiness I call it as cook on board a vessel, then the galley is so small, I should think it is no larger than a good sized packing case so that when you are inside your back touches that of the galley while your head is bent (or I should say you are stooping over the stove which is frightful from the heat if for nothing else[)]. The days run 150 miles.

April 1st Last night I washed the trousers but as I expected they are spoilt in colour. The breeze still continues with us, sometimes strong, sometime weak, but as can be seen we have made headway. St. Helena passed in 8 or 9 days as quick [as] a steamer does it, which is not bad, in 5 or 6 days we shall be on line & I hope we shall pass & get in the north east trade's without any calm, we have had the south east trade's on the side. This day's run 200 miles.

April 2nd Today is my birthday my 21st too, how little do they think at home that I am spending it here, on the wide ocean, amongst strangers[.] the Captain said he would make some dough but would not let me when I went to fetch the flour so I was too late, however we are having bloaters to sea, such little things I am speaking about for I am obliged to do so, for I have not anything else but to write my thoughts[.] I had hoped to spent my birthday at home, ay will they not be surprised when they receive a letter from America instead of the Cape, I have a good letters of introduction to people in America & hope to get on. The days run 150 miles

April 3rd This day has nearly passed and nothing of importance has taken place with the exception of my spoiling about 3 lbs. of rice by boiling it in salt instead of fresh water, the boy told me to half fill the kettle with water & I innocently put in salt instead of fresh water fortunately told him of it when I found it out & he got me more in time of dinner, so much for being parsimonious as regards water, always ringing in your ears "be careful of the water", right to certain extent, but when I think they have only 8 casks on board & I & Mr. Perrott made in one year out of the vineyard 11 casks of wine (same size as we have on board[)] 3 of brandy beside 4000 lbs. of raisins, I think they brought too little, why, I think I & the Captain are the only two persons who wash every day, (the others only once a week) I had to cook this morning a flying fish (that flew on board in the night[)], for the mate, & I am told they are fine eating, when I get one I will try it, I am making good progress with my French can read it far better than speak it, hope Mary Alice can do the same strange how I wish that girl educated, but suppose she spends her time at the door same as Lizzie did with some nice young man, My poor mother how often I think of her, I am sure I feel the effect of her prayers night & morning I think of her may God help & comfort her in her affliction[.] I've been so unsettled that I could not write home & let her know my troubles & this adds to hers. I wish I was at Boston that seems my one desire at present, but when I get there I shall probably wish myself on board, I dont think I shall go and see Tom till I am settled, I am firmly resolved if I can do without it never to depend on relations again, I think it is the worst thing a young man can do <u>so I think at present</u>[.] I may have to change my mind before long, well I must stop for one day. The days run is 150 miles.

Sunday April 4. But how little like Sunday to me, if anything I have more work to do that day because everybody has extra & better food that day, going very slow today scarcely doing anything compared with other days however must take it has [sic] it come, the day is very hot with not a cloud in view, pitch coming out of the seams in the decks, which causes you frequently to stick to the decks[.] I was barefoot saving my shoes and it was dreadfully hot, obliged to seek a cool spot in the shade. The days run 150 miles.

April 5 Again am endeavoring to scribble a little, but dont know whether I can do much or not for I have had scarcely any time for the last 3 or 4 days. For the last 4 or 5 days the run has been 150 miles, it is very singular <u>if correctly</u> the captain says it is he ought to know. About 5 o'clock this afternoon the boy came running to the companion & sang out Mr. Sheriff (the mate) the fat is boiling over in the galley. Mate & myself was in the cabin looking at a caross & two feathers the Captain had brought at Cape the (Captain) asked me if he had been "taken in" when the cry was made I ran up & found we had a narrow escape of being burnt at sea a distance of 8 or 900 miles from the nearest land (St. Helena) the water butt was near & they threw water on & succeeded in getting it under the flames the boy said came out of the door, & smoke a sailor said nearly suffocated him, however I found the galley a nice mess. How astonishing it is how ignorant sailors are of things on shore, the question was discussed between the Mate & Captain what quality of potatoes could be raised from certain piece of land the mate persisting even to obstinacy that 5 bushels could be raised from 1 square yard of land, I tried to point out to him that that quantity placed side by side would cover twice that amount of land, but to no purpose he would not be convinced, so I let him alone. April 5th run 150 miles.

April 6th The galley is nice and clean this morning having been scraped by the sailors. Yesterday I was up for the second time to the cross trees, bye the bye that reminds me that when in Cape Town I was so disgusted not being able to gain employment (if I have not mentioned the circumstance before) that I went on board the "Gondola" to see if I would like to go to sea, well the mate of the vessel who was then in charge did everything to disgust me with it, the day after I went on board it was the owners son's wedding day & had to decorate the ship of course with the flag & he was drunk & sent me up to the truck on buttons at the very top of the mast, first was the foremast, well after a great deal of trouble I succeeded, & the height was something dreadful, with nothing but a rope as thick as your finger to hold on by, well no sooner had I come down than he sent me to the top of the mainmast, which is some 20 ft higher & it is all very well when you have the ratlines or rope ladders to go up with but when you have to use your legs & literally swarm up a greasy rope, certainly you have a rope but it is dreadful for one not accustomed to it & not knowing how to use the different ropes to best advantage however I had nearly succeeded when the halyard slipped from my mouth & I had to go all the way down again, the same the next time, the third time when I got to the top of the degallant mast I scarcely [had] strength to hold on with, shaking in every limb, heart fluttering and pulse beating high, though not afraid in the least, I considerably mortified & annoyed to think that I could not succeed so I fastened to a stay & came down & told the mate who seemed astonished I had not done what he told me, sent another or rather young man up for he was 20, he went up like a cat, I went with him but stopped when I got up to the degallant mast, however it disgusted me fortunately with the sea, so I am instead on my way to America. The days run 140 miles.

April 7th The breeze has sprung up a little & we I think have made a better run than yesterday and are nearing the line rapidly, strange not seen a vessel yet, I hope & pray we have no calms on the line, from where we are not far off. Captain shewed me the chart & I was surprised to find how close we were to America. The day has been very good 170 miles. Today I have scarcely done anything for last night I asked the Captain in our conversation, if he would allow me to work on deck, with the sailors & not to go in the galley & in the morning was surprised to find the boy there, I have been learning French nearly all day occasionally a little job to do.

April 8th Learned the Mariners Compass, the points are commencing at North going East, North, North by East, North North East, North East by North, North East, North East by East, East North East, [East] by North[,] East, East by South, East South East, [South] East by East, South East, South East by South, South South East, [South by East.] that is half the other half is [South,] South by West, South South West, South West by South, South West, South West by West, West South West, West by South, West, West by West [sic], West North West, North West by West, North West, North West by North, North North West, North by West, North & between these points are what are called half points. After midday, the breeze sprung up & caused u[s] to go along nicely hope to have a good run tomorrow. The days run 150 miles.

April 9th The breeze kept us all last night & is still with us, up to 12 oclock we made 200 miles a very fair days run approaching the line fast, Today and yesterday called away at this point & wishing to resume writing forgot what I was about to remark in fact I had not hardly an opportunity till tonight Saturday [sic]

April 10th Saturday Today scarcely any wind towards noon we were almost becalmed making very great headway in the afternoon rained heavily & setting sail to catch what little breeze we could the sailors had no chance of getting fresh water to wash their clothes in, one or two have everything dirty. Had some conversation with mate about Masonry & I really think when I can afford it I will be one, the benefits they derive from it must be extraordinary—now if I went to Boston being a Mason, the Masons there would not allow me to starve till I succeeded in obtaining a situation. Abe frequently spoke to me about Masonry & advised to be one when I obtained my majority. Plenty of time to think about it. Still no sign of any sail, it seems as if we had the ocean to ourselves. I hope we shall make a quick passage & when I get there I am told I must be careful & not get drugged by the Yankees, they are great hands at it. The days run 160 miles.

Sunday 11th Was awaken this morning by the cry "sail ho" & on

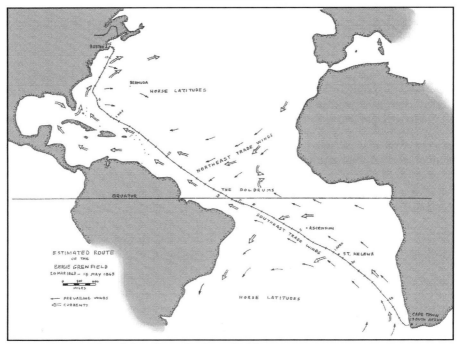

Estimated route of the *Bessie Grenfield*

turning out saw a schooner homeward bound, an hour afterwards a bark appeared in an opposite direction, bound the same way, we are now in the track of vessels from South America to England. Rained very heavily for about an hour & managed to save a great quantify of water—9 pm—How suddenly has been the change in the weather, from a calm it came on squally & such a gust of wind came that we were obliged to shorten sail. Oh how she did go for a few minutes almost on her beams end to stand on deck was like standing on the roof of a house, till she was releived [sic] of her sails. I say <u>we</u> for I helped as much as I could. but I knew no more what to pull on, to loosen, to let go. the only thing that I could do was to follow & pull when I could. I told the Captain after all was over I never felt such a fool in my life before. so out of place, it did run awfully, my sow wester mackintoch [sic] on, & trousers rolled up to the knees. The days run 140 miles

April 12th Last night it rained so hard that I was obliged to put my cap on in bed (the roof leaked just over my bed) to keep my head dry a perfect calm this morning, the breeze sprung up a <u>little</u> about 10 oclock but made very little headway. I don't know how much for the Captain cannot take the sun.

April 13th Last night it rained more than ever, coming through the roof so much that I had to put my oil skin on the bed to keep it dry but still had to lie on top so hot it was This morning saw a steamer for about an hour & calm being still was with us the captain wished very much to have possession if only for a week, well really it is annoying this calm, scarcely moving. Yesterday we saw the Benetta fish in chase of the flying fish, like to catch some, be a change of diet, likewise saw 7 or 8 Stormy Petrel <u>on</u> the water a thing rarely seen, the sun is not visible today at 12 o'clock

April 14th Last night was caught or rather it came on board itself the largest flying fish that anyone had seen, it measured from tip of tail to nose 12 1/2 inches, I measured it myself, the captain offered me the wings but stupid forgot them till it was too late they were dry so would would [sic] not stick but if placed in a book when fresh caught they will. To show what a calm we had for the last [illegible-2?] days we have only made 20 miles & that from 5 am to midday. Ok yesterday I saw the first shark at a distance, leaping out of the water chasing something or other likewise the Benetta again I've tried to catch some but no use[.] I believe whose fish would outstrip anything so quick are they,

April 15th The breeze has again failed us very tantalizing certainly, and we are again becalmed. Last night a large shark followed us, he shone like phosphorous he smell the meat that we were towing.

April 16th Oh this is dreadful weather the ship not moving an inch the potato peeling thrown overboard yesterday still by us at least they look them, I may be mistaken, however the sea is like glass & the sun is so hot the pitch oozes out of the decks if I put on a pair of boots & walk the pitch tears the soles off, if you are without it scalds the feet & that is the predicament I am in my feet covered with pitch. The largest shark ever I saw, I saw last night & though the Captain & myself fired 20 shots at him his hide was too thick for a rifle ball. Porpoises too I have seen, large unwieldy brutes to all appearance, but if of the same kind I saw coming out, they can be quick if they choose. I made mistake for the Captain told me we made 22 miles. Saw another shark this afternoon with the pilot fish a most curious fish that constantly accompanies the shark & pilots him in his wanderings. He is a fish with deep blue & black alternately.

April 17th Almost becalmed going about 2 miles per hour, really if we stay another week here we must go on short allowance of water & a person drinks very much this hot weather, to keep up the supply of perspiration. Had some shark for breakfast, the mate would not eat any, though far from religious, he seems to follow the Mosaic Law (Lev 11c and 9 v[)] in which it says fish without fins or <u>scales</u> is unclean, the shark has the former but not the latter, however it is better than pork which he eats clean or not- 12 o'clock- thank God the breeze has sprung up & we are going again, I hope it will continue all night. The breeze came out & went off most provokingly though it rained most dreadfully enough to allow catch 11 1/2 casks.

Sunday 18th 12 o'clock Sunday out today & not across the line up to 11 oclock. The breeze has been with us since 6 oclock & I hope it will take us across. I spoke to the Captain & said I wished to keep watch with the mate so last night I was up till 12pm & 4 to 8. I felt rather sleepy there but could not sleep this morning- so hot. Today I had what the sailors call "sailors pleasure at sea" turning my box inside out brushing my clothes & airing them but I could not do altogether what the sailors call ["]pleasure" i.e. read old love letters for I am sadly deficent in that commodity. Crossed the line this afternoon been going very slow, but better than the last week. Days run 60 miles. Hope now we are north of the line we shall have the northeast trades. the wind is from that quarter now

Monday 19th The winds made its appearance in the first watch last night & we have been bowling along ever since so much so though we went slowly all yesterday we have gone 130 miles up to 12 oclock every bit of canvas was set excepting lower strin sail. Another sail passed us last night, likewise a large shoal of porpoises strange thing that if one of those things are hit or shot all his companions will pursue him for his blood, got the harpoon ready so if they come

31

again they may get it. How strange it is the feeling is strong up on me respecting self education, I've got to be the subject of conversation in the ship, every moment I have to spare, French, French nothing else consequently I have made great progress, I only require to have someone to speak to & then fasten or clinch in memory that which I have learned in my book. This morning the watch on deck made so much noise washing down that they awoke me an hour before time so could not get to sleep again & turned out and learned French, I hope Mary Alice is trying to improve her mind how I would like to see her & all at home once more, but I will not go & be a burden to my relations any more if I can help it how uncomfortable my mother (God bless her) would be if I did I had two passages offered me to England in steamers too if I would go but do not at present repent what I have done the only regret I have is not having written home for so long a time & being obliged to leave my watch behind me however I hope to redeem it bye & bye for I hope by the help of God to make headway in the world, & when able to do so, come & see them at home.

20th Not anything but the usual ship life occurred today going rather slowly still thankful to say we are going for if ever there's a thing that is tantalizing or annoying it is being becalmed at sea on the line deck so hot to walk or sit on, below or the house on deck nearly the same though of course in shade sea smooth as a mirror & a tropical sun pouring down upon you making you perspire so much that though you have a woolen shirt on it literally trickles down you into your boots if you have any on if not on deck, not in the least exaggerating, for it happened with me, so hot that the pitch ran out of seams on deck...(a leave is missing here so it sounds funny) up to the keyhole in water & be dry inside, he last night was very anxious often on deck in all the rain & wind, the vessel almost on her side he pushed her so, nearly all her canvas set, it was all set except when they expected a squall & then they took in one or two small sails he so anxious to get out of the region of calms at this moment the vessel is pitching & tossing so, with the water coming in occasionally over the bow it is no easy matter to write I can tell you, you are first one side of the perpendicular & then the other & then from side to side, we hope to make the 4000 miles up today. Some vessels when they go at this rate in dashing the water from their bows groan & roar like a bull but this water go so smoothly that she seems to cut it like a knife, Let the reader of this if ever there should be one look not at the writing but at the reading. Days run 130 miles Not a cloud scarcely to be seen in the heavens. They really seem to be as brass run 106 miles [second distance listed for the 21st Last night was a dreadful wet night & quite a fresh breeze, which caused us to bowl along at a tremendous rate from 7 to 8 or 9 to 10 knots an hour today pulling on back stay fall (captain my authority) the confounded rope broke & I & another came down I on the edge of a water cask & he on a soft part of the body, I don't know how he felt, but as regards myself, It was rather sore & queer. Yesterday my work was knocking the rust of[f] the iron work. Today baled out the boat, any little odd job like that, the captain is very kind indeed to me, he gave me paint yesterday to paint my box with, which I bought from the Carpenters without painted, Yes though a packing case formerly it has made a very good chest it being lined with tin, it might be.... (A leave is missing I think he has not sent it)

Part II
Continuation of my log on the *Bessie Grenfield*

April 22nd The breeze is still with us and we now say we are fairly in the North East trades, & the reason we did not make so much as I expected yesterday, it was because the wind lulled & I did not know it, but today we have made it up, for we have run 200 miles, a very good days work.

April 23rd, 24th, 25th Today is our 4th Sabbath out I have only to-day found time to write in my log, for the last three days being so tired, when in watch below that having so little time to spare (try to get all the sleep I could) that it has been a question with me which I should do, devote it to French or log I decided in favor of the former as I do not wish to lose ground again no knowing how useful it may be to me in the States or Canada. Many times I have been studying the whole 4 hours & go on duty faint & sleepy, for if my mind holds good & God spares me, I will well educate myself, I have the good example of an uncle, but hope to be without the pride he had, if I should succeed. It is very discouraging to find that I am only at the foot of the ladder, when I left England expecting by this time to be a long way up, but as I said to the Captain last night I have gained a little experience in the world (& it will be no loss) Well my uncle, though he had which I have not (a trade) still he was 25 when he began to educate himself how well he succeeded I need not say, but poor man he had his faults same as every one else & what I saw wrong in him may I have the resolution & strength to avoid. Thursday night we parted our flying jib stay, the breeze was so strong & how they manage to splice it again though a moonlight night I cannot tell, I could not have spliced that wire rope in daytime much more at night & when I examined it in the morning I was astonished it was so well done. Saturday night we saw what the sailors said was a whale close by the ship but I could see only a dark moving mass on the water, he did not blow or anything like that, Sunday night we saw a nautilus or Portuguese man, it was very similar to a bubble, in fact that is the only thing I can compare it with. Today I have studied too much nearly worn out, the captain says he does not believe in studying too much so he told me not to do it & gave me another book to read called "The Fall of Palmyra" when I have time.

April 26th The breeze still holds good, having made over 1180 miles this week very firstrate work indeed (see log) in fact we begin to find a great change in the weather. The nights getting chilly & cold but beautifully clear so clear a person can read well by them Distance run for the last 3 or 4 days in pocket book.

April 27th This morning very sleepy about 4 oclock fell asleep whilst speaking to the mate who said I should be a nice fellow to be entrusted the lives & property of other people, quite true, but not being accustomed to turn out in the small hours of the night, it is to me a strange thing. Today & yesterday had the pleasant job of scraping out the long boat. Oh such little things it all seems to be so different to what I am accustomed to, it makes me very wretched sometimes but what "cannot be cured must be endured" & I know the captain & mate gives me as little to do as possible, especially dirty work, but any work I would have to divert my mind from what must soon occupy it, that is about what I am going to do at Boston if I shall succeed in obtaining any employment or not & how I shall get on. The breeze is still with us having made 200 miles again today, & as we are approaching the American coast fast, so do we get in the track of vessels bound to the West Indies, saw this morning two vessels bound that way. Some one was kind enough to steal my pipe out of the boat today, but whether the Captain or anyone is playing me a lark or not I cannot say, but I know if the former has it I shall get it again, if he has not thrown it overboard, which some would, for I had no business to smoke when working. Now the voyage is drawing to a termination I can give some idea as to know I have liked it. Well as a voyage I have enjoyed having a kind Captain which is everything, if he had been otherwise, it would have been miserable work for me but more & more is he growing kinder towards me having told me that on our arrival in Boston I may stay on board till I get a situation which is very kind of him, I think, then again we have had very fine weather indeed, which is a necessary accompaniment to a pleasant voyage <u>five</u> <u>days</u> <u>clear</u> <u>blue</u> <u>skies</u>. glorious sun risings & settings (which are only seen in the tropics) so beautiful that it has often astonished me, but why astonished me when I think that all things which came from the Creators hands are perfect. How often I have seen the feeble attempt of artists to paint or pourtray a sunset but if anyone wishes to see one let him come here in the tropics, such beautiful colors, such soft tints & shades, so well intermingled, that tell's but that such can only proceed from Divine hands. Saw today two boatswain (birds as they are called why I know not only that they have tails like marling spikes (a tool sailors use when they are splicing ropes a piece of iron an inch thick, a foot long gradually tapering to a point) while writing two more passed.

April 28th As I am writing one of the most glorious risings of the sun has taken place that I have ever witnessed, first is the first streak of light, then the clouds glow with a brilliancy only known here getting brighter every minute, till it seems as if the heavens are all melting, then the upper rim of the sun is rising as it were out of the sea, so bright that it is impossible to look on it. Today I went up to topmast yard or some other such things, up above or aloft. I went with the mate to fasten the top sail which had got adrift. I felt very comfortable up there, for I suppose I am getting more accustomed to it.

Ap 29th Today the Captain had commenced making ready his cabin for harbour by painting it all over (they say it's for that purpose so I had to help him, I say him for he did it himself for he is very particular about his vessel. I happened to mention the other day that I could paint, so he gave me the two life bouys to paint on them the vessels name & I say that I felt more at home with that than amongst the ropes, what a continuance of fine weather we have, it is rather too fine we now are going through the water about 3 or 4 knots an hour which is very slow as regards the vessel, but quite quick enough when you are bathing over the side as I did about 5 oclock with a rope around my waist to prevent me dropping astern the sailors sing out "Leave the key of your chest before you go" I was astonished that the vessel was going so quick for when I went over I thought I should be able to keep up with her but I soon found out the value of the rope & of the bath too for I was dreadfully dirty, quite ashamed of myself, but the captain said that was nothing, sometimes they never wash for a week I know the mate does not. The sea weed from the coast has been for the last 2 or 3 days passing us in great quantities but not having anything to put it in cannot get any.

Ap 30th This is the last day of the month & we have now been 39 days out and has [sic] they consider 60 days a very fair passage we have so far made a good one, not being more than 2000 miles if that from Boston, as we get nearer so much greater is my anxiety, oh that I may soon drop into a situation is my earnest desire Another sail today to all appearance a bark & I believe she brought the wind with her for half an hour back we were scarcely moving but after that we went at a very good pace.

May 1st Another month has come & we are still at sea & nothing but the dull monotonous sea life occurred, the breeze we had yesterday has died away, but the Captain expected it would for we are now in or about the calm belt of the Tropic of Cancer but it is certainly very tantalizing when we are within a good weeks sail of our destination.

May 2nd Sunday Another Sunday has come, the sun this morning rose gloriously but brought no wind with it, but at that time a fire fish came along side very much like a salmon the mate very nearly succeeded in getting him on board with the granis (an instrument like a toasting fork but shaped like a harpoon at the ends) but there is a saying that you may as well be a mile as an inch, it would have been a very nice breakfast something out of the common but fates ordered it to be otherwise, we were not to get it. The day is fast waining & as a proof of Gods protecting mercy at about 5 oclock I feeling rather dirty & being Sunday no work being done on board the vessel that day, I had a bath in the sea, I jumped overboard from the bulwarks (a height of 9 feet) 3 times & had not been on board many minutes when a cry of "Shark there's a Shark" & when he came under the stern he would not have been less than 12 or 13 feet long a tremendous fellow if I had been in the water, then there would have been a termination of my earthly career everyone on board saying what a narrow escape I had had, true the shark may not have seen me but they only who have had the escape can understand the feeling I now have truly God has been merciful unto me & another reason has he given me to be thankful unto him, I cannot help here remarking, that having spoken to the Captain before going overboard, he said there might or might not be a shark about but he did not think so has [sic] we had a piece of pork on a hook overboard in hopes of catching the fish we saw in the morning, if there had been a shark he would have come to that, however before I went in, as much as people may ridicule the idea I breathed an inward prayer to the Almighty to protect me & I believe he did answer my prayer, however there the proof was & I am grateful to him. Quite a calm today scarcely 40 miles we believe the current drifted us that much certainly there was no wind.

May 3rd After two days nearly calm, breeze has again sprung up & now I hope we are going to keep it all the way to Boston. We are going through fields of sea weeds which is the only break in monotonous sea, sight of blue water, the weed is of a very dark ochre color when seen at a distance, frequently there glides by pieces of large as our vessel as our vessel in one small piece yesterday I for the first time saw the sea adder a very young one about 9 inches long. I never knew before that was a species of snake except in the heated imagination of some newspaper editor.

May 4th Yesterday saw the 9th sail it was an American bark it looked very well indeed being under full sail & broadside on, this morning the breeze has come upon us in its old style, we are now going about 10 miles an hour & nearing the coast rapidly I hope to be there in a week & then the tug of war commences, I think if I do not get a situation with the letters of introduction I shall make for Thomas but I have forgotten his address & I do not wish to write home till I have got a situation.

May 5th Today we have nearly a headwind which has caused us to alter our course to nearly north instead of northwest, heavy seas coming right ahead causing us to pitch & toss as if she intended to dive under several times have I seen the water within an inch if not level with the bulwarks. Saw a brigantine homeward bound going at a tremendous pace for the wind was for her fair.

May 6th Last night I was troubled with earache but resorted to my old remedy, ammoniac or hartshorn & lint which is a certain cure burning much at first but giving afterwards great relief. If anything the vessel pitched more this morning from 6 to 8 seas white topped with foam & -not mountain- but hillock high for that phrase like many more is exaggerated no doubt the seas rises very high in a storm but never <u>mountains</u> high certainly thank God it has never been my lot to see it.

May 7th Today my earache is better but still rather painful—otherwise I am in good health. The weather continues rather unfavorable the head causing the vessel to pitch & toss much still & though we have had a good breeze it is like a bull running at a gate she is making very little more than 4 miles an hour. Yesterday I gave the longitude & latitude to the boatswain & he having worked it out said we were 930 miles a great way yet but I suppose we shall be in in 3 or 4 days.

May 8th The breeze last night was more favourable & the sea having gone down we make more progress. Last night just before tea the mate having some caulking to do, the tar was placed on the fire

& while the boys were out a sea came causing the vessel to pitch, capsized the tar everybody was at the door in a moment, the smoke was something like a chimney on fire, really if there is such negligence going on it is probable the ship may be burnt, no one knows the consternation it causes amongst a ships crew an occurrence like this, it may be very trifling in itself, & we may think so when it is over, but it is not pleasant to have the least shadow of a chance of being burnt so far from land.

Today (Sunday 9th) the breeze has increased to a hurricane or very near whistling in the shrouds & rigging & making a great noise, the sea rising fast & the vessel plunging very much but we received a warning in shape of the porpoises, a great shoal of them going along at a tremendous rate, for they say that they always run away from or before the wind. Oh, I never saw such a shoal in my life, hundreds of them diving in & out of the water as if they were in chase of some thing but they were only playing. I suppose all I know is that the wind came not an hour after them strong had to take in sail & make the vessel snug. The vessel rolled so much that it caused the bands of a water cask to give way & it leaked & though it was Sunday—necessity is law—we had to bail it out into another one.

10th There has been wind & rain all night quite a hurricane, blowing the sea higher than ever likewise the ship more slanting, double reefs in mainsail, foresail, topsail, the flying jib boom, jib, square sail, degallant sail, and royal all snugly stored in also main top sail, the vessel pitching water over her bows, everything wet & cold- I never felt but once I think the cold so much since I left the Cape or England coming out of a warm climate you do so. This must be a dreadful coast in winter, the sea & wind rises so quick.

11th Today thank God the weather has changed the sun came out so nice & warm it was quite refreshing, Oh after all there is nothing like the blue sky, but then we are never contented in this world if we have one thing we desire another. About midday there came another lot of porpoises, but in the opposite direction, so if the rule holds good we shall have a fair wind, it is in fact blowing that now a little I am progressing nicely with my French though I am now in the most difficult part. 5 pm The above rule did not hold good for we are becalmed. Oh I am getting sick & tired of this—I regret patience is a thing I do not possess—but must learn. Today is 50 days out.

12th Last night in our watch about 11 oclock a breeze sprung up (contrary to porpoises) & we are now dashing along at a fine rate, hope to spend Sunday in Boston harbour. This morning saw another sail but have ceased counting them as they are getting numerous now, they never come close enough to speak to them. The weather all day has been very fine & a nice breeze carrying us along nicely. Caught a nautilus & was astonished at it being such a curious thing, like an inflated bladder, being full of gas or something like it.

13th We are now approaching Boston quickly. Saw another sail today, a sure sign of the proximity of a port. Next Sunday being Whitsuntide, hope to spend it in harbour we got up the cable out of the hold- a nasty job indeed the anchors on the side everything ready The night are cold but thank God short—7 1/2 hours—& I wear a warm pair of socks my poor mother knitted for me—God bless her I wonder how she is, she little thought when she knitted them that they were to keep her youngest son warm at sea, I have only one pair Abe gave me two, but one some how or other in passing through Lizzie's hands found its way back to him & I never got it again, the pair I have is marked 1 & 3, what a long yarn to spin as sailors say about a pair of stockings

14th Last night my watches were the 1st and 3rd or morning watch ie—8 hours on deck & it was a fearful night blowing & cold enough too in the bargain! though I had two coats on I felt it & in the watch below the wind increases so much that all hands for the first time since we left had to turn out & shorten sail going ahead at a tremendous pace 10 miles an hour the sea's was dreadful & as they broke the phosphorous made everything light, not knowing much about seamanship the Captain sent me forward to look out for vessels & being under the sails all the wind came out of them on me it was very cold indeed The Captain told me when I turned in to be ready to be called out & I had boots & everything else on & when he called me tired as I was [I was] the first of [the] watch on deck

14th [sic] The weather has moderated & we are still going quick we shall make a good days run of it hope to be in late tomorrow night. The sea has rapidly changed its colour from a bright blue to a dark green for we are approaching land, saw them heave the lead for the first time result 55 fathoms or 200 feet [55 fathoms = 330ft], high as All Saints Church. Yesterday painting the ship ready for harbour, looks like a new pin.

15th I said that the last night previous was bad but Oh I shall never forget it, last night was worse, Oh I understand now the sufferings & trials of the sailors, we today & yesterday have had dense fog so dense that the Captain did not know where we were the thunder rolled & lighting flashed & the rain fell in torrents in the first watch & worse still there were lights under the lee that denoted danger it was a light ship on a sand bank, Oh it was awful the lightning flashing, blinding everybody for a moment & making the night as it were darker than before, orders being issued so rapidly no time was given for their execution, it was piercingly cold my hands have not their warmth yet take my writing now & compare it when that are all right, now they are as stiff as bones. All day it has been foggy, but just before noon the sun appeared & we got a sight & found out where we were. This afternoon seen two fishing schooners & they told us where the land lay, & gave us some fish (cod) a great treat & no mistake, it is no joke for a Captain to come to a strange place & have dirty weather.

Sunday I am thankful to say we have better weather today, though last night it was bitter cold & my fingers were very stiff & cold, but they are better this morning & I am able to write better too, we have just sighted land & I have for the last half hour been heaving the lead for we got in shallow water quick on a bank hope to end this eventful voyage today or at least tomorrow. 1 pm The pilot came aboard just now & has taken charge & having a fair breeze we are going on nicely, we have passed I could not tell how many, say 50 since we sighted land, it is a long sandy beach with scarcely any vegetation on leaving that on the left with its lighthouse we are crossing Boston Bay now being about 4 mile off, probably be in by midnight, now really become anxious as to my being able to get a situation, I wish I knew Thomas's address as I might be compelled to write, however I am determined not to do so if I can possibly help it. Sunday night at 1/2 past 10 cast anchor, my sensations then I shall not attempt to describe. The Captain has promised that I shall stay on board till I am settled.

Finis

-

John arrived in Boston on May 16, 1869. He apparently visited some relatives and traveled around the United States working for a railroad. He married Clara Hardy in San Antonio, Texas on Feb 14, 1879 about 10 years after his arrival in the USA. Their story continues in Chapter 8.

Chapter 5
Polly's Poem

Inside covers of John's log, copied by his sister Polly.

Inside Front Cover

I never knew a mother's love
   Yet happy were my days
For by my own dear father's side
   I sang my simple lay's

Savannah's tide dash bravely on
   I saw wave roll o'er wave
But in the morning when I woke
   I found I was a slave

He died & heartless strangers came
   They closed o'er him his grave
They tore me weeping from his side
   And claimed me has their slave.

Inside Back Cover

Connubialities

When Adam slept God from him took
   A bone and as an omen
He made it like a seraph look
   And thus created woman

---------- " ----------

He took this bone not from his pate
  To show his power more ample
Nor from his feet to designate
  That on her he might trample

---------- " ----------

But 'neath his arm to clearly show
  He always should protect her
And near his heart to let him know
  How much he should respect her

---------- " ----------

He took this bone, crooked enough
  Most crooked of the human
To show him how much crooked stuff
  He'd always find in woman

Bennett Heap (left), his wife Frances Heap, John Bennett (my grandfather), George Heap, and his wife Polly Bennett Heap (John Bennett's sister) in San Antonio.

Chapter 6
Letter to Aunt Polly

John wrote to his sister Mary Alice (Polly) in England a very homesick letter June 10th 1872. The envelope was addressed to: Miss Mary A Bennett, Barlow Street, London Road, Derby, England. On the side it said: The postmaster will deliver (please) this to whom it is directed.

New Orleans
New Orleans, Mobile and Texas R.R.
June 10th 1872

Dear Mother and Sister;
I do not know if it is like "sending coals to Newcastle, but this is the latest style of note paper called the "Dolly Varden". Now Polly prepare yourself & receive another complaint. You will see how necessary it is to write often, from the tone of your letter received yesterday it is evident that you must have written one which I have not received, therefore I would like you to answer that and this— answer my questions Polly dear and then you [know] how disappointed I was in not receiving the long promised photographs. It is really selfish on your part to keep especially my mothers from me so long after I have asked and persuaded you who have her with you every day gazing on her face. You cannot I am sure realize how much I yearn for so much as the faintest shadow of a glimpse at it, why? why? Are you so unforgetful of your promises, why put my patience to such a severe task causing me to plead, yes again I say it plead for it every time I write. it is really too bad, too mean, where is the object and what is it why you cannot grant my request, or are

you indifferent to anything I say, do you think it tend & strengthen the tie to bind me to home by such conduct, at any rate, I want you to explain yourself and say if I am to expect it or not. Now Polly do answer me and induce Mother to send it, common politeness if <u>nothing more</u> demands it. Sorry as I am to use such expressions to one I love so much. and Polly don't let Mother run away with my letters anywhere till you make notes of my questions so as to enable you to answer them. but I have told you so often. God knows I don't like to always be writing in such a strain, it is neither profitable to myself or you. Your last letter (not dated) with one in from Will, left England on the 24th of May and reached me on June 7th. Just 14 days on the ways, and considering it is 4 days journey to New York it was the quickest passage that I know of. The other one must [have] either been lost in the Post Office or in the Atlantic. it never reached. The last one that I received was in the latter part of April and if you had not written this last, I suppose I must have waited considerable longer. So there is another augment in favor of writing more frequently. It was over 6 weeks between [sic] and your last one, and I wrote 3 weeks ago tomorrow waiting a week to see "if something would turn up" from you and it did. I shall expect another in two weeks from this. Polly, what is Andrew doing with Abe and has he a permanent place, better wages. I cannot imagine what particular branch he is following. I hope they will agree and where is Will working. I forget if you told me he was living in Derby. Is he at the station. Does Lizzie (Abe's wife) feel offended at my not answering her letter direct. I don't know if I persue the right course in answering all my correspondents in one letter, but I have written directly home so long that I would feel doing wrong did I discontinue it but after this I intend answering every one even if I enclose it in the same envelope so that they may have no excuse for not writing. Polly, how is the town built up around Barlow Street. You have never told me. you know it nearly 8 years ago since I left and there must be a great improvement since I left. You remember there was a large open field at the back of the house, Crossby's I think. I think you told me that street at the top of Barlow ran through where Curtiss's house stood, or this side of it, and what have they done with that large field we used to cross on our way to the station, is it built over yet, or does it belong to the Midland, or Suntan or North

Western. And then all those gardens over the bridge between the Midland and their New Branch to London. Is Elche's park still in existence or has it been swallowed up. I suppose with Litchurch on the London and Litchurch on the Osmaston Road the people at the park must soon clear out their residence will no longer be suburban. Bye the bye, what is the number of inhabitants last census in Derby—tell me something about the improvements in Derby. Whether Saddlers Gate, Walker lane, Rothan Row and all those dirty thickly inhabited pasts of Derby have been fixed yet, Whether the Markeaton Brook has been covered in yet, or does it wind its dirty, slimey, sluggard way to the river as in times of old, an offense to the eye as well the nose. where are all the friends of my youth scattered to? I am afraid that I should find few that I know if I were to return to England. You promised to ascertain the addresses of many who have come to this country, but it must have slipped your memory I guess. Where is my uncle that came over to the states. What is he doing, where is Higgins, and Walters. What part of the states are they in. I would give something to hear from them. When I was in Detroit nearly two years ago I thought I would go to the Post Office for fun, and see the young lady letter deliverer and ask her if there was a letter for me not having the remotest idea of such being the case, and she handed me one purporting to come from one Wm Anderson, and he said if I would go to such an address I would find him, he having understood from some one that I had arrived in town which was the case. now there was a boy of that name in the telegraph with me in Derby. I hunted for him for hours, but failed to find him. do you remember my speaking of him at home. He used to live [on] Liverage Street opposite the back door of the yard where my aunt Ann lived. Oh where are now the playmates of my youth. I often think of those happy days, Ive seen none such since. is my old school master alive yet. Ive given you so many questions to answer, I am afraid you will never get through them, or if you do wont I have a glorious long letter. I was pleased to receive a letter from Will. I wish his houses were sold, and Charley's too, I would be pleased still more if they were on the way out here to the United States. I still think they will do well in this country, and from the tenor of their letters (at least Will's) they seem likely to come at last but I do not forget "there is many a slip between the cup and the lip", and I am dubious and doubtful till they are actually on their way. I am afraid if they come through Canada (which of course they will if they wish to see Tom & Sam and its being as near and short a route to the West) that they may be induced to cast their lot, I hope not for it is in West and if Will does settle down to farming, I do want to get some land along side of him, and then for the first time I shall have some fixed place, some one of the many states in which I may say I belong to. Kansas is my favorite state though Iowa and Nebraska are very good ones. The winters are too long though there still not as much so as Minnesota, Wisconsin and Michigan. Illinois is filled up. and I don't think—[end of existing letter]

In 1998 John D. Bennett and his family looked in Derby, England for Barlow Street, but found the buildings there had recently been torn down.

Chapter 7
Harry Bennett's English Report on Clara Bennett
Pearsall High School, February 11, 1941

It is because of this report that we have history of Clara Bennett that otherwise we would not have. Thank you, Harry. (Harry Bennett was her grandson.)

Clara Hardy (Bennett)

Clara Hardy Bennett was born November 10, 1859 in England.

After living in England eighteen years, trouble began to appear in her family. Her mother died and only a short time later, it was talked that her father was thinking of remarrying one of Clara's cousins whom all the family hated. Clara told her father what she had heard and he replied that it was not his intentions to do so yet, but in the future, he was certain of remarrying.

All the family left home, Clara went to live with her sister Emily and her newly acquired husband and four children. Will Cumberland had formerly been married to Lucy, another sister of Clara's. It was a death bed request of Lucy's that Emily would marry her husband and be a mother to her four children. She had joined her husband's and sister's hands and made them promise. A year or so after Lucy's death, the marriage had taken place.

At this time Dr. Kingsborough was in England telling of the wonders of America. Clara and her sister pictured America like they had always pictured Heaven. Finally Will and Emily decided to come to America and requested that Clara come along.

Clara had landed in America before her father was even informed of her intentions. They had left Liverpool with their friends, Mr. and Mrs. Mírgetrod, on the ship *Nevada*. [She entered the US at Castle Garden, New York on May 1, 1878.]

The trip was all very exciting to Clara, especially when they encountered two or three fogs and the ship's fog horns had to be blown.

After several days journey they ran into a storm and no one was allowed on deck because waves lashed furiously across it. Side boards were put on the tables so meals could be served. During the storm, Clara became deathly ill and was put to bed for three days.

After arriving in New York, they boarded a train headed for San Antonio and because of their large group, there being fourteen in all, and their lack of finance, they had to take day coaches. Sometimes it was possible to get their meals on the train, but most of the time they had to get off. Since the train was open, the children were always smokey and always several had bloody noses from falling off the benches in the trains. Clara was terrible ashamed of them and would give them a scrubbing every chance she had.

The children had never seen negroes in the "Old Country" and they were amazed at their sight. Every time they ate a meal, they would sit and stare and refuse to eat. When they again boarded the train, the children would have to be lined up to see if they were all there.

Clara Hardy Bennett

Clara ate her first cornbread on this trip. When her brother[-in-law], Will, saw some cornbread cakes, he thought they were a type of muffin they had in the Old Country. He proceeded to take a big bite and was dumb-founded. He asked the waiter what it was and after being told, he said, "I beg your pardon but I will have to spit it out".

When they arrived in San Antonio, Clara also saw her first ox teams.

They rented three rooms in what is now the Gunter Hotel, then an adobe building. Here they stayed five or six weeks while looking for land to buy. It so happened that Mr. Mírgetrod and Will Cumberland bought adjoining pieces of land. Clara boarded with William Bennett while a home was being built. The Mírgetrods lived in three rooms on one side of the house and Will and his wife in three on the other side. They all ate in the same dinning room.

Meantime Emily, William's wife, had written to John, her nephew who was in St. Louis about an English girl down here. When John Bennett came to San Antonio, he asked of the whereabouts of this English girl. Thus Clara and John were introduced.

Before she met John, Allen Jackson took her to prayer meeting every Sunday. She had had a date for the day when she met John, but he asked her and she went with him instead. When the unfortunate Allen came with an extra horse to take her, she had gone. He went on to prayer meeting alone and when it was over, he went up to Clara and said, "I've got the horse Miss Clara. I suppose you will ride home with me." Clara excused herself and Lizzy, a relative of John, went home with him instead.

On the way home John told Clara he had bought some land in Frio [County] and that he wished for [her] to marry him.

When Clara and John arrived home, Allen was waiting. Clara had now both her beaus to deal with. She waited and waited, but Allen would never leave. Finally John left and kissed her good-bye. Allen fumed because he said in his several years of going with her, she had never kissed him that way. Clara took Allen's ring from her finger and calmly offered it to him saying, "I like you as a friend but I can never marry you." He flung away the ring and left, to be seen no more.

The marriage was talked about by both relations, and the next day John, Clara and both their families went into San Antonio to get their license.

The clerks in the license department asked for the contracting parties. "John and Miss Clara--. It can't be Cumberland, that's her brother-in-law's name. Wait a minute, I'll go and see." Clara was rather disgusted at his not knowing her last name was Hardy.

Their marriage took place only three days after he had met her.

When they came to Frio [County], both his and her people came along with them. They had to camp on the way, but could not find water. Finally the men found a pond nearby and brought them water for coffee. Next morning they packed up and drove all day only to find themselves again at the pond where the water had come from. The women were certainly disgusted when they saw a cow, several days dead, lying in the water, and it was only the day before they had made coffee from it.

Most of their party had to walk because the wagon was so heavily ladened with lumber and camp goods. They took their first drink of water in Frio County from Mrs. Dawson, then recently arrived from Sweden. Because she had not yet learned English, they had difficulty in making her understand what they wanted.

Frio was still a frontier, Pearsall being only a sheep camp.

They pitched camp on the greenest spot they could find when they arrived in what is now Derby. The next day they built a shelter made of logs and the small amount of lumber that they brought along. That night it rained a terrible flood and they found they had built their shelter in a pond for the water rose about two feet. Everything they had was soaked

John and Clara then moved to another location and threw up a shelter and began work on their home. The men quarried sand rocks and plastered them with adobe. The roof was covered with the few boards brought from San Antonio. It took six months to construct a little two room house out of this material.

Clara described entering her home like entering Heaven, even though she had no stove, no chairs nor even a mattress. And a mattress they did not have until their neighbor showed them how to make one of shucks.

Once a month all the families would go to San Antonio to buy groceries taking a week to make the trip. On one trip they were caught in a blizzard and they had to stop and build a fire to heat bricks so they could ride the rest of the way in a little comfort.

When Clara's first child, May, was about fourteen months old, she experienced an awful rain. As she sat on one side of the adobe room, she noticed the wall cracking and when John came in, she called his attention to it. They only saved the wall by propping it with long poles.

One day, four engineers came to their home and ask if they could spend the night. John learned that they were railroad men and he was delighted. He soon found out they were going to construct a railroad through that country. He inquired for the job and received the work on the division between McCandless Hill and the river.

The next day, John went to San Antonio and sold his five hundred sheep and took up civil engineering for the next six years.

It was during this railroad building that Clara was given her first stove by Mr. Burn, a contractor.

After the division was finished through Derby, John, Clara and May moved to Cotulla. They put May on a blanket while they set up camp not very far from a deserted home. Presently the baby started screaming and they found her covered with fleas. They moved camp in the middle of the night and went to the next division. They later found out that the house was deserted by the people because of the great infestation of fleas.

While John was working with the railroad, they rented their home in Derby to some Kings. When Clara returned home, she was thoroughly disgusted. The Kings had had a cowpen in the front of the house and a pig pen in the back and the cistern was filled with trash and cans. That night as she slept, she found out that the Kings had left their house alive with bed bugs.

Meantime John went on into Mexico with the railroad and worked away, off and on for six years. When the first train was to go into Monterey, he sent for Clara. It was a big "to do" for the Mexicans. All the men and women were there as the big engine puffed into the town very slowly. Clara recalled hearing the senoritas saying, "Pobrecito. Esta muy cansado." ["Poor little thing. She is very tired."] The Mexican women even took pieces of coal in their hand-kerchiefs as a curiosity.

Clara and John stayed in Monterey for two months, then they returned home where he took up the work in the Derby depot and post office. The rest of their lives they lived in Derby in the original house they had started out in.

Clara, Sidney, John

Chapter 8
John and Clara Bennett

Starting in the 1870s John bought several thousand acres in Frio County on the north side of the Frio River. It was still a frontier with occasional Indian trouble. The soil was red sand, except for a caliche deposit near the north end, and the caliche deposit had a natural lake that was later named for my sister, Betsy. The land was covered with prairie grass as high as the stirrups on a horse, according to family legend. Later mesquite trees moved in, and now any land not under cultivation is brush country.

In about 1881 John went to work for the International & Great Northern Railroad as a surveyor from north of Derby, Texas to Laredo. He also surveyed railroads from Laredo to Monterey, Mexico, and from there to Torreón and to Tampico.

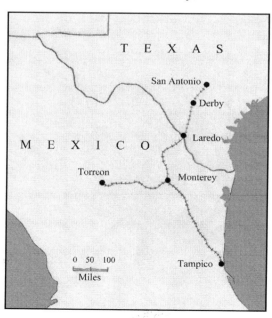

John and Clara had five children: May, Ella, Lillie, Harry, and Sidney. She found several of them in Mexico after visiting Grampa at the end of the railroad.

John Bennett at the Derby depot

May

Aunt May was married to a man named Richter, and they lived in San Antonio. He was a house building contractor. He was the first man I heard of who put a tree on top of the house when it was finished. Aunt May got sick and was in a hospital in San Antonio for a long time, a Catholic hospital. There was a Catholic nurse who took care of her. When they finally brought Aunt May home to Derby the nurse, Cecil, came with her. The hospital sent someone to Derby to get her back. Grampa wouldn't let them take her back. She lived with Grampa and Grandma for a long time, and finally she married a man named Corey. One time my sister Betsy got real sick, and everybody said she died. Cecil gave her an injection of strychnine in the heart and it revived her. That's the reason we all became so attached to the nurse we call "Aunt Cecil." She is buried in the family plot in Pearsall next to May.

Ella

Aunt Ella married Roy Howell. Roy and his brother had a store in Derby. After Uncle Roy got out of the business of running the store he became an oil leasehound. He would deal in land leases in the vicinity of oil wells that were being drilled. He would offer a certain percent of the lease to the landowner and a percent to oil companies, and he would keep a percent for himself, so he got a free interest in any wells that were drilled. Later he ran a store in Wichita Falls. They would take off a month at a time and come to Derby with their daughters "Tookie" and Clara Elizabeth. We would have big swimming parties in the lake on the farm. After John and Clara Bennett died Aunt Ella inherited their house and lived there till she died.

Harry

Uncle Harry was a farmer in Derby all his life. He married Maude Howard, of Pearsall. When he died Harry's farm was divided among his children Howard, Hardy, Bernice and Cathleen. For a while I courted Frankie Scott in Pearsall, while Uncle Harry's son Howard courted Frankie's sister, Ellen Scott. After our date I started walking home. Sometimes I walked almost to Melon (about five miles), then Howard would come along and pick me up and take me home.

Lillie

Aunt Lillie married Otis Cook. He had something to do with an ice house in Kenedy, Texas. Later he was a federal fruit inspector, part of the time in Laredo. He inspected the shipments of spinach and onions. Aunt Lillie and Uncle Otis lived across the road from Grandma.

Sidney

Sidney was my father. There is more about him in a later chapter.

Sidney Lionel Bennett, Sr.

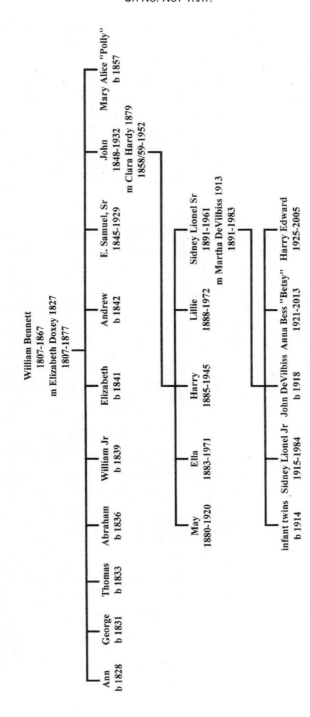

Bennett Family Tree

The House
Grampa built a two room house out of red sandstone that was quarried out of a hill on his property. The walls were 15 inches thick. Grampa continuously added onto their two-room house. He built the house in a "T" shape, two stories, with sections added onto each side of the stone rooms. The roofs were guttered so the rain water would run into a cistern. There are lots of old roofs in the attic, apparently a new roof was added for each addition.

Wells
He drilled several wells in the yard, and put a big tall windmill over one of them. The well had a "Fullen-Johnson" [Fuller & Johnson] pump engine that ran off a hotshot battery and a Model "T" coil. It had a suction valve run by the vacuum from the cylinder. Those things were all over the country. If you had a windmill you had a Fullen-Johnson pump engine.

Working for the Railroad
One night there was a knock on the door and there were four men from the railroad who wanted to spend the night. They talked to Grampa and before you know it they hired him as a surveyor to survey the International Great Northern Railroad from just below Moore, Texas down into Mexico. Grampa Bennett gave the railroad right of way on all his property, which went from north of the present town of Derby down to the Frio River. (He also gave a piece of property down on the river that was made into a state park, and that operated as a state park for many years. It was finally sold.) Derby is at the intersection of Interstate Highway 35 (formerly US Highway 85) and Farm to Market Road 1583, and is nine miles southwest of Pearsall in south central Frio County.

Now Grampa came, according to information that we found in the Handbook of Texas, moved to the site in 1879 and surveyed the International Great Northern Railroad from Moore to the Mexican border, passing through Lenore. Lenore was the first name of the Townsite of Derby. Grampa took 160 acres of his property and he laid out this town of Derby in 1907. He had two main streets through town that were for businesses, and all of those lots were made 25 feet wide because that was the standard width of the lots

59

that were used in England for businesses. Now the lots that were for homes, he laid out as 50 feet wide. They were on each side of the railroad.

Railroad Spur
Back in those days when Grampa was so influential with the railroad he had them build a spur off the switch at Otley, Texas out into his field. That was so they could load spinach into the trains. That spur caused another excitement because back in the early days the railroad was trying to promote the sale of land in South Texas. They tried to get my daddy to let them park a train full of prospective land buyers in his spinach crop so they could see the prospects of farming when they woke up in the morning. (He wouldn't let them do it.) Then they built a fine hotel at Catarina in the most God-forsaken part of Texas. They would take the land buyers down there and they would sell them land at Catarina, that had only cactus and rattlesnakes, but no water. Recently most of that land belonged to former governor Dolph Briscoe.

Steam Engines
Now you know back in those days the trains had steam engines, and they had to have water. Now Grampa Bennett built a dam across the Frio River on the railroad company's property, that dammed the Frio River up and made a little lake there. They pumped water out of that lake up onto a little hill that was on the south side of the river where they had a water tank that they used to fill the train engines with water. Now you see the trains had to stop there at the river in order to fill up with water. Now it was kinda up hill a little bit all the way to Derby. I can remember lying on the bed there listening to those trains as they'd start up that hill. You could hear them trying their best to get up that hill and you'd hear them spin their wheels. And the first thing you'd know, they'd back the train back up and then come at it again and get a running start to see if they'd get up that hill.

That dam is still on the Frio River, it never has washed out. The dam backed the water up and that's where on the south side of the river they made that Frio State Park that Grampa gave the state. Back years ago we used to go swimming in that river and we'd climb up the tree that was leaning out over the river. Course that tree was covered with poison ivy, and we'd climb right on up through the poison ivy. I guess when we'd jumped out of the tree and went into the river it washed the poison ivy off us, so we never did get poison ivy. We used to do a lot of piddling around in the river. It was the silliest thing in the world 'cause we didn't know whether there were under water logs there, we could've broke our necks. When you were kids back in that day you didn't have too much supervision and you ran kinda wild.

Dividing the Land

Grampa eventually divided his land up. He gave the land on the west side of the railroad and the highway to his son Harry Bennett. Then on the east side of the highway and on the south city limits of Derby was Grampa Bennett's house. Now his house was not in the city limits of Derby. He had some land that surrounded the house that was part of the homestead. East of the railroad was my father's strip. It ran from just south of the city limits of Derby clean down to the Frio River. Now east of my father's strip of land, there was another strip of land that belonged to Lillie Cook, my father's sister.

Sidney, Lillie (foreground); Ella, Harry, Clara, May, neighbor (back)

Her piece of land ran from the Farm to Market Highway 1882 south of the Frio River. East of that piece of property was another strip of property very similar to that that ran from south of that road and was close to where the Derby cemetery was. It ran from there to the Frio River too. So the land was divided between Uncle Harry, my Daddy, Aunt Lillie, and Aunt Ella. There is an awful lot that I don't know about what happened, and there is nobody to ask. So I'm giving you information that is to the best of my knowledge.

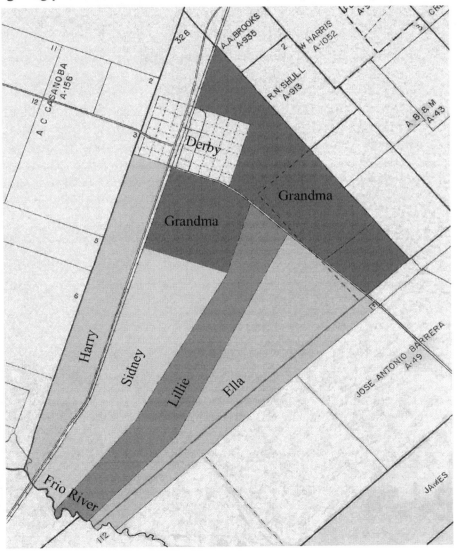

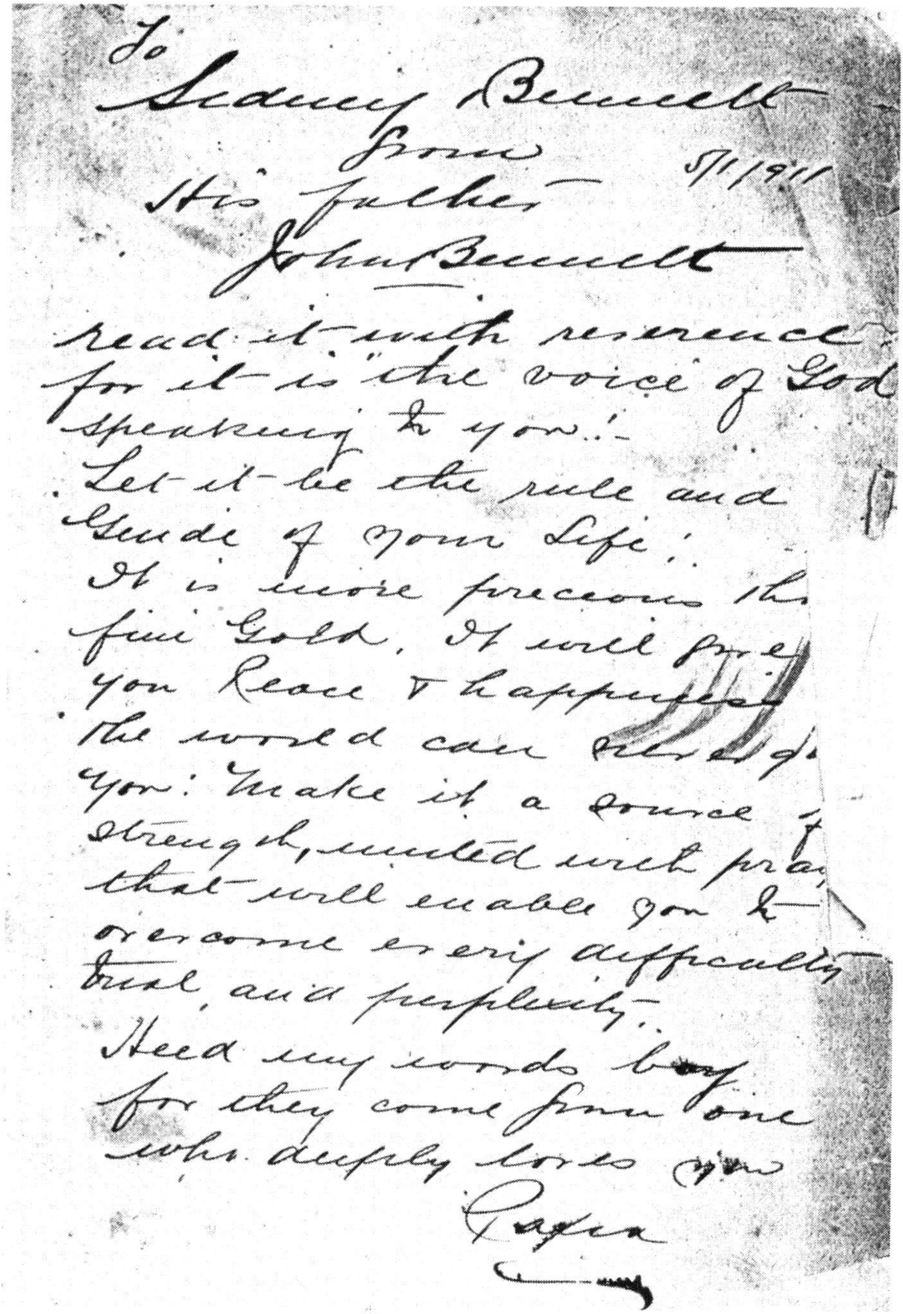

To
Sidney Bennett
from 5/1/1911
His father
John Bennett

read it with reverence
for it is the voice of God
speaking to you:-
Let it be the rule and
Guide of your Life:
It is more precious th
fine Gold. It will give
you Peace & happiness
the world can never give
you: Make it a source of
strength, united with pray
that will enable you to
overcome every difficulty
trial, and perplexity.
Heed my words boy
for they come from one
who deeply loves you
Papa

Dedication page in Sidney Bennett, Sr.'s Bible

Good advice from John in Sidney's Bible

Above: Sidney on horse

Right: Sidney in 1913

Chapter 9
Derby

History of Derby

This article that was written up in the Texas Handbook says that Grampa changed the name of the town from Lenore to Derby because that was the name of his hometown in England. It says it was an emerging farming community in 1935 and there were eight large artesian wells in the community which were used to irrigate fields of cotton, as well as onions, spinach, carrots, beets, and a variety of other vegetables. In 1936 the community had an estimated population of 50 people. They had two general stores, a cotton gin belonging to Grampa DeVilbiss, three filling stations, two schools, two churches, a Post Office, and a depot. In 1990 the population was still reported at 50.

Stores

Years ago, Aunt Ella, my daddy's sister, and her husband Roy Howell built a house in Derby. It was next door to Uncle Roy's bachelor brother Jack. The two brothers had a large general store in Derby on the west side of the tracks. In fact, there were two large general stores in Derby. Now on the east side of the track was another big general store, and it was named Benavides. I remember that store very well because it was in existence after Uncle Roy and his brother Jack Howell's store closed. You could buy nearly anything that a person needed in these two stores. There were barrels of beans and all kinds of grocery type stuff all over the store. There was even the conventional pot-bellied stove where you could get warm when you were cold.

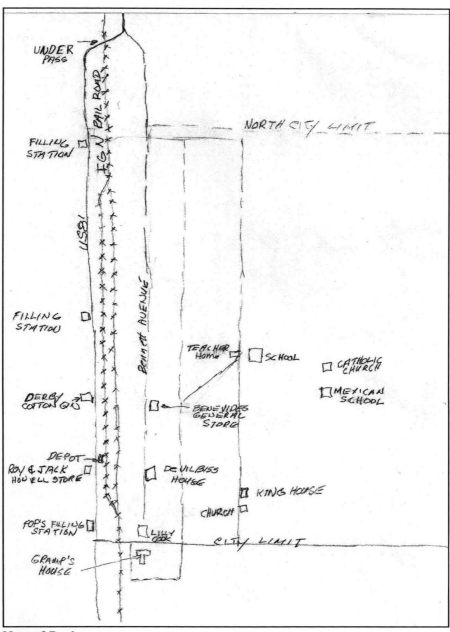

Map of Derby

Teacherette
The old Benavides store was on the way from Grandma Bennett's house to what they called a teacherette. It was a nice little house that was built there for the school teachers to live in. The teacherette had a big water tank, probably three feet in diameter by eight or ten feet long, on wagon wheels. They would take the tank to the well to fill it up. It had a hydrant and one tin drinking cup which everyone used.

Schools
We had a school there that was two big rooms (we only used one of them) and then there was another one-room school, oh, three or four blocks away that was built for the Mexicans. They had a Mexican school and a white school. I went to the white Derby school thru the sixth grade. The schools also had water tanks on wheels. During recess time the boys would all dig tunnels under the school. We had a horse pen out back where our horses stayed during classes. Sometimes we even got to sit in the windows while we were studying. They were big windows that were cool when the wind blew.

Churches
There was a Catholic church in the town, and a Protestant church that was built by my two grandfathers, and it was more or less a community church. At the Derby church Grandma played the organ. We would all stand around and sing. We had a Sunday school teacher for the adults, and of course we kids had to sit in the adult class. He was a Baptist, and he taught hellfire and brimstone. Oh Lord, he had me scared to death. His name was Mr. Mills. We had a preacher there by the name of Carmichael. Times were real hard back then. Daddy wanted to give some money to the church, but he didn't have any money to give. So he butchered a hog and gave the meat to the preacher.

Light Plant
Grampa had a Delco gasoline light plant with big batteries in glass containers. It was in a special house to house the engine generator and all of those batteries. Whenever the charge would get low the electric generator would start up and recharge the batteries. His light plant was in the front yard, about half way to Aunt Lillie's

house. There were wires running to his house, Aunt Lillie's house, and the Derby community church. His house was wired for 32 volts.

Windmill

Derby had a cemetery, which Grandpa also donated the land for. They called it the Mexican cemetery and it was about a mile east of the town. And incidently, there was a windmill up there near that cemetery that had good water, and that good water was one mile from where Grampa and Grandma's house was. And when Grampa was building the railroad in Mexico, poor little Grandma would get her two buckets and she'd go walk that mile to that windmill and get good drinking water and bring it back. There seems to be a very peculiar thing about the shallow water situation in Derby. There was a ridge that kinda runs North and South through Derby. On the east side of that ridge was good water, on the west side of that ridge was terrible water, and most of the town of Derby was in the terrible water section. They had a lot of dug wells about 100 feet deep there where people who lived there tried to get decent drinking water, and they really couldn't. They used to load up their wagons with barrels and drive down to my Daddy's house on the farm where he had this good artesian well. They would haul water from there a mile back to Derby for their consumption. They brought steel barrels that had the top cut out of them. They would lay a board on the top of the water to keep it from splashing out. Of course, since the water in Derby was not fit to drink and people relied on cisterns to hold the water that was caught on the roofs during rains. Water is what killed the town of Derby, because you could not get good water, and the people finally just moved out.

Filling Stations

Now Derby supported three filling stations. One of them used to belong to my father, Sidney Bennett, and he had a partner named Ben Speer, who ran it. Mr. Speer ran the filling station for a long time. Now Ben Speer was kin to my brother Sidney Bennett's wife. Her mother was a Speer. There were two more stations in town, one about half way through it, and the other was on the north end. Two were just ordinary filling stations. The one in the middle had a grocery store attached to it. And it did furnish some groceries for the population around there.

Aunt Lillie's Fire

I can remember when I was a fairly young kid Aunt Lillie's house caught afire and burned up. Now it was just across this Farm to Market road from Grandma and Grampa's house. Uncle Jack and Uncle Roy's store was still standing and it was empty. So they tore the store down in order to get the lumber to build a house for Aunt Lillie and Uncle Otis. That house is still standing; today made out of that lumber out of that old store.

Donkey

Derby had quite a population of Mexicans and every one of them had a donkey and a donkey cart. Now there were so many donkeys that they just ran wild all over the townsite. In later years they became such a nuisance they rounded them up and shipped them to Mexico.

Wells and Tank

Grampa was an engineer who had an obsession with water, probably because they had such bad water in Derby. He drilled several water wells on his land. One was on what would become the boundary between Sidney Bennett's land and Aunt Lillie's land. That well I believe was 600 feet deep, and went to the Wilcox sand. I can remember back when I was a kid they had a big pump house over the well with an engine in it and a belt that drove the pump. The pump pumped water into a brick tank, probably 200 feet by 200 feet, lined with brick and covered with stucco, with sloping walls and probably five or six feet deep. They would take water out of it to irrigate the fields. In 1918 he completed a deeper well, as noted in the next chapter. There was a blacksmith shop by the tank. Every farm back then had one.

Depot

After Grampa finished surveying for the railroad he was the depot agent at the Derby depot. At one time you could catch the train there. Later they stopped passenger service at Derby (except for Grandma), but the train would still stop for delivering and picking up freight. Derby shipped quite a lot of farm crops. There was a post beside the track where they would hang outgoing mail in a mail sack. When a train came along it wouldn't stop, but it had a hook which would grab the mail sack. For mail going to Derby they would just throw a mail sack out the door as the train went by. They also had a telegraph, but it was just for railroad business. The depot was heated by coal, which the railroad had on hand for burning in the locomotives.

After Grampa got too old to run the depot a man from Dilley named McLain was the agent. I don't remember much else about him, except that I helped Mr. McLain build a pea sheller that worked like a clothes wringer.

During the war they moved in a train car and set it on ties on railroad property near Grandma's house. Mrs. Kingsley became the station master and lived in the train car

Grampa at the Derby depot

Chapter 10
Sidney and Martha

Grampa Bennett built the original home on property he owned in Frio County. After having built the railroad into Mexico, I guess he thought he should lay out a town on his own land. He named the town after his hometown in England, "Derby", Texas. He completely surveyed the town into streets and lots.

Soon John Wesley DeVilbiss, Jr., son of the Methodist preacher of Texas history fame, moved his family to Derby, their house being about a quarter mile north of John Bennett's house. John DeVilbiss built a cotton gin in Derby and ran it for many years. Naturally the Bennetts and the DeVilbisses got to be friends, especially the Bennett's son Sidney and the DeVilbiss daughter Martha.

Courting

Now the DeVilbiss house was built up on posts (piers) and stood about 2-1/2 feet above the ground. It had a front porch on the house and a porch swing. Now Sidney, my father, would come courting Martha, my mother. Martha's two young sisters, named Ledell and Helon, would crawl all the way under the house so they could get under the front porch swing where Mother and Dad were courting, just to hear what was going on. They were brave, stupid, but curious girls because that part of Frio County, Texas was known for its rattlesnakes.

I had heard very little about the courtship of my parents except I heard that Dad owned a buck board and a pair of beautiful black horses. They were riding west of Derby and a mountain lion crossed the road in front of them. Now, I would like to tell you a good story

Martha and Sidney Bennett

about what happened, but I was so young when I heard the story. There are always two reasons for not remembering, you were too young or you were too old to remember. For some reason, my parents never did tell us kids about their courtship. Sure must have been dull because you know your parents never did anything interesting.

I do remember my Aunt Dime (Helon), she was called that because when she was little and up to her mischievous self, one of her brothers offered to sell her for a dime. That name stuck until the day she passed away, about 96 years young, the last of Mother's siblings. After all, her name was Helon <u>Young</u>blood.

Now when my young sister was due to appear, Mother thought it best to ship me over to the nearby farm where Aunt Dime and Uncle Earnest lived. This was known as the Lilly farm and Uncle Earnest ran the farm, complete with the farm store.

Now people tell me, I don't believe it, but this seems to be where I first obtained my notoriety. I raised so much hell Aunt Dime and Uncle Earnest had to take me back home in the middle of the night. Maybe that is the reason Mother never would let me whip my sister when I knew full well she needed it. From there my mind does put together many worthwhile thoughts.

Raising a Family

Sidney and Martha were married on November 1, 1913 in San Antonio. In 1914 they had twins, a boy and a girl, who died almost at birth. Later on Sid was born; he's my oldest brother. Then, of course, there's me, John D., and then there was Betsy, my sister (Anna Bess Bennett), and finally, in 1925, my youngest brother, Harry. We were four kids, and I don't remember us having much trouble getting along with each other when we were young. Seems like we played together pretty good. But of course the thing that I remember most about our early years was Sid. It seems to me that kids, as they grow up, they know older people better than they know the younger people. So I know a lot more about Sid than I knew about Betsy and Harry.

Moving the House

There is gobs of stuff that I can tell you about Derby. I can't really put a time frame on some of it, but I believe the tale about Dad buying Uncle Roy's house in Derby came maybe before we kids

Our house

were born. Uncle Roy could see that Derby was not going to grow into a big metropolis so he and Aunt Ella sold their house to Dad. Now Grampa had divided up the land that he had bought between his kids, Ella, Lillie, Harry and Sidney. Sidney, my Dad, had inherited a piece of land south of the old Bennett homestead down to the Frio River about two miles away. There was a hill about half way to the river and off the railroad to the east about a quarter mile. There was eventually a railroad siding there named Otley. Dad decided that his house that he had bought in Derby needed to be on that hill on his land. Now Dad's oldest sister, May, was married to a man named Richter, who was very handy at building houses and stuff. You understand that I am recalling from memory what I thought I had learned of things that happened before my time. You know, I don't know what happened to Aunt May's part of the land unless it was part that I remember that Grandma had. It could be that Grandma got that back after Aunt May died. It will be hearsay too.

Anyway, Dad decided to move the Derby house to his hill on the farm. That was a big job as Mother and Dad were still living in the house during the move. I believe I remember hearing the figure of six months for the move. The house was placed on large skids and was dragged the distance. A windlass would be installed in the direction the house was being dragged and mules would go round and round until the windlass took up all the cable, then the windlass had to be reinstalled, the cable let out, and the process would be repeated hundreds of times. I do remember Dad saying the time came when the house had to be moved across the railroad. Now Grampa was a railroader so he knew what to do. The only thing was it took time to cross the track. They got the house all ready for the skid across the track and while in process of crossing, the train came. Now this is where I inherited some of my hard-headednesss and determination.

The train had to stop and wait and wait and wait. The train engineer told Dad that if he didn't clear the track, he would run the train into the house and knock it off the track. Dad said "Go ahead". The train waited some more, maybe a day or so?

Finally the house was set up on top of the hill about three feet off the ground on mesquite posts, facing south toward the river.

The Deep Well

Back in 1918, which was the year I was born, and probably after the house was moved to the farm, Grampa decided that he needed a water well on the farm, about 400 yards south of Dad's house. Grampa was an engineer who was determined to get water for the farm. He had already drilled several wells on the farm but he never did get the water that he wanted. After six months of hard drilling with a cable tool rig, they finally brought in a well in the Carrizo sand down about 1750 feet deep. That well flowed 1000 gallons of water a minute and at the time it was drilled, it was the second best well in the state of Texas. It had a 60 foot head on it and the water was 98 degrees the year around. Later we used the water to heat the slab of the house.

The well was never closed in and was made to flow under the highway and under the railroad to Uncle Harry's farm which paralleled Dad's farm, but was separated from it by the railroad. Sometimes it flowed over to the east to Aunt Lillie's farm which

Drilling the deep well

Uncle Roy at the well

paralleled Dad's farm on the East.

A large pipe was installed on the well which made it flow up on the hill that Dad's house was on. From there an irrigation ditch carried the water by gravity north into a natural pond. From there an irrigation ditch was installed with a sluice gate allowing the water to go to Aunt Lillie's farm. The tank at the well was the best swimming in the world and people came from all around to go swimming. Especially Uncle Roy's and Aunt Ella's kids, Tookie (Ella Francis) and Clara Elizabeth, who would come back to Derby to Grandma's house and spend a large part of the summer. All of the cousins, aunts, and uncles would go swimming every day. As Grampa use to say, "Oh the years of my youth." This place was Paradise.

Now back in those days they foresaw the fact that the water table would eventually drop. They cased the well and down about 15 or 20 feet they put a "tee" in the casing. Years later when the water table dropped and they weren't getting as much water as they wanted they dug a cellar around the well and installed a centrifugal pump with a horizontal shaft. They put in a sloping floor that slanted up to the ground where there was a big engine. The big engine ran the pump by a long drive belt. I think the engine was a Cooper-

This Bessemer engine had two cylinders, ours had one

Bessemer with two flywheels about six feet in diameter. It didn't have a spark plug; it had a rod sticking out of the end of the cylinder. You would heat the rod with a blowtorch until the engine was running. They had a little gasoline engine that ran an air compressor. They would use the compressed air to start the big engine. You hand-operated a valve to put the compressed air into the cylinder at the right time to turn it over. That little gasoline engine was the joy of my life. Later I build a little car that was run by that engine. I would drive it all over the hill.

Howard Bennett operated the pump. I could hear that thing all night long. Years later electric power was available and they built a 3-phase power line down to that well. They put in a 25 hp 3-phase electric motor to run the pump. My daddy had electricity before most of the houses in that part of the country.

The Farm
On the farm, there were several houses that my Uncle Mibe (Mother's brother) had built for the Mexican families that worked for Dad. After dark, the men who had been working all day, would go down to the tank to take their baths. Being as our house was only

77

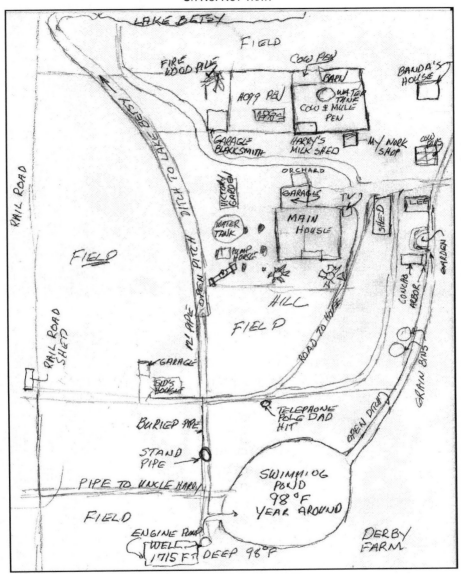

The farm

a few hundred yards away, we could hear the men singing while they bathed. I thought their voices were the prettiest I had ever heard.

Concho

Concho Valdez and his wife Chona lived just down the hill from our house. Their house was built very close to the ditch that flowed around our hill on the way to Aunt Lillie's farm. They had three children who were my first playmates. Their names were Chon, Adrian, and Lodia. Concho's house was just two rooms. One large room, which is where they slept, and then a lean-to type room on the back of the house that was the kitchen. There was a stove in that kitchen and Chona kept a stack of flour tortillas on the back side of the stove where it didn't get too hot while she was cooking her beans and other tortillas on the top of the stove.

The irrigation ditch in 1943

I must have eaten a million of Chona's tortillas. On the back side of the big room was a brush arbor. It was not 10 feet to the ditch full of that 1000 gallons-a-minute water flowing by. They dug a bypass loop ditch that flowed through their garden and then back into the big ditch. They had the most bountiful garden there ever was.

Under the arbor was a large table that had benches on each side. The ground was sandy and always moist so it was as cool as it could be. They always ate outside unless the weather was cold, and then they ate in the kitchen. All the yard was shaded with large mesquite trees. Chona thought I was another one of her kids. I loved it there.

Concho was the same age as Dad and had worked for him as long as I could remember. He was a fantastic mechanic and his job on

John D and Sid about 1921

the farm was to keep all the machinery running. Of course there were practically no tools to work with. I hung around with Concho and he taught me the basic mechanics that I knew and gave me the desire to always be doing something mechanical. He was my mentor and my protector. In later years when I was supposed to be helping Concho rebuild a tractor or peanut thrasher and we were down under the big shed that Dad had for the machinery, sometimes I would get pretty tired and sleepy. I would take a nap on some of the bales of peanut sacks that were always there. Concho would always be listening for Dad who would be riding his horse all over the field. Dad always whistled one note, repeated endlessly. When Concho would hear Dad coming, he would shake me and tell me to wake up because, "Your Dad is coming." I thought that Concho was just about the finest man there ever was.

Merry-Go-Round
Uncle Otis Cook was my daddy's sister's husband. He was pretty much of a mechanical-type man. He had a lot of things that intrigued me. He had a little automobile that was junked out there on my Daddy's farm, over close to Aunt Lillie's farm. They used to

Sidney Jr. (front) Sidney Sr., John D, and Martha about 1920

have a big blacksmith shop where they had a water well that went down into the Wilcox sand. This old car was called a Metz. It had a chassis with a four cylinder engine in it. There was a propeller shaft that came off the back of the engine and went to an aluminum disc, and I think that aluminum disc must have been at least two feet in diameter. The face of that disc was at least a half inch thick. It had ribs on the back of it to rein-force it. Whenever the engine would run that disc would spin. Behind that disc was a shaft that was perpendicular to the axis to the shaft that went up to the engine. On this thing was a fiber wheel that must have been about eight inches in diameter. You could slide that wheel from one side to the other. On each end of the axle that the fiber wheel was on there was a sprocket and a chain that went down to the rear wheel of the Metz automobile. The rear wheel of the Metz stuck out there like a normal tread on a car, and then it had a long hub that came back towards the body of the chassis and on that hub was a sprocket and that chain worked on that sprocket, one on each side. I don't remember if it had a differential or not, but I do remember that shaft and I remember that fiber wheel that you could slide back and forth. Somehow you could disengage that aluminum disc from rubbing on that wheel. I'm not sure but what the disc could be moved forwards or backward a little bit to make the contact. If you had that wheel right at the center of the disc when it

Packing and loading spinach at the Otley siding

was turning it wouldn't turn the wheel. But as you slid the wheel out towards the outside edge it would roll the wheel forward. That would make the vehicle go forward. If you got on the other side of the center of rotation it would make the vehicle go backwards. That was the reverse. That was the only gearshift it had, sliding that fiber gear backwards and forward. That really intrigued me.

Well one time I decided I wanted to make a merry-go-round up in the yard. So I got the rear axle out of this old Metz. Now that rear axle was a piece of steel that was maybe an inch and a half in diameter. On each end of it there was a solid spindle. The Metz wheels had ball bearings that operated on this spindle. Well after so long a time I was able to get that axle out of that old Metz automobile. I took it up to the house. In the front yard on the west side of the road that came up into the yard there was a spot under some trees. We stood that axle on the end in a hole and poured concrete around it. So there that axle was sticking up in the air, and the top end of the axle was maybe 3½ feet off of the ground. Well, we put the wheel back on it, and there we had a wheel that would spin on that vertical axle. Then we got a piece of board about 1 x 12, must have been 20 feet long. We put it across the top of the axle and tied it onto that wheel so that that board could be spun around and around like a merry-go-round. On each end of that board we had a 2 x 4 that was nailed on that 1 x 12; it was about a foot or so from the end. You would hang your legs over the top of that 2 x 4. When you spun around the centrifugal force would want to throw you off the end of that 1 x 12, but you would hang your legs across that 2 x 4 and that's what kept you from flying off. I'll bet you we turned that thing a million rounds. On the center of the 1 x 12 we had another 2 x 4 nailed across it so we could have a kid or two pushing on it to supply the power. We kids would get on that thing and ride it and ride it, and see if we could turn that thing fast enough to sling some-one off the end of it. It's a wonder we didn't get killed on that thing, but we had a lot of fun with it. That old axle I think maybe to this day is stuck in the ground down on the farm.

Sidney, Sr.

Pop started farming about 1913. In about 1930 he became one of the first farmers to grow peanuts in Frio County. He also grew cotton, watermelons, spinach, and onions. He irrigated them by flooding the fields from irrigation ditches. A railroad spur was built out into his field. He rode all over the farm on his horse, though he was crippled. Pop could whistle only one note (pitch), but he whis-tled it over and over all day long.

Honesty Lesson

We would go on vacation to the river at New Braunfels or to the Frio River at Concan. When we went to Concan we would stay in cabins at Neil's Lodges. Concan is in the edge of the Hill Country, and the river is fed by cold, crystal clear spring water. The river has a rock bottom and made great swimming. The whole family would go up there—all of my cousins, probably 50 of us. Daddy was always afraid a storm would come along and cause a flood that would wash us all away. Everybody else had a good time, but Daddy was miserable. When I was about eight or nine years old we went there in Uncle Otis' big old flatbed truck. When we got ready to go home I dreaded the uncomfortable ride, so I stole a pillow out of one of the cabins. When we got home and Mother saw what I did she made me mail the pillow back. Woo, did I get a lecture!

Accident

One day Sid drove to Dilley with me riding in the back of the Model "T" pickup. He turned real sharp to go into a parking spot and I was thrown out and landed on my head. It knocked me out for several hours. When I came to, the doctor wouldn't let me sleep the first night until the knot went away. It's a wonder we ever grew up.

Sid, cousin Mary Francis, John D (both photos)

Chapter 11
Derby School Days

Eating with Grandma

The best thing about the Derby school was that the schoolhouse was about six blocks from Grandma Bennett's house. I got to go to Grandma's house every day, at least the first year that I was in school, to eat my dinner. We would eat in the dining room, just Grandma and me, at that big old table. She used to have a tablecloth on the table and another one on top of that where she kept the food covered while it was waiting to be eaten. This second tablecloth not only kept the food warm, but it also kept the flies off the food.

Now Grandma used to make an apple pie on the top of the wood stove (pie-by-the-yard). She would roll out a large piece of pie dough that was real thin. Then she would cover half of the dough with a very thin layer of pie filling. The second part of the dough would be folded over the first part and then the edges would be mashed together. This was cooked on top of the wood burning kitchen stove, just like Chona would cook her tortillas. It was Heavenly. If Grandma let me see the pie, I wouldn't eat anything else. She would hide the pie in the tablecloth so I couldn't see it, and then when I came in from school to eat she would say "No pie today, Johnny. You will just have to eat your dinner." Naturally I was crushed, and then very reluctantly would eat my dinner. When I was finished, she would start rooting around in the tablecloth and then say, "Why, I do believe I have found a piece of pie." You know I fell for that line every day. Boy, I loved my Grandma.

Harold Crawford

My good friend Harold Crawford was my same age and he stayed with his grandfather in Derby. His house was just next to the community church, about two blocks from the school. Harold's grandfather was an old man so Harold's mother let Harold live with his grandfather, just to keep him company, and help him do what he could. Mr. King was a bee man. He had the neatest work shop because he made all of his bee hives and frames. After school Harold and I would go to Mr. King's shop and build all kinds of things. They had a table saw, that I never did get to use, but it was powered by an old one cylinder popping willy engine. Harold and I loved to play in that shop. Harold's daddy was named Charlie Crawford. He was well known in Frio County as the windmill man. He installed windmills and repaired them for everybody, because windmills were very important at that time. Harold and I went all through school together. I kind of lost track of him for years but when I did find him years later, he had been voted man of the year in Abilene, Texas, had his own airplane and owned 34 Firestone stores.

School

The Derby school was an old two room schoolhouse. My first grade teacher was named Miss Steinball. My brother Sid was sitting in the Derby school when Harold and I went that first day. Naturally we were scared. Sid said that a puddle of liquid appeared on the floor that day. I can't remember who was the most scared of Miss Steinball, Harold or me. We sat next to each other. At recess, the boys would all go and dig tunnels under the school. The floor of the school was a couple of feet above ground, and being as we were all very small we could navigate around under the floor with great ease. We built all kinds of tunnels under the school. It is a wonder it didn't fall in on us. Then we would have to go wash our hands. There was a pen for the horses at school where our houses stayed during classes. Sometimes we even got to sit in the windows while we were studying. They were big windows that were cool when the wind blew.

Remember, I told you that none of the Derby water was any good. The school hauled the water for us in a tank wagon. There was a hydrant on the back of the wagon and all of us drank out of the same tin cup. The toilets were two outhouses, one for the girls and the other for the boys.

I inherited a trait that nearly killed my mother. I could not spell, never could, and never will. She would school me on my spelling words, morning and night. When I was old enough to have spelling, mother would take me to Derby in the car. Mother would give me my last lesson as I got out of the car and then she would cry all the way home.

Martha about 1932

(Thank God for Larry Johnson, director of research and my boss while I worked much later for Sun Oil Production Research. I said something about not being able to spell and he said the nicest thing that has ever been said to me. "John, we did not hire you to spell. We have other people to do that." My spelling is so bad that I can spell the same word three different ways in the same sentence.)

One day I was swinging on the back door of the Model "T" on the way to school when I fell out of the car and Mother ran over me. Fortunately Model "T"'s are light, and Derby sand roads were soft and I didn't get hurt. All the Derby kids either walked to school or rode horseback.

There were six grades taught in Derby. In the seventh grade you got to go to Pearsall school with the big kids. The bus to Pearsall was called the Chicken Coop. It looked just like a chicken coop. It was just about the size of an 8-foot bed pickup truck. The back was all closed in with heavy wire and boards and had two bench seats. There were roll-down curtains to keep out the cold, wind and rain. The entrance was from the front, just like present day school buses but I believe both doors were open like the UPS trucks now. Boy, it was cold and airy. I just couldn't wait to be old enough to ride the bus.

Scooter

I designed a scooter made from a board with skate wheels under it. It was like a modern skateboard except that it had a seat and handlebars. I used to ride it home from the store in Derby. I would ride it down the highway and pick up cigarette butts that I found on the road. Sometimes I would find one that was still smoking, and I could smoke it on the way home.

One day Dad came in and told Sid (my oldest brother) and me that he was having an "airplane" built for us to ride to school in. You know that the airplanes were very new and we didn't know what to expect. All we knew was that he was having it built at a blacksmith shop in Pearsall. The day finally came when he brought it home. It was a two-wheel gig (buggy) with a nice seat on it and the bottom of the seat would raise up making a place for us to put our lunches and books, as we were flying home, literally, with our one horsepower horse. Man, were we in style and the envy of everyone.

Dad

Our own buggy and being raised on the farm, it was no chore to hitch and unhitch the horse. The back of the buggy had a place under the seat where we carried our horse food for the day. Our own pickup truck.

Filling Station

Just across the highway from Grandma's, Dad and Mr. Ben Speer had built a filling station. It was a place of two rooms and a kitchen for the Speers to live in. I remember there was a Kohler light plant to furnish lights for the operation and run the air compressor. After all, any respectable filling station had to have free air and water for the cars, and believe me, they all needed it.

The Speers had two sons. One was named Ben and the other was Toppy. Ben went all through school with me. After a few years of running the filling station and store that was in it, Pop and Mr. Speer came to the parting of the ways. Mr. Speer loved his spirits too much. Pop took over running the filling station and hired a man named Sacadeus to run it for him. Mr. Speer took over the filling station on the north end of town.

The Store
Mother and Dad decided they had to do something more with the filling station. They had Sacadeus helping them, and I delivered groceries all over Derby to the Mexican families in our gig. I had stripped the bed off the gig and now it consisted of two tongues, the axle and two wheels and a little platform built on the two tongues so I could stand up and ride like Ben Hur. I delivered the groceries standing on the platform with the box of groceries between my legs, always taking the corners on one wheel. Sand would fly everywhere over the groceries and me. We ate dirty groceries in those days. Having to haul drinking water in barrels, who could waste much water for washing groceries? Just shake off the excess loose dirt before taking them in. Most of the Mexicans hauled water from our flowing well in open barrels with a board floating on top of the water to keep it from sloshing out. That was about 1-1/2 miles one way.

Mother decided to put in a Mexican food restaurant in the back of the store in the rooms where the Spears had lived. She would only run it on Saturday night. Ventura, Chona's mother, lived there on the farm and was the world's best cook of Mexican food. I know, I was raised on it. She and mother would cook the food on a kerosene stove. People would come down from Pearsall and the room was full every Saturday night. Times were hard then, but she made things go. Mother later said that the only money she made was enough to buy her boys suits.

One day, we will never know why, but Mrs. Speer came up dead. We think she took a whole lot of aspirin and that did her in. After that, Mr. Speer moved out to the Richey Ranch and lived in the guest house. In the mornings, he would drive the Chicken Coop, picking up kids on the route and those who came to the Derby school to get on, and then deliver them to school in Pearsall. On the return trip he took the bus home to the Richey Ranch, which was the end of the run.

I would ride that bus, after all I was in the seventh grade. As we would round the corner at the Humble gas station, I would dream of someday getting a job at that station and becoming the auto mechanic who could fix anything wrong with a car. I could give instant analysis of what was wrong with that car.

All this would keep my attention until we went in front of the Gilliam house. There the girl of my dreams lived, of course I never told her. Every time we drove by, I looked for Vera Pan. I thought she was the prettiest girl I had ever seen. She had another guy on her mind and didn't even know I existed. I used to even ride my horse to Pearsall on Saturday just because I knew she and her boyfriend would be riding horses around town. Hardly ever could find them.

John D in the seventh grade (holding sign) at Pearsall (1930-31), Mr. Sterling on the right

Mr. Sterling

When I was in the seventh grade in Pearsall we had desks that had a hole for an ink bottle. Mr. Sterling would have us do math problems on the blackboard. I never could do as well as he thought I should do. He would say, "You are so dumb I'm going to knock your block off with an ink bottle!" So much for political correctness. He had a crippling back injury that kept him in pain all of the time. He was mad and mean all of the time.

Model "T"

In my delivering of groceries, I had noticed a lot of old Model "T" Fords sitting around. They were junk and more junk. One of the kind Mexicans gave me my first Model "T" Ford and I promptly stripped off the body. Who needed a body on a car when there was a perfectly good seat on the top of the gas tank? That made the car light and fast. You could run with thin tires. Tires were the reason most of the old cars were junked. Tires cost too much. Now Dad had a filling station and stocked tire patch. I guess Dad thought that he was selling an awful lot of tire patch because it sure did disappear. Even the candy case got robbed on the way to robbing the patch supply. Dad was either awful good, dumb or blind. He never did see me. I could patch a slit in a tube that was six inches long. Put a patch on the inside and a patch on the outside and you could make a tire that would stay on on most any corner going full speed. Boy, that was living. Barney Oldfield didn't have a thing on me.

One day I rounded a corner so fast that I threw that 30 by 3½" tire right off that clinched rim. I was in my stripped-down car coming back from a grocery run. I stopped so fast, jumped off the car and grabbed the tire to let the air out of it. It was blown up as big as a football and I didn't know if Dad had enough patch in the store since I had borrowed the last from him. The tire was saved.

I became the Model "T" expert of Derby. I believe to this day that I can draw every part of a Model "T" from memory and almost put the exact dimensions on them. I used to go to Dilley to the city dump to get my cars. In the old days everything from cars to garbage was dumped at the city dump. You would take a wheel off this one, a tire off that one, search the gas tanks and find a little gas. You didn't have license plates, insurance, or even driver's licenses to worry about. Just crank up and drive home another chariot. People shop for new cars now days; I went to the dump and

Betsy, Sid, John D in the snow!

drove one home for free. I drove home my first one when I was about ten.

I had cars that I underslung, cut off for a short wheel base, with four exhausts coming straight out of the hood, making the most beautiful four stacks of flame 18 inches tall, and the most lovely music. Who ever had time to even think about such useless things as sports? That was for kids that didn't know the joy of being a grease monkey.

During the war, my Dad was very patriotic, he sold all of mother's extra cooking ware that was aluminum or steel and all of my 17 Model "T"s that I had stacked on a hill on the farm. He even sold the one that had the two speed Ruxel rear end in it. He ruined my life. I will never be the same again, but I loved him anyway because he did it for me and George, my sister Betsy's husband. Must have helped, we both made it home from the war.

Cadillac
When I got to be a little bit older, when I got out of school, I would go to Grandma's to play. My Uncle Otis Cook had an old 1916 model Cadillac car that had a flat truck bed on it. I could remember how the whole family would get on the back of Uncle Otis's Cadillac and off to Dilley we would go to Sunday School and church at the Dilley Methodist Church. Those were great times.

Finally the day came when the old Cadillac was put in Grandma's barn. Everything centered around Grandma's house when we were kids. I would sneak out to the barn and ooh and aah over that wonderful piece of machinery. It even had a built-in air compressor to air the tires in case of flats, and there were many. There was a shiny knob on the dash used to pump air in the gas tank so the gas would go to the carburetor. To start the engine, you had to pump up the gas tank with air pressure. After it started, the air pump would keep up the job. I believe it even had a pump that pumped grease to all the fittings so the Cadillac could be greased from the driver's seat. Man, how I loved to study that engine. It had four cylinders that were separated and with a brass cylindrical water tank around each cylinder. There was brass all over it. What a car.

I guess that Uncle Otis thought the thing had died, times were getting hard, and my heart broke one day when I slipped into the barn to study that masterpiece. It had been stripped, the engine taken apart and all the brass had been removed. They might as well have removed my heart too. The remains of the bones of that picked chicken were drug out behind the barn, even behind the cow pen, and it didn't even get a decent burial.

I would go out there every afternoon after school and work on it. Finally I decided that I was going to get that beautiful transmission out of it. That box was a great big thing and had the two gear shift levers on the left side. I just couldn't let something that beautiful to me just lay there and die. How could I get it out? It had the wheels off and the frame was sitting flat on the ground. I had to get under the car to work on the transmission, then the idea hit me: Tunnel under. After all I was a schooled expert on tunneling. We learned that in Derby school.

I dug the tunnel where I could work on the old car. All I had was a pair of pliers, a Ford monkey wrench, a hammer and chisel. I worked on that thing at least two years, all the time gaining in my knowledge of mechanics. I had Concho as a teacher. He had taught me the wonders of how to split a nut with the chisel when you didn't have the proper tools.

Frio River Flood
In about 1934 we had the great Frio River flood. It was so great that it floated the railroad track off the embankment and out into Dad's

field. When that happened nobody could cross the river, even on the railroad bridge. (During smaller floods people would drive their cars across the railroad bridge.) About that time a barnstormer flew down in a single engine monoplane. It had a front seat that was wide enough for two people to sit on and a rear seat with room for

Frio River flood

one. He came down and landed in Pop's field just north of the house and south of Betsy's Lake. He landed parallel with the rows. There was a band that came out of San Antonio, and was supposed to be going south. He ferried them across the river, one musician at a time. They landed in a field just north of Dilley. I helped him; my job was to hold on to the wing when he would rev up the engine and turn around in the plowed field. He took all of the band members and their instruments across. I never will forget when he loaded up the bass fiddle. He finally got them all across. He stayed there for a day or two taking people across the river. Then one day came the payback. He got me in that airplane and flew me to Pearsall. He landed in a field out close to where the cemetery was. We went into town and he bought my dinner. I thought I was the biggest thing that ever was. Lots of aviators were called Mac, back then, and I wanted to be called Mac.

Railroad crew working the flood

Turkey

We had an old turkey on the farm that hated Betsy. It roosted on top of the chimney. Any time that turkey saw Betsy it would fly down to where she was and harass her. One time Betsy was way down by the well and the turkey flew several hundred yards to attack her. We finally cooked the turkey for Thanksgiving one year, but nobody could eat her.

Cousin Mary Frances with the turkey

95

Chapter 12
Christmas at Grandma's

Grandma's was the center of everything exciting to me when I was young.

Light Plant
Besides the fun of exploring the old Cadillac that belonged to Uncle Otis and building stuff in Mr. King's work shop with Harold Crawford, there was Grampa's Delco light plant that was located out in the front yard between Grampa's house and Uncle Otis's. Electricity had finally come to Derby and the light plant was no longer run. There it sat in all of its glory with those big glass battery cells, 16 of them. One had some little balls that would go up and down according to the electric charge of the batteries. Actually, depending on the specific gravity of the liquid in the cell, a different colored ball would rise. These balls would indicate the gravity of the cells and thereby show how much the cell was charged up. I spent a lot of time studying the whole system and I became fascinated with electricity.

Windmill
Grampa had a windmill that still stands to this day. Trees have all grown their limbs up through the tower but there it stands with the windmill head still sticking up through the trees looking like the king of the roost. The blade is closed off or tied down so the direction of the wind shifts the tail around but the blade is always turned 90 degrees to the direction of the wind. This action keeps the blade from turning but every once in a while, the wind will suddenly shift and will catch the blade before the tail has had a chance to respond and the blade will spring into action. The windmill is no longer hooked up to the pump. The well is no longer in use at all. Grampa

use to have a bunch of cattle and they had to have water, wind or no wind.

To be sure there was water, Grampa had a Fuller and Johnson Pump engine. It could be hooked up to the pump rods and the windmill disconnected. This engine would even run on kerosene. It had a big fly wheel with a handle that was used for a crank and when the engine would start, the action would make the handle retract. To start it you would check the dry cell batteries to be sure the charge was OK and see if the coil was buzzing when it was supposed to. Then you would slowly hand crank the engine until the pump rods were lifted and then with the crank going over top dead center you could crank the engine real fast as you prayed it would start. The weight of the pump rods would make the engine run fast after it had passed dead center and it would start.

Clara Bennett

Water Tank and Cistern

Grampa had a great big wooden water tank with the bottom about three feet off the ground. The sides of the old tank were gone when we were kids and only the bottom was still there. It must have been 10 feet in diameter and was the center of activities for all of us cousins. There was also a cistern in the yard that must have been 10 feet in diameter and 15 feet deep. It was all lined with brick. Where the top of the cistern came up out of the ground, the side walls gradually tapered inward so that the opening to the cistern at the top was no bigger than four feet in diameter. A thick wooden deck was built on top with a trap door so you could climb down the cistern on a ladder to clean it out. This was my job on at least one occasion. There was a hand pump mounted on the top deck to pump water up with. As I told you before, the surface or shallow water was no good, so you used rainwater to wash your hair and water the plants. Grandma had hundreds of plants and I was always pumping water for them.

Bathhouse

Now the bathhouse. No self-respecting Englishman would have one of those filthy things in the house. There was a separate building for the bathtub and the kerosene-heated hot water heater. This building was connected to the main building by brick sidewalks at least 20 feet wide, and bricks completely encircled the house. A milk separating room was in the same building as the bathtub. The hot water heater served the washroom for the cream separator parts wash up.

Milk

Grandma had a bunch of cows. She would milk the cows and bring the milk into the separating room, and I would crank up the separator. The head would spin at a terrific speed, and the cream being lighter density than the milk would be separated by centrifugal force. The milk came out one spout and cream out the other. She put the cream in a 10 gallon milk can. When the can was full, off to the depot it would go to be shipped off to San Antonio to market. Next thing you knew, off to San Antonio Grandma would go shopping. She had a lifetime pass on the railroad.

Milk separator like Grandma's

One day she went in to the dispatcher in San Antonio and said, "I want to go to Derby." He said, "The train doesn't stop in Derby." She said, "I'm Mrs. John Bennett." He looked it up and said, "Oh." The train stopped in Derby and the conductor took her to her door.

Electricity Book

Grampa gave me a book named *The American Boys' Book of Electricity*[2]. How I loved that book. I studied it all the time and learned all kinds of good things. I found out that with a light bulb, some wire, and a "hot shot" battery like that used on the Fuller and John-son pump engine, I could make the light bulb work. I found out that with the same battery hooked up to the Model "T" coil on the pump engine, you could knock the fool out of yourself. One day Grampa came home from the Depot and opened the iron gate. I had hooked the Model "T" coil to the gate. When he opened the gate, he learned how much I had learned about electricity. Poor Grampa thought it was wonderful.

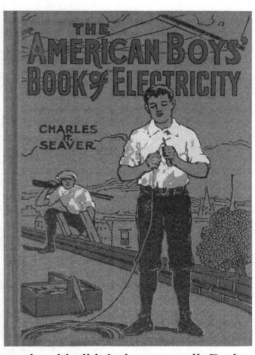

Radio

He used to have an Atwater Kent radio. It was battery operated and it didn't do very well. Derby was too far from San Antonio to receive a good signal. My book showed how to make radio antennas and I made all kinds of antennas and we would hang them in the windows in his house. They never did do any better, but he made out like it did.

---

2 Charles H. Seaver, *The American Boys' Book of Electricity*, (Galveston: David McKay Co, 1916, 1921.)

Model "T" Coil

Then the devil of DeVilbiss went to work. A little knowledge is a dangerous thing. One day Grampa was sleeping in his chair—at least he made out like he was. I very carefully untied his shoes and slipped my Motel "T" Coil wires in his shoes and then laced them up again. When I turned on the electricity, poor Grampa danced all over the room. He should have whipped me but he thought that I was smart. From then on, I was trying to get everyone.

Grandma's Cat

Well the old devil was working again, and with all those cousins, I knew that some of them were going to get hot pants from my Model "T" coil. Grandma had some chairs with wooden bottoms with lots of holes in them and I had very carefully woven wires in the seat of one of them. Some of them got it, and in a lull of the rejoicing at my success, Grandma's favorite house cat came to see all the excitement. To this day I will swear it was not me that threw the switch. My dear deceased brother Sid, he threw the switch. I had merely loaded the gun. That poor cat, the fur stood straight up and started flying out its body.

When we realized what had been done, all the cousins immediately went into a prayer meeting. We were all church members and knew the power of prayer and we sure tried to do our best. The next day, that poor cat was as dead as it could be. That shock took up all nine lives of that cat in just a second. We found the cat out in the yard out under the big water tank table. I don't know who took it out there and nobody ever told Grandma.

The Model "T" coil was an excellent toy. We always had one hooked up so if someone leaned on the car and we hit the switch, the wire that drug on the ground completed the circuit and the victim was fried.

Christmas

Christmas came. All the cousins were up there. The toys for all the cousins were always ordered out of Sears catalog for our Christmas. Poor Grandma had read to me a hundred times about a little steam engine in the catalog. I would go get the catalog and she would read. When the toys came, they were always put in the parlor behind the piano and then the door was locked. Fortunately, we knew where the key was hidden and we all had our toys practically worn out before Christmas. When time came, Uncle Otis and Uncle Roy would put up the Christmas tree in the parlor and someone had to stand guard when the candles on the tree were lit. Boy what a Christmas! Grandma would cook her famous lemon pies and mince meat pies. To become the wife of a Bennett man, it is necessary for the girl to carry on the tradition of making little lemon pies.

Lemon Pie Recipe[3]
Here is a recipe for the lemon pies from my nephew's cookbook, modified for modern cooking methods:

Lemon Curd:
6 lg. lemons, juice & rind   ¼ lb. butter
3 c. sugar
6 lg. eggs or 7 med., beaten to blend

Grate rind from all the lemons; then juice them, making sure there are no seeds. Put lemon juice, lemon rinds, and sugar in a medium sauce-pan. Bring to a boil. After mixture boils and thickens to the consistency of syrup, remove from heat. Add hot mixture, a very small amount at a time, to beaten eggs, beating well. Return to heat and cook until thick like pudding. Remove from heat and stir in butter, mixing until melted. Store in refrigerator. Prepare your favorite pie crust or use Bebe's Pastry Dough recipe. Roll out on floured work surface. Cut into small rounds with pastry cutter (these should fit halfway up the sides and on the bottoms of regular-sized muffin tins.) Place dough into muffin tins and press. Fill each pastry with one heaping teaspoon of Lemon Curd. Bake at 400° until dough is browned, 10 to 12 minutes. Cool slightly and gently lift out.

---

3 Pie recipe from: Blue Bonnet Café, *Still Cookin' 80th Anniversary Cookbook,* (Kearney, NE: Morris Press Cookbooks, 2009), 146-147. Used by permission.

Bebe's Pastry Dough for Lemon Tarts [4]

3 c. flour   1½ c. Crisco

1½ tsp. salt   9 T. ice water

Mix the flour, salt, and Crisco together with a pastry blender or fork until a coarse meal is formed. Add the iced water one tablespoon at a time until incorporated, being careful not to over work the dough. Refrigerate the dough for at least 1 hour. Roll out on a floured surface and use as described in the Lemon Pie Recipe.

By Betsy Kemper

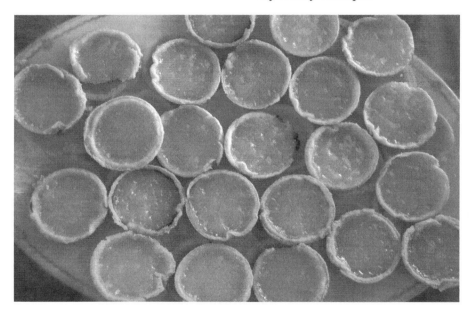

---

4 Pastry dough recipe from: Blue Bonnet Café, *Still Cookin' 80th Anniversary Cookbook*, (Kearney, NE: Morris Press Cookbooks, 2009), 167. Used by permission.

Grandma's house in 1959

Chapter 13
Life on the Farm

Canning

Back when I was just a kid we had a big canning operation at Grandma's. All of the female relatives and all of us kids would get together there. We had a big operation. They would can up a whole bunch of tomatoes, putting them in cans, and sealing them. The cans always had a hole right in the middle of the lid. After they put the cans in the cooker they cooked those things until they were all well and done. Then Uncle Otis took his soldering iron and soldered up that hole in the middle of the can lid to seal it. We didn't know then that that was a poisonous thing to do. We have read in later years where this bunch of people in a boat were trying to go across the northern part of Canada. They got locked in the ice and couldn't move, and they all died. Later they found out why they died—they died from lead poisoning from food that had been canned and the hole sealed up with a soldering iron. Luckily none of us ever had any trouble that we know of from that food they used to

Mother on the back porch

105

put up down there. Boy, it was a big occasion. It was a fun thing when they'd do all of that canning at Grandma's.

Slaughtering Hogs

There was another thing that was a big operation. When it got cold it was time to slaughter a hog. The railroad boxcars had big boards called "drain boards" that were about three feet wide and as long as the door was wide. They would put one in there to block the bottom of the door. When the car was loaded to that level they'd put another board in there and block the next three feet. They could blow grain or corn or anything they wanted to in that railroad car for shipment. They had a lot of those "drain boards" around. We used them when we were kids because when we'd dig our caves we'd lay those drain boards across the top of our cave and that was the ceiling.

When it came good old winter time it was time to butcher a hog. They'd get out a great big old cast iron kettle that they used to put the clothes in on wash day. Well that kettle served lots of purposes. When it came time to butcher the hog, they would throw all of the extra fat meat in the kettle. Course the fire would get hot and it would cook the fat out of the pork, and they would call what was left "chicharrónes". It's kinda like eating the white part of bacon. Well they put all of the fat meat into that big pot. They'd heat it up and boil it until they got all of the grease out of it. Later on they'd put pork, hams, and things like that in a barrel. They'd completely cover that meat in the barrel with rendered fat (lard). It was a liquid and they would use that fat to cover up the hams. They could keep hams for a long time smothered in that fat.

Well, slaughtering hogs was quite an occasion. One of the men would hit the hog in the head with the blunt end of an ax to kill it. I can remember them putting the old pig down on one of those drain boards. They'd throw scalding hot water on him and wash him off real good. Then they had a big knife and they'd scrape him and that'd cut all of the hair off of him. They'd wind up with nothing but skin. Then they'd butcher the thing and cut it up. Eventually they made sausage out of him, and stuff like that. When they'd make sausage they'd grind that pork all up, and course they had to add all of the sage and all of that stuff they usually put in it. I imagine the ladies know what goes in it. They'd make the sausage, and some of it they'd put in the entrails. They would take the entrails out of the hog and they would scrape the entrails and it would look like clear skin. They'd put that on the snout of the sausage stuffer. It had a crank with an auger in it. You'd put that sausage in the top of it and turn that crank, and it would squirt that sausage out through that snout and it would fill that entrail full of sausage. Then ever so often they'd take a cord and tie it up tight around the entrail and it would separate it into links. On the back porch they had a pipe that hung down a couple of feet from the ceiling. It was probably eight feet above the porch floor. They would tie the sausage up on that piece of pipe. I don't know what in the heck kept it from spoiling. I think they smoked it before they hung it up. I don't know too much about that part of it.

They also would make a slab of sausage, maybe six inches wide and maybe a foot long and maybe an inch thick. They'd cover that slab of sausage with cheesecloth and then hang that slab up on the pipe. I remember seeing that stuff hang there, it seems like all winter long. When they needed some sausage they'd cut off a piece of that slab and cook it for breakfast.

40 Mules
My Daddy had a big pen, and he had 40 mules. That is a lot of mules. The pen was on a sloping hill. Why in the world they ever did it the way they did, I don't know. On the bottom end of the hill was a big barn. They'd put cottonseed in the barn, and all kinds of feed for those mules. They had a great big old round cement tank in the middle of the mule pen. It must have been at least 15 feet in diameter, and it had walls on it that were maybe four inches thick. I guess those walls stood up at least three feet high. There was a pipe that stood up in the middle of the tank and had a float. Whenever water would come in through the valve at the bottom it would run into that tank and the water would rise in that tank and raise the float up. After it got so high the float would close the water off. That's where all of these mules drank, out of that water tank. Oh, I've gotten in that tank a jillion times to work on that valve and fix it. Oh, I hated that place!

Now you can imagine feeding all of those mules. They had some feed racks in the middle of that mule pen. They were shaped like the letter "X". They were nailed together about three feet off the ground and the upper part made a place where you could throw hay. It had slots up there and the mules could reach up there and pull hay through those slots and eat and eat, and did they eat. That doggoned pen sometimes would get a foot deep with old hay and mule manure and cow manure and everything else. When it rained I had to walk through that mess. Oh, Lord, I hated it! I hated it with a passion.

Milking Cows

Why my daddy didn't have sense enough to put the cow lot up on the upper part of that sloping hill instead of down on the lower part I don't know. That's where the cows had to be milked—down in that milk pen, where we had the calves. They'd be out there in the mule pen and we'd bring 'em around to the part where the milk pen was. The calves would run up to the mama and start sucking the milk. Well, what you were supposed to do is put a rope around the calf's neck and tie him off so he couldn't get to the cow. Then you could sit there and milk her while she was eating out of the feed trough. Well, that was a lot of trouble. Gosh, that was a lot of trouble. I was pretty strong back then and the little old calves weren't very big, so I'd just turn them upside down and put them in that trough. They'd be laying in that trough with their feet up in the air just a-bellering and raising all kinds of hell. Then the cows would get all excited and they wouldn't let the milk come down, and I had a terrible time milking. They would kick me. Oh lord, they would kick! I'd get mad and I'd hit them with the bucket. I had more dents in the milk bucket than you could imagine. And the flies, my gosh! They were not by the millions, but billions. We had more flies than we have national debt. Oh, Lord! Before I'd take the milk in the house, I'd have to reach down with my hand and scoop out all of the dead flies so Mama wouldn't see them. Sometimes they'd give me a reprieve. I'd have a date and I'd want to go on my date kinda early. Well, I was supposed to milk, and Mama would say, "Well, just turn the calves in with the cows." So, I'd do that and I'd be happy.

You know, I was a little older than Harry. I had to do some things that Harry didn't have to do. You see, he went to high school and took a course in agriculture. I didn't take a course in agriculture; I wasn't interested in agriculture. He found out that you should have a milk shed with a nice concrete floor. It should be on top of the hill instead of at the bottom where all of the drainage ran through it. And you should have a water hose to wash the thing out so it would be nice and neat. That's the reason he turned out to be such a good farmer and I didn't.

Milk Cooler

Back then they didn't have any refrigerators. So, on the back porch they had a milk cooler stand. Now visualize the top of this milk cooler stand having a galvanized pan on the very top of it, maybe three feet long and two feet wide. It had sidewalls that came up about three inches. Now, set that galvanized pan on a wooden shelf the size of the pan. And the wooden shelf would have boards that would come up on the side as high as the sidewalls of the pan were. Now, if you visualize this cooler having about three shelves, and each shelf being separated by the height of a milk bucket, maybe a foot. Then on each corner there would be a leg that attached to the top of the cooler and sloped own to the floor. The side walls on the milk cooler kinda sloped out. The second shelf was a little wider and longer that the top one, and the next shelf was a little wider and longer than that. So you had four posts that held this thing up. Then they would wrap a piece of cloth like a bed sheet around this contraption. The sheet was fixed so that it came clean to the top, and it folded over into that pan on the top. They'd set some bricks in the pan to hold it in place. The sheet would come on around, and they overlapped it in the front. If they wanted to get into the compartments they would open the sheet up and hold it back like curtains. They would slide pans of milk in there. That's where they kept the milk until it had sat there long enough for the cream to rise to the top. They had to keep it cool to do that, and what would keep it cool is they would fill that top pan full of water. The water would soak up that sheet and go over the top and gradually soak down that sheet clean to the bottom where they had another pan down below. They cooled that milk by evaporation of the water. They did a lot of that back in the early days because that was the only refrigeration they had.

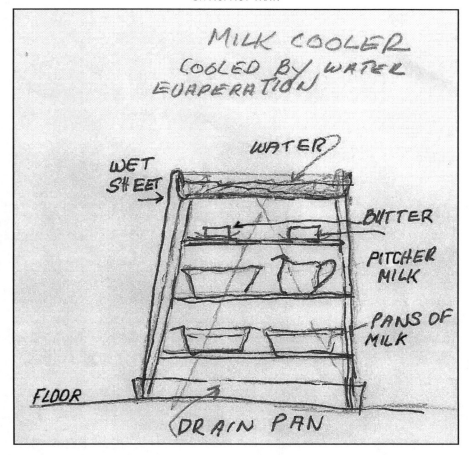

I remember that I had a gallon jug made out of a clay. There was a place almost to San Antonio where they manufactured these jugs. Everybody had to have one of these jugs 'cause that's what you put your drinking water in. Now the outside of the jug was covered with several layers of burlap. You'd wet that burlap, and as the water in the burlap would evaporate away it would keep that jug cool. Pretty good refrigerating system. That was the same principle that they used on the milk cooler.

Carbide Plant

We had a carbide plant. Whenever you wanted to find out what was new in the country you went down to Sidney Bennett's farm, 'cause he had it. We didn't have any electricity, and he needed some lights.

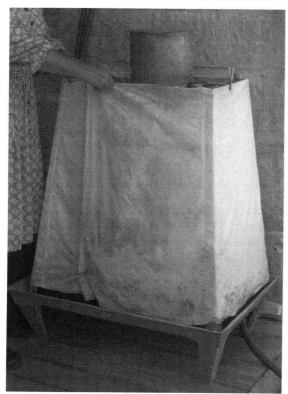

Milk cooler similar to ours, except ours had wooden legs

So he had installed a great big carbide plant there in the yard. Carbide is a rock (calcium carbide) that reacts with water to form acetylene gas. It is very explosive. Besides gas, the reaction also created a white sludge (calcium hydroxide, or caustic lime). Acetylene burns with a very bright, white light.

The carbide plant had a container about four feet in diameter and it must have been eight feet long. It was all buried in the ground, except about six inches that stuck up out of the ground. It had a big lid that you could raise up, and expose all the guts down there. Now in this big container, in the bottom of it was water. Above the water was a container that you put carbide in. On top of this carbide container was a cylinder, a dome that went over the top of it that would float up and down. The floating dome contained acetylene gas. The carbide made the acetylene that burned to provide light in the house. As you used it up, that inverted dome would gradually settle down. The bottom of that dome was in the water, so the gas couldn't get out thataway. Being as the dome was turned upside down the gas was captured in there. So that made a floating reservoir. As you burned the gas out it would gradually settle. When it got down there so far it would hit a trigger mechanism that was on the container that held the carbide. The trigger mechanism would

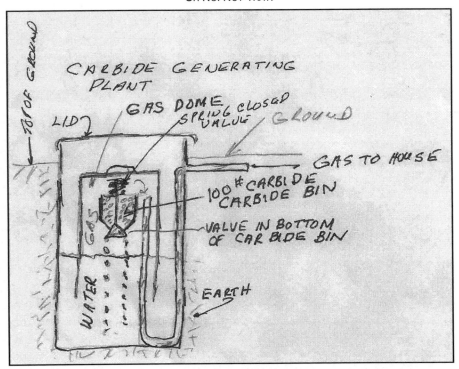

drop a little of the carbide out of the bottom of the carbide container into the water. It would make more acetylene gas, and the gas would cause the cylinder to float up again. So the cylinder was constantly floating up and down. The weight of the cylinder created the pressure to push the gas into the house and it also served as a storage tank for the gas. It worked real good. You'd put a hundred pounds of carbide in that thing and it'd last a pretty good while. Eventually you'd use all of the carbide up.

Whitewash

Dad was a farmer, and he wanted the farm to be perfect. He didn't make much money, and nearly all the money he earned he spent on beautifying the farm. Dad didn't want a weed to grow up underneath a fence anywhere on the farm. He wanted it to be a showplace. We had the house sitting on top of the hill. That hill at one time was a flint rock hill. Some of those flint rocks were as big as six inches in diameter. Dad built four posts, two on each side of the driveway, where you drove up under some big trees, and two on the

112

far end of the yard. Those were all on the south side in front of the house. When you crossed the Frio River bridge, which was at least a mile away, you could see that house sittin' on the hill. We didn't have any great big trees at the time, but they were growing.

We used lime from the carbide plant to paint the trunks of the trees. But mostly, Dad wanted every one of those big rocks that lined the yard painted. When you'd come across the Frio River on the bridge and you looked up there it looked like a cemetery, and all of those rocks were tombstones. To me it was hideous, 'cause I had to do the painting. As time went on Dad decided that he wanted to get rid of the little rocks that were on the hill, so they'd mark off a place maybe ten feet by ten feet. My job for the weekend was to rake all the rocks up in that area, pile them up and haul them off, to where it was nothing but a nice smooth spot. The next weekend I'd have another spot marked off for me that I had to clean up. Then eventually Dad decided that he would like to have some grass. But he didn't want Bermuda grass, 'cause he was afraid that it'd wash down in the field, and that would be terrible. So he decided he was going to have St. Augustine, because we had lots of water. He had dirt hauled out of the field and put up where the house was to plant that St. Augustine grass. He must have hauled hundreds of wagon loads of dirt up there. So we had St. Augustine grass all over the top of that hill.

Orchard
Then he decided he wanted an orchard, so he planted some citrus trees. I'm telling you we had lemons that were at least six inches in diameter. And we had grapefruit trees that grew grapefruit six inches in diameter. And we had pomegranate trees that grew great big pomegranates, but I don't think anybody ever ate those. And we had tangerines and oranges. The well was flowing all of that water and we just irrigated all of that stuff on the hill. To keep the trees from freezing in the winter time Dad would have dirt stacked around the trunks of the trees maybe two feet high. That would keep the trunk from freezing. We had some beautiful trees up there.

Hogs
We had hogs. Lord, I hated those hogs! Like I said, Dad spent an awful lot of money making that place beautiful, hauling all of that

dirt, planting all of those trees. He'd get in debt. When he did there was only one way to pay out, and that was to raise hogs. In my life-time he did that at least twice, maybe three times. He'd get a bunch of hogs and start raising them. I had to take care of the hogs. I was a midwife to the hogs. I've delivered more hogs than you can shake a stick at. I'd reach up in that old sow and grab ahold of those pigs and pull them out. Oh Lord, I've delivered lots of hogs! That's the reason farm boys knew all about the facts of life. They'd put a post out in the middle of the hog pen and wrap burlap sacks around that post. We'd soak that burlap with old crankcase oil. Boy, those hogs would come up to that post and rub up and down and rub that crankcase oil on their skin wherever they'd get itchy, and that would take care of the itch for them.

Dad wanted his hogs to have the best. So we had two barrels, and every day I had to put corn in the barrels. It would get in there, and it had water in it, and it would sour. Stink, my gosh it would stick something terrible! They liked that sour corn. I remember one time they had a hog pen out parallel with the mule pen, on the west side of the mule pen. Another time he put hog pens under the big shed, and I had to take care of them down there. It's no wonder I wasn't a farmer.

Chickens

We had a chicken coop. You know farmers have got to have eggs to eat, and Mother had a bunch of chickens. You'd go in there and get the eggs, and when you'd come out you'd be covered with fleas. I hated it with a passion. You'd go to get the eggs, and then you'd have to be defleaed. Mother used to have a 22 rifle. She was a deadeye shot with that 22. It was a single shot 22, and whenever she wanted a chicken she just went out in the yard and shot its head off. Other people used to put the chicken down on the ground and put a broomstick across its neck and stand on each end of the broomstick, and pull up on the chicken's feet until you pulled the neck in two. Oh, it was gruesome.

Watermelon Stand

Before I was in high school I would sell watermelons. I had a stand that straddled the fence. I would get 10 or 15 watermelons and sell them for 30 or 40 cents apiece to people who came down the highway. If I sold some watermelons I was in high cotton.

Pear Burners

In Derby there were lots of prickly pears. Huge ones. The cows loved to eat them, but the thorns were a problem. Cousin Lottie was the bookkeeper for a Mr. Woodard. He built pear burners. A pear burner had a tank you could put gasoline in. You pumped it up so the pressure made the gasoline come out through a flexible hose with a burner on the end. The burner was a pipe with a straight section and then a coil which wrapped around the straight section. You would set the gasoline on fire and the fire would vaporize the gasoline that was still in the pipe. It would make a flame that shot out about three feet. You would use it to burn the thorns off the prickly pear so the cows could eat it. Every farmer had two or three pear burners. They are probably propane now and use a smaller burner.

Fires from the Railroad

One of the biggest fears Daddy had on the farm was fires caused by the railroad. The train cars had journal bearings. The end of the axle

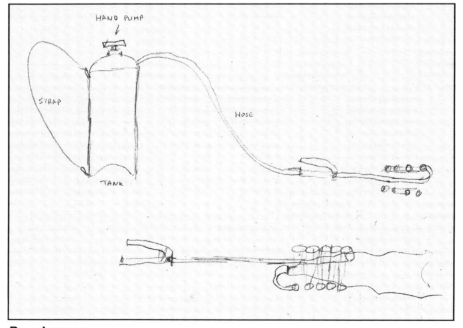

Pear burner

went through a metal box that was filled with cotton waste. The train crew stuffed cotton waste into the box and poured thick heavy oil on it. The oily cotton would lubricate the bearings. There were lots of hobos back during the Depression, and they would take the cotton waste out of the journal boxes and use it on their campfires. The unlubricated journal boxes would get extremely hot. When a train went down the track the hot boxes would throw off sparks and set the fields on fire.

Storm Cellar

Daddy was also scared to death of storms. Being crippled, he couldn't move very fast if a storm came. He built a storm cellar out of concrete out beside the garage. It stuck about three feet above the ground and went five feet below. One end had concrete stairs and a strong door. It was a nice shelter.

I played a lot in the storm cellar. I took a base from an old Singer sewing machine and mounted a table top on it. Then I had a little electric motor mounted on it with a drive shaft with several pulleys on it. I had a belt that ran the butter churn. I had to churn butter nearly every day. The motor also ran a grinder and some other things.

I never will forget one time Daddy was sitting in the bedroom during a storm. A strong wind blew a piece of tin off of a shed and it sailed right toward the window where he was sitting. Just before it reached the house it sailed up and went over the roof. I can still hear him saying, "I like to got my head cut off."

The Bank

Pop would go to Dilley to see Mr. Forrest Avant at the bank to ask for a loan. He couldn't walk, so Sid would go into the bank for him. It was like begging. Sid, bless his time, sure hated to do that. Pop would get $15 a week to live on and pay the farm hands.

Workshop

I had a workshop on the farm. It was an old house with a lean-to on the side. I had some old blacksmith equipment and a wrench, a hammer, a pair of pliers, and a chisel. A light switch in the kitchen in the main house turned on the yard light and my shop light.

116

Whenever my parents wanted me to come in, about 11 o'clock at night, they would turn my lights off.

Car with Bicycle Tires

I took the front axle of a Model "T" to Dilley and had it cut in two, and 18 inches or more removed. Dad took it back to Dilley and had it welded back together. Then I took the front wheels of a Model "T" and drilled the hubs so I could put bicycle spokes in it and mount bicycle wheels. I was so proud of those wheels. I put more Model "T" wheels on the back and made a little car. It had a motorcycle frame and engine in the middle. A motorcycle chain went to the rear axle. The whole car was about 6 feet long and about 3-1/2 feet wide. The frame was made of 1 inch galvanized steel pipe. I rode it all the way to Pearsall and back. In my triumphant return to home I was speeding too fast. I went around a curve on the farm and the wheels collapsed. Broke my heart.

Shed

That's about the main thing that went on, except for rebuilding the thrashing machines and the wagons and hay bailers. We did that under a big old shed. Pop had a huge shed with a big roof. Below the edge of the roof was an airspace of about 18 inches, and then below that there were eaves about 36 inches wide that stuck out on the sides. There was a huge block of wood—the trunk of a live oak tree that was our workbench. An old drill press was mounted on one of the posts.

The shed was built with big, long cedar posts that still had the bark on them. We'd go out there and get some of the cedar bark off of it and rumple it between our hands. Then we'd put it in brown paper and roll up a cigarette. The shed had a little platform built on top of the roof trusses where we could go and smoke our cedar cigarettes. It's a wonder we didn't die.

You can understand why I never was in sports. I went to high school in Pearsall, and I rode the bus home. I had to get home in time to take care of all of my chores. And I had a lot of chores. So I didn't have time to stay after school and indulge in sports. I had to get home and tend to my work. Nearly everything about that farm I hated. But in my dreams today nearly all of my dreams are centered back on that farm.

Chapter 14
"Dumbest Farm Boy That Ever Lived"

With a title like that from a boy's father, how could he possibly succeed at farming? In fact, who wanted to succeed at farming? My two brothers did.

My oldest brother, Sid (Sidney Jr.), was studying to be a lawyer. He was studying in San Antonio, living with my Aunt Bess Ward, mother's sister, and driving one of the finest Model "T" Fords there ever was. It even had an electric starter and had pretty good pick-up. At least some of the old family pictures had some pretty good lookers in them but we don't talk about that any more.

I got pneumonia and almost died, so Sid came home from school and never did go back. Law wasn't his thing. He was a farmer, and I will always think, the world's best. He stayed home and started farming some of the land that belonged to Grandma.

Jobs on the Farm
Me, I had to do all kind of jobs on the farm. I had to chop wood and bring it in for the stove and fireplace. I was supposed to bring in kindling so mother would have something to start the fires with and enough wood to keep the fires going all day and night. The wood was mesquite, which is very hard, and the kindling was mesquite bark and twigs. How my mother could start fires with the sorry lot of kindling that I would bring in for her, I do not know. I probably caused her to cry a lot of times besides the times when I couldn't learn my spelling.

I've told you how I hated milking cows and delivering pigs and dealing with mule manure. Now, Dad thought that I was a dumb farm boy. I was a dumb farm boy all right, because I never studied agriculture in high school under Ray Chappel like Harry, my younger brother did. After I went off to A&M college, Harry found out the cow pen should be up on top of the hill with good drainage, a milk stall, a separate pen for the calf, and even a cement floor with a hose and a drain trench to wash out the manure. He topped it all off with a milk shed and with sides to keep out the blowing rain. You see, Harry was smart, and when he went to A&M, he made excellent grades. One day he called Dad and told him he was coming home to farm. See what a little education would do for you.

I had to get my own education when it came to farming. I found out that if I drove a nail straight up in the cultivator tongue and watched the shadow cast by the nail, it was time to go eat when the shadow was the shortest. We had mule-pulled cultivators that had swinging stirrups to put your feet in. When you were cultivating cotton, you were supposed to swing the cultivator arms so you would not plow up the cotton. Now in my striving to broaden my education, I already knew I wasn't going to be no stupid farmer. If I plowed up the cotton on the end of the row where Dad could see it, he would throw me out of the field and make me go help Concho work on the farm machinery. Dumb me.

Farm Equipment
Help Concho I did. We had a baling machine that had to be rebuilt. It had 4 by 4 by 3/8 inch angles on all four corners of the baler and they had to be replaced. Each angle had to have at least 20 holes drilled in them and some were at least 3/4 inch size. Now that was a heck of a task for an old man and a small young man to do. We started out with the only tools that we had. Electric hand drills hadn't even been invented yet. We would take a punch and hit it as hard as we could. Then we would use a hand brace, like you use to drill wood with, and a great big old steel bit like was used in the hand-turned blacksmith type post drill. That was work.

Concho and I made a hay baler that was excellent. We must have made a million blocks for the baler because if you didn't drop those blocks just at the right time, that baler ram would eat those blocks up like it was hungry. (A block was a wood piece that fit between the bales of hay.) We were always rebuilding everything that ran on the farm.

We rebuilt entire mule-drawn wagons, making new beds with wings of wood, and replacing the original axle tongues with pipe. The wagons had to be in first-class shape to haul the heavy loads of un-thrashed peanuts to the thrashers. Equipment that was needed on the farm that Dad didn't have, Concho and I built.

This was when Dad began to believe that there might be something other than farming that I could do. I talked him into buying me a 1/6 horsepower electric motor which I have to this day. I got the parts off a bicycle and put the big pedal sprocket on the shaft of the fly-wheel of the blacksmith drill. The electric motor ran the rear wheel of the bicycle with a belt. The tire was removed and the rim made an excellent pulley for the belt of the motor. The bicycle chain was from the rear wheel to the drive sprocket on the drill press. We now had one of the finest electric-driven drill presses ever on a farm.

Dad was one of the first farmers in the area to plant peanuts. Every year it was a job to rebuild the peanut thrashers. We made parts and I learned to work very fast. When they thrashed peanuts, the peanuts were plowed up, turned upside down to dry. When they were ready,

Dad's first peanut thrasher, about 1933

all the farmers around would rent out their wagons by the day to haul the peanuts. In those days the thrasher stayed in one place and the peanut vines were hauled to it. The thrasher would have its rear wheels chocked, the tractor would be unhooked from the thrasher, turned around and lined up so the belt could be used to run the thrasher by the tractor. This was a very time consuming job, and meantime the cost of the 6 or 8 wagons hired by the day was going on. If the thrasher would break, Dad would say, "Hurry, don't you know how much this is costing while you are fooling around?" I got where I worked very fast.

Then came the day that Dad said, "I have got to have another thrasher and a tractor, but I can't afford to buy the thrasher and the tractor, too." The next chapter has to be treated special. That was back in 1934, my junior year in high school (10th grade).

Chapter 15
Peanut Thrasher
1934

This thrasher is very important for the effect it had on modern farming machinery. If your knowledge of machinery consists of running a fishing reel and you do not understand what makes the line leveling mechanism work, then this chapter on peanut thrashing may be too complicated for you. You may skip it with a clear conscience. (I couldn't spell that word and had to ask my tutor and helpmate. Without her, the spelling would be so bad you couldn't read this. When I am really stuck is when I can't spell good enough to be able to look the word up in the dictunary.)

Dad now had faith in Concho's and my ability to do unusual things, especially since the hay baler. One day he said that he needed another thrasher, but you can see by the date, the country was right in the middle of a terrible depression. He said that he thought he could swing the thrasher, but he didn't know how he could get the tractor that was necessary to pull and run the thrasher.

I remembered that Aunt Ella and Uncle Roy Howell had a big seven-passenger Buick that wasn't in use any more. I remembered the glorious transmission that I had salvaged from Uncle Otis's 1916 Cadillac. I remembered the Model "T" Ford that I had installed a Chevrolet transmission in backwards so it would serve as an over-drive. All things were possible to a young mind. I said, "Pop, I think I have a way. If you could get Aunt Ella's Buick, I believe we could make it pull the thrasher and at the same time run the thrasher."

Well, Dad bought the car for $200. It tore me up to have to take that

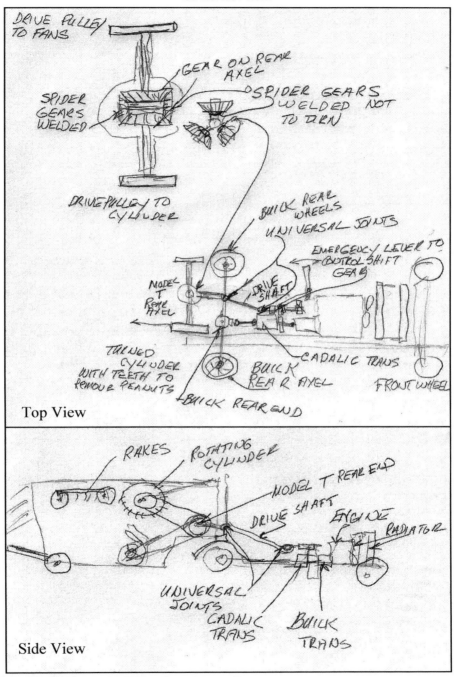

Modified Buick-Cadillac thrasher puller

beautiful car body off the chassis. It had those nice little pull out jump seats that folded into the back of the front seat. The upholstery was a smooth velvet. The windows were all intact. Concho and I saved everything forward of the instrument panel, even the clock.

The peanut thrasher arrived. We stripped the back axle and iron wheels out from under the thrasher. We stripped the front axle and iron wheels and the tongue out from the front of the thrasher. Pop must have gotten a refund on those expensive parts because I never remember seeing them on the farm again. The back axle was replaced with a Model "T" rear end, complete with balloon tires. The drive shaft housing was removed and discarded. The hole where the drive shaft housing was bolted on to the rear end housing was capped.

We found the backbone section of a large plow, a large piece of steel that was probably 2 inches thick by 4 inches high and long enough to span the Buick chassis from one side to the other. We mounted it just directly above the Buick's rear axle. The thrasher was made to pivot on this beam just like you see 5th wheel trailers mounted on a truck today.

Now the Cadillac transmission was mounted just behind the Buick transmission with a short drive shaft. A new drive shaft was cut to hook the Cadillac transmission to the Buick rear differential. We had reworked a Massey Harris tractor transmission previously, and had removed a splined shaft and a slide gear and the mating gear. The mating gear was installed on the front of the Cadillac transmission and the splined shaft with the sliding gear with its shift collar pointing toward the front of the Buick was mounted on two bearings, with part of the splined shaft projecting through the rear bearing. The shifting collar was fastened so when the emergency brake lever was pulled up, it shifted the slide gear to be in mesh with the lower gear. This is essentially what I believe was the first power takeoff on a transmission.

Now comes the tricky part, a power shaft drive. We mounted a Model "T" rear axle inside the thrasher. The spider gears had been welded so both rear axles had to turn. In other words, no more differential. The drive shaft was cut off so the universal joint was just above the king pin of the thrasher-Buick connection. Another universal joint was put on the part of the splined shaft behind the bearing of the splined shaft. A drive shaft was cut with a slip joint to go between the two universal joints, thus connecting a power train from the Buick engine, through the Buick transmission, through the short drive shaft to the Cadillac transmission, up through the slide gear on the splined shaft (when the hand brake was up), then through the first universal joint, through the drive shaft to the second universal joint, to the Model "T" transmission in

Peanut thrashing crew

Sacking peanuts

the thrasher. Pulleys were added to the Model "T" rear axle, one side driving the thrasher cylinder and the other side driving the shakers and the fans.

The merit of this self-propelled thrasher was its power. It could negotiate any sandy field in Frio County by putting both transmissions in gear. It had eight speeds forward and eight speeds backward. The balloon tires would ride the sand with no effort. You could go 30 or 40 miles per hour down the highway and drive out into any sandy field, shift gears, pull up the emergency brake lever to engage the power take off and you were thrashing.

The usual practice of thrashing was to pull the thrasher to the field with the tractor, chock the rear wheels of the thrasher, disconnect the tractor to turn it around, and then line up the belt to drive the thrasher. When the pile of peanut hay behind the thrasher got so large that men could no longer be able to throw it back with pitch forks, the thrasher would have to be moved forward again. With my machine, you could shift gears and move in minutes.

When haystacks 300 feet long began to show up in Frio County the tractor companies sent their engineers to the field to see what was going on. If I had only known about patents then, it would have been worth more than all my 65 other patents together.

Unloading peanuts from wagon to send to thrasher. Pop would say, "Hurry up, Johnny, and fix that thing! Can't you see all of this bunch of men is costing me a lot of money when they're not working?"

Removing thrashed peanuts from thrasher. Note pile of peanut hay in the background.

Repair man waiting for something to break

Chapter 16
Siblings

Sid

My brother Sid was two and a half years older than I am. Sid and I used to sleep together. We slept in a big old room that was on the west side of the house. And we had a double bed. We'd get in that bed and we'd draw a line down the middle of the bed. "Don't you dare put a finger or a toe across that line!" Cause if you did that was reason to fight. But we got along pretty good. We didn't fight very much. I really loved my brother Sid. He was good to me.

Sid was my teacher. Everything I learned about girls I learned from Sid. You don't discuss things like that with your sister or your younger brother. But I learned an awful lot from Sid. Back in those early days when I was courting the girls I didn't even know how to kiss a girl. So I said Sid, "Tell me how you kiss a girl." He said, "Oh you just put your lips together and put them against hers, and that's it." Well, that's really about

Delma, Sid and Lionel during the war

the only instructions I had on how to kiss a girl. Sid and I did a lot of double dating. You see in those days we only had one car, and the car that I remember so well was a Model "A" Ford. I would work on the farm all week, and on the weekend Dad would give me 60 cents and the car. My date and I would spend 25 cents apiece for a movie, and that left 5 cents apiece for a drink. I would drive, and I'd have my date in the front seat, and Sid would be in the back seat with his date, and going and coming I'd get instructions on what to do from the rear-view mirror.

Oh, Sid had lots of girls, my gosh! But he had one of them that lived way out in the country named Lorena Foster. The one he was most interested in was Delma Cude. Well, now Delma lived on a farm down the road. You go to Melon, Texas, and go two or three miles west and you run into a road that sorta parallels Interstate Highway 35. It went from Pearsall down to the Leona River and on out to Divot. Well, Sid dated Delma.

I remember one time he was dating her and I was driving and I had on a new suit. Oh boy! I was diked up. I had already taken my date home and we were going to take Delma home. Well, it was raining like the dickens. There was a slough that ran across their farm, and to get to Delma's house you had to cross that slough, and you couldn't get there if there was too much water in that slough. But there was another way around that went sorta the back way that Sid and Delma knew about, so we went that way and came to her house by the back road. Well, we come to a gate and it was raining like the dickens, and somebody had to get out and open that gate, and who do you think had to do it? It was me! So they insisted I take my pants off so I wouldn't ruin my new suit. So I took my pants off and went and opened that gate and drove through it, and then I put my pants back on. That was some deal. Man that was a long time ago. But Sid taught me everything I knew.

Sid was crippled. My daddy was crippled, and Sid took after my daddy, having this thing called Charcot-Marie-Tooth. Daddy wanted to be sure that we had exercise. So we had a table in the living room, a big old round table, and it had a center trunk that come down, and at the bottom it had four legs that spread out kinda like the feet on a chicken. So Dad wanted to be sure that Sid exercised because he thought maybe it'd keep his strength up, being as he had this disease. He didn't want to make Sid feel too bad about it, so he made Betsy and me (and I don't remember if Harry got in on the deal or not) but we all had to lay down on the floor and put our toes underneath the legs on that table and do situps. Boy we had to do a lot of exercise so Sid would retain his strength. Eventually Sid had to wear braces. That caused lots of problems for Sid. But Sid never did complain about being crippled. Now, my daddy, he complained about being crippled. He wanted a lot of stuff done for him, and in later years I built him all kinds of stuff to help him. Such as an exercise machine and a rocking bed and a device that would raise him up and put him in the car when he was farming. I did a lot of things like that, and Dad expected it. I guess that's one reason why I got to be a pretty good mechanic, because I was building things for Dad. But Sid was more gentle about the thing. He kinda accepted the fact that he was crippled. Sid didn't complain about it.

I went off to A&M in 1935 and graduated in 1939. When I was off at A&M in my freshman year, why Sid and Delma decided they would run off and get married. I didn't know that Sid and Delma had gotten married until it was all over. Sid didn't have any place else to take her, so he took her home. And she got my place in the bed. Anyway, Dad used to always tease Sid when they came to the table to eat. He used to always tell Sid, "Now put a quarter on the table to pay for your wife's dinner." Bless his time. He had a lot of duress, but they made it pretty good I guess. Eventually Sid built a dinky little house on the farm that had one bedroom and a kitchen and a bath. After Sid got married he started farming some of Grandma Bennett's land. He was doing pretty good on that. Sid and Delma had a son, Lionel, born in

Sid's house on the farm

1937, and another son, John Scott, born in 1945.

Betsy

My sister Betsy was three and a half years younger than I am. Betsy and George Kemper from Pearsall were childhood sweethearts. Sid's little house on Daddy's farm was about a block away from the house that Daddy lived in up on the hill. The road going to Daddy's house passed right by Sid's house. Well, George would come down to see Betsy. Now George was a wild one in his young days. It seems that Sid had a clothesline strung across the backyard and there

Betsy

was a water pipe that come from the well down below and flowed up on top of the hill. There was quite a dirt bank on top of this water pipe. George would drive down to see Betsy and he'd tear through Sid's backyard, run underneath the clothes line, jump over the top of that pipe to get up to the house where Betsy was. Lord, he was wild. He was <u>wild</u>! He was the kind that after he got in the Army Air Force he would fly his airplane under a bridge. I don't know how he ever lived as long as he did with the activity that he did in his younger days.

George found out that Betsy was going to be in Pearsall one weekend during the war and he was in the Army Air Force in Arizona or somewhere out there, and durn if he didn't get to Pearsall before she

132

got to Pearsall, and she was just coming from San Marcos, where she was going to school.

Back in the time when Betsy and George were in high school all of the students in her class were supposed to write a report of some kind. I don't think George wrote the report, and they had to have that report to graduate. Being as George didn't write the report he decided that he wasn't going to let anybody else have a report, either. So he stole all of the reports and put them down in the bottom of a dry dug well. I think, maybe before it was all said and done he had to retrieve all of the reports out of the bottom of that well so that all of them could graduate. The school told George he couldn't graduate, so the class rebelled and said that they wouldn't graduate either, then. The school gave in and they all graduated.

Betsy and George married in 1943 and had a son in 1944, the first of four children.

Harry

My brother Harry was seven years younger than I am. There's an awful lot that I don't know about my younger brother, Harry. You see, the problem was that I was gone. When you're gone tending after your own business you don't have time to worry about what your young siblings are doing. Anyway, he eventually got into the service. When he did they sent him off to school, to Cincinnati or somewhere up there. He found a young lady up there and they were pretty much in love. This young lady moved down to San Antonio, and used to make Harry an awful lot of cookies. That relationship hasn't been discussed too much in my presence. I don't know about the outcome of it, but I know that eventually they broke up. She was really after Harry, and I think it scared him.

Eventually Harry got sent on over to Germany in the ordinance department during World War II. Harry started to A&M to study chemical engineering. One day he called home and said he was through with school, he wanted to farm with his father. He came home to farm, and eventually formed a partnership with his brother Sid. At one time they owned about 5000 acres and were the world's largest producers of peanuts.

Harry about 1932

We had a cousin name Eddy Youngblood. Harry and Eddy were really a pair. It seems like Eddy would get a girl and Harry would try to take her away from him. Eddy would drop out and Harry would lose interest in her. Eddy would get another girl and Harry would try to take her away from him. Finally Eddy introduced Harry to JoAnnelle Waggoner. She was a school teacher teaching school in Cotulla, Texas. They got married in 1958 and they have one son named Bill.

Dating

I can remember that I used to date Dorothy Wynn. I thought she was really something. And I'd even go up and spend the night with the Laxons 'cause they lived two houses over from Dorothy Wynn. That way I could go see Dorothy when I didn't have a car. After I courted Dorothy Wynn for a long time I started courting a girl by the name of Frankie Ethel Scott. There is more about that in the next chapter.

Chapter 17
Senior Year in High School
1934-1935

That was the year I had arrived. I had a girl friend named Frankie Ethel Scott. My brother Sid had taught me everything that I knew about girls. He was always singing "Frankie and Johnny were lovers".

I had been going with Frankie before my senior year started in high school. Frankie's mother was named Ethel Scott. She was the high school math teacher and knew that I wanted to go to Texas A&M and study engineering. She also knew that I did not have enough math to be able to get into A&M, so she taught me, on her own, the extra math that I needed for the entrance qualifications. Everybody loved Mrs. Scott. She died at a ripe old age of close to 100.

I wanted to get some mechanical drawing in high school and it was not offered. After all, Pearsall

Frankie and Johnny

was a school that turned out farmers, not engineers. There was a nice young teacher named Miss Bloodworth who was the art teacher. I kind of had a crush on her and they hadn't even made the movie about "Mrs. Robinson", or I might have been tempted. She said that she would teach me mechanical drawing in her Art class. I took it and she let me do anything I wanted in class. I made a few drawings and then I made a drawing of an old fashioned spinning wheel. It looked pretty good, so I asked Miss Bloodworth if I could rig up a little electric motor and make a lathe out of it. There was a lavatory between her art room and a room that Chemistry was supposed to be taught in. There was a sink in the little room and a shower for chemical accidents and glass doors between the art room and the chemistry room. I set my homemade wood lathe up there. I brought mesquite wood from home on the school bus to have material to build the spinning wheel. The wheel was about 14 inches in diameter and had all the features of a real old fashion spinning wheel. It had the tread pedal, bobbin and the works. I made the only A I ever made in high school. Poor Miss Bloodworth thought that I was going to give it to her but I gave it to Frankie, and some years later, their house burned and there went my mesquite spinning wheel.

Now, I had been able to acquire at the Dilley city dump a most fine Model "T" Ford coupe. It had all the glass, a little trunk in the back to carry your spare tire, jack, hand air pump, extra inner tube and tools. With a little work, it had an electric starter. It had a push out windshield with two little arms on each side to hold out the windshield. What a car, and no payments. When I got through, it ran great to take your girl for a leisurely drive in the country.

One Saturday, I had been thrashing peanuts out east of Pearsall and came into town driving my Buick-thrasher, and stopped at Frankie's house. We had a date that evening so I asked her if she wanted to ride down to the farm so I could leave the Buick-thrasher and then I could get my fine practically brand-new-from-the-city-dump Ford coupe and we could go ride in the country. Now the Buick-thrasher only had the cultivator seat that was used for the driver so Frankie got on the overhanging gas tank, sat down, and away we went.

We got my new car and had a nice little ride in the country, going out to the Leona River picnic ground. Now the roads were rough and the Ford gas tank was up over our feet. It would never pass Ralph Nader's safety standards now. Being as the car was new from the dump, not new in years, the gas tank suddenly developed a leak and all our gas was leaking out and it sure was a long way to town and no traffic in sight. I told Frankie to put her finger over the hole to stop the leak and I would try and find something to save enough gas to get us back to town. I looked and looked and could find nothing. Finally I saw my spare inner tube in the trunk. I got that and on the opposite side of the tube from the valve, I cut a hole so we could pour gasoline in the tube. We got the tube about 3/4 full and let the rest run on the ground. What to do, what, what to do? We had the windows rolled down and the windshield pushed about half out, after all that model had not come out with air-conditioning. By pushing the tube into the passenger side window, I hung the tube on the windshield bracket. When you are stranded, you do the only thing you can do, evaluate and expedite. By taking the gas line loose from the tank (that model used gravity feed, as fuel pumps had not been invented yet) I bent it out to toward the inner tube hanging on the side. We lifted the hood on that side and tied it down. The only thing left was hooking the gas line to the tube. The Lord smiled on me and I took the air hose off the pump and forced the end over the gas line. By removing the valve core in the tube, the gas came gushing out until I screwed the air hose on the valve stem.

Needless to say and with much praying, we drove home from our leisurely drive. Mother was in town and had called the Scotts that she wanted to ride home with me when I went. I left Frankie, picked up Mother, and then I had to make arrangement for another trip to the store (dump) for another gas tank.

It was an exciting year.

John D, high school graduate (11th grade)

**Pearsall High School 1935 graduating class.
John D (third from left on back row).**

Chapter 18
College
1935-1939

"Those wonderful years" that I still dream about: can't find the classroom, forget to go to class, that lesson I forgot to prepare, pop quiz, pop quiz, and still more pop quizzes, no money for nothing so you would sell the use of the picture show card for 10 cents.

After that initial shock of those terrible upperclassmen, they could be tolerated. I will have to admit that when this 17-year-old country boy got off that train in College Station that first night and all that

Southwest Texas A&M Club, John D (middle of second row); Aggies wearing boots are seniors

bunch of upperclassmen with their belts starting hollering and trying to hit us with belts, if they could catch us, I was pretty scared. After that, I fell in to the routine of being my assigned upperclassmen's orderly, having to clean their room, go to the post office and get their mail, get their laundry, smuggle food out of the mess hall if they were too lazy to go get it themselves. Even those square meals we had to eat, let your upperclassmen eat your dessert, all that "YES SIR!" baloney, not being allowed to study in your room after taps and having to go to your upperclassmen's room. You had to be in your room when the study time started, couldn't sit on your bed, couldn't talk to your roommate, couldn't play a radio, you sat at your desk and studied. If you didn't have any studying, you looked at your books, not a magazine. It was hell, but the discipline was good for you. If you didn't pass your grades, a report was sent to your company commander. We were in military units, you were called in and reprimanded and just so you didn't forget, a board was forcefully applied to your posterior extremity. Even with all this help, I stilled flunked Freshman English and Chemistry.

Courting
There were no girls at A&M when I got there. So I continued dating Frankie in Pearsall. On Saturday morning I'd get out on the highway at College Station and stick my thumb up in the air and, by george, I'd get to Pearsall in time to have a date on Saturday night. And then Sunday I'd turn right around and hitchhike back to A&M. So Frankie and I went together pretty good my freshman year in college and everything was fine. Then came the sophomore year. Frankie was just a year behind me. She went to a college in Cisco, Texas, It was a Christian church school. I know that a boy named Hardy Van Ratcliff that used to live with them and deliver papers, he worked for Mr. Scott. He went to that school, too. I thought things were just rocking along pretty good with Frankie. So one day I up and stuck my thumb up in the air and hitchhiked to her town to see her. When I got there I found out she wasn't there. She had been seeing somebody on the sly and had gone home with him for the weekend. So that broke us up and that was the end of that romance. We were friends after that, but we didn't date anymore.

Pattern Shop

I had a job in the machine shops all four years of college, and it was my salvation. I could work any time I wanted to and became acquainted with the other boys who had those "student assistance jobs." My job was in the pattern shop working for Mr. Fleming. You would think he was hard, but he really was a softy. The student who had been working for him the longest was always the reference goat. This boy's name was Russell. If any of us underlings did anything wrong, we were "pulling a Russell". This job was the most enjoyable thing in my whole college career. We did such things as taking a real good card table and covering the top with pieces of different colored wood veneer to make the Texas A&M seal. When they were finished, after our spending untold hours, they were sold, usually to some college professor for five dollars. You know, come to think of it, there was football (whatever that was) going on but I couldn't afford that, and I was being paid to do what I loved best. I never saw any football games when I was at A&M.

Color Blind Test

Just before I finished the sophomore year, Colonel Washington had me take a color blind test to see if I could get a commission in the Army. Col. Washington was the U.S. Army supervisor of the cadets in my branch of the service (Coast Artillery and Anti-Aircraft Service). He had Sergeant Gill give me the polka dot test to see how I could identify colors. The test was a book with many pages that were covered with colored dots of various sizes. Different colors were placed so it would show, say, a seven, if your eyes were normal for that particular color, and if you were color blind for that particular color you would see, say, a one instead of a seven. Each page was arranged to test you for a particular color. I was just reading through that book like I could read.

When I got through, Sgt. Gill told Col. Washington that I had flunked the test. The Colonel said, "Sgt. Gill, you take Bennett back in there and show him exactly what the number was on what page in the book. When he knows how to read that book give him the test again." Well, there were too many pages for me to memorize the test, not that the Colonel would cheat, he just wanted me to pass the test. I went home at the end of my sophomore year knowing that I was not going to get a commission because if you didn't pass the color blind test, no commission.

When the summer was almost over, Col. Washington wrote me and said that the Army had changed its requirement, and it now used the colored yarn test. If you could pick up a red yarn when you were told to do it, or a blue yarn, etc., you were in. I was elated, I passed the color blind test. I would be offered a commission in the ROTC.

My Only "A"

I flunked English the first time I took it. When I tried again in my junior year I was going to have to make a talk in my class on some subject of my choosing. The whole grade was to be on the talk and we had a good bit of time to prepare for it.

I decided that my talk was going to be on the hydromatic transmission, and titled "The Fluid Coupling." It was a brand new invention and as yet it was only talked about; no one understood how it worked. Mr. Fleming let me make a model of it in the wood shop and I was even paid for making it. The model would come apart so you could see how it fit together and how it worked. I gave my speech in English and demonstrated with the model. Everybody was so impressed with that model that I got the only "A" I ever made in college. They finally put that model in the M. E. shop display showcase.

Milner Hall

My sophomore year at A&M I lived in Milner Hall, which was right between Sbisa Hall and the Bookstore. Milner Hall was a real old dormitory. It was a peculiar built thing because it had an atrium in the middle of it. Some rooms had outside windows, and others had windows on the atrium. The rooms and halls had wood floors.

I had two roommates. One was Owen Watkins and the other was J. Ferdinand Reed. We had triple deck bunks in our room. J. Ferdinand Reed thought he was awful beautiful. I used to get so mad at him. He'd get up in front of the mirror and flex his muscles and look at his beautiful body. But he did have a beautiful sister, and I liked her. Anyway, Ferdy would take a five gallon bucket and he'd fill it full of water. He'd dissolve maybe 3 or 4 rolls of toilet paper in that

Sophomore year at Milner Hall, 1936-37
John D (front row, fifth from left)

water, and it'd kinda make a mush. Then he'd slip out at night and go find somebody and drown them out in the middle of the night. Oh my God that was a mess. Then they would drown out Ferdy. We made him sleep on the bottom bunk because if anybody got wet it was going to be the person in the bottom bunk. The person on the top bunk, they couldn't throw the water that high. And the person in the middle bunk was pretty safe. I slept in the middle bunk.

I decided I was going to protect us from being drowned out. I was always piddling with electricity. (Don't try this at home!) So I got me a 15-watt light bulb and mounted it on the wall right there, almost in my face where I slept in my bed. It was hooked to 110 volts. Then I slipped one wire from the light around the wall to the hinge on the door, and used the hinge as an electrical connector. I went from there down to the door knob. The other wire went to part of the door latch mechanism. I took a bare wire and wove it back and forth in the cracks of the wooden floor, just outside of the door where you couldn't see them. Well, somebody would come and want to drown old Ferdinand Reed out. Well, they'd take a coat hanger and start sticking it in that door to jimmy the latch. It would shock them and they would drop their bucket of water. They had ahold of the doorknob, which was one wire, and they were standing

Bedding drying out at Puryear Hall

on the wet floor, which was the other wire. Boy when they stuck that coat hanger in there the light would flash on in my face. You'd hear them drop that bucket and go off a-screaming. You know it's a wonder I didn't electrocute some of those people. The Lord had me by the hand, then, and I never did electrocute anybody, but I sure gave some of them a large charge.

Reed, Watkins, Bennett 1937-38

Owen Watkins

I still communicate with Owen real regular through email. But Owen and I ran around together. We traveled by air of course, stick our thumb up in the air and catch a ride. We went back to Houston quite a few times to visit his folks and date the girls. We even hitchhiked one weekend up to Llano. He had some kinfolks

J. Ferdinand Reed

Owen Watkins and a girlfriend

up there named Watkins that were in the leather business, and we went up there to see them. We traveled all over. We made numerous trips to Navasota because Owen and I were very active in the Methodist Church, and there was a preacher there named Carlisle that was real good to us kids. His wife would cook cookies for us, and what not, and Owen and I spent a lot of time over there. We used to have this Epworth League. It would meet in College Station one Sunday and the next Sunday it might meet in Navasota. Then the next Sunday it would meet in Huntsville at the Methodist Church or might meet in Bryan. We met all around like that, and naturally, being as there weren't any girls at A&M, we still met girls around that we'd go see. We had a pretty good time. We could have had a whole lot better time if we'd had any money, but we didn't have any money. So we went where the food was free and had a good time.

There was one young lady from Navasota, the daughter of a dentist named Johnson, and she wanted to dance. She wanted to go to one

First review – 1937

of those Aggie dances in that big old Sbisa Hall. (Sbisa Hall was a big dining room that would feed several thousand boys at a time. The whole corps would eat there; they would march in in formation.) Man she wanted to go up there bad. I told her I couldn't take her to one of them dances, I couldn't dance! She said, "I'm going to <u>teach</u> you how to dance." Well she taught me one step. So we went to the dance and I danced that one step. That's the only step that I ever learned in my entire life.

Professor Wingram's Coat
When patterns were made, there was always a fillet placed where two pieces intersected, so when the item was cast in iron or brass, the fillet would minimize stress. The way we would get the wax to make the fillet was to use extruded beeswax to lay against the two intersecting planes, and then it would be ironed with a hot tool shaped sphere of the size the fillet was wanted. To get the beeswax extruded into about a 3/16" diameter extrusion, we had a piece of pipe with a fixed plug in one end, the pipe would have a hole drilled in the side of the pipe the size of the extrusion was to be, cold beeswax was placed in the pipe cylinder and then a wooden dowel of the correct size was used as a plunger to compress the beeswax

146

and force it out of a hole. It was a very difficult thing to do.

Now, I was a third year mechanical engineering student with a fine "student labor job," and was allowed to do anything in the shop that I wanted to do. I decided that the wax press had to be improved. In the first place, the piece of pipe cylinder should be heated so the wax could be extruded out easier. There needed to be a heating pot for the ball-shaped fillet tool so it could be heated too. There needed to be a lever action for powering the piston that compressed the beeswax. So I built a wax extruding machine. All done and ready for the experimental run. The mechanical engineering professors knew their students real well and the word got out that I was about to try the tool. One of my favorite professors was a little late coming and the machine had been plugged in awhile getting warm. I didn't have any thermostatic controls on it. It was a cold day and he had come in with a very long, fuzzy coat on. By the time he had gotten there the machine was hot. "Let her rip," was the word. I pulled down the lever and that hot beeswax shot out of the hole and went straight for Professor Wingram's fine, woolly coat. It went all over that coat. Even with all that, he passed me on the subject he was teaching.

Fort Crockett

That summer I attended ROTC Camp at Fort Crockett on Galveston Island. The fort had several 12-inch rifles. (A rifle is a gun barrel that is longer than 25 times as long as the bore of the gun.) They also had some anti-aircraft equipment on which we trained. They had a base hospital at the fort. I got to try out the hospital one day as I was swim-ming in the Gulf and ran into a Portuguese-Man-O-War. That thing put me in the hospital for several days and gave me a chance to check out the nurses.

John D

147

Guns on A&M campus; 1938. Buildings are Chemistry (left), Petroleum Engineering, Power Plant.

Anti-aircraft gun at Fort Crockett

Puryear Hall

In my junior and senior years I was in Puryear Hall. I was in the coast artillery anti-aircraft, but the cavalry was across the courtyard in Law Hall. We would sneak oranges out of the mess hall. Then we would make a slingshot out of an inner tube by attaching the ends to each side of the window sill. We could shoot oranges across the

148

12-inch rifle at Fort Crockett. Gulf of Mexico in background

Calisthenics at Fort Crockett

courtyard (where the sheets are drying out in the picture on page 144) and put them right in the door of the dormitory across the courtyard. Of course the cavalry would shoot back.

Graduation

My senior year, I was First Lieutenant of our Coast Artillery Battery, second in command. My cousin Maury Riggan had sent me to school my junior year. Times were hard. My last semester, Dad said, "Son if you don't make it this time, you are through. There is no more money." I went to the Dean and told him what the situation was. He allowed me to take 24 semester hours the last half of my senior year, all of them engineering subjects.

Demonstration of the use of the paddle

My first six years of school were in a one room school, so I didn't get a good background. I'm dyslexic, too, so I had a terrible time in college. I had to have 24 semester hours to have enough hours to graduate. When it came time for the final exams, I had to raise every subject one letter by the final exam, except Steam Lab. I had to raise it two letters by the final, and that meant I had to make 100 on the final. Finals counted 1/3 of the grade. I was in bad need of grade points. Steam Lab was the last exam.

I didn't buy any graduation announcements. I studied and studied. As the saying goes, "A man knows what a man has to do," this boy knew what he had to do. You know when you have done it, and I knew I had done it in every course except Steam Lab. I knew that I had missed one part of one question so I only made 95. Mr. Charlie Crawford, head of the mechanical engineering department knew my predicament. Bless him, he said "If he made 95, I will give him 5 and we can graduate him and get rid of him".

I couldn't stand it before the grades were posted so I told my good friend Fritz, "If I make it will you wire me at home?" I immediately hitchhiked home 250 miles to Derby. I couldn't stand it and turned around and hitchhiked back. In the meantime Fritz sent the telegram that I had made it, and Mother and Dad almost beat me back there. I was graduating! I got out with exactly the required number of grade points. I walked across the stage to get my diploma, opened the tube, there was a note, no diploma. "Come down to the administration office and pay your chemistry breakage bill of 35 cents and you can pick up your diploma."

At least 20 years after I graduated, my wife Wynona and I were in Fred's Barbeque in Richardson, Texas. I worked for Sun Oil Production Research there in town. Professor Crawford came in and saw me. He didn't say a word to me, but turned and told his wife, "Honey, this is the man that I said couldn't graduate back in 1939, but he did it anyway."

Senior Year, Class of '39

Bugle stand

Second Platoon, "A" Battery, Coast Artillery

A visit from FDR. He was glad to visit what he called the "Agricultural and Military College of Texas".

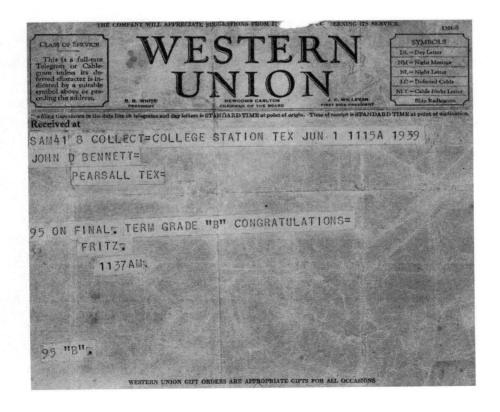

Chapter 19
Important Events of 1939

Methodist Conference
While still in college, my religious training was greatly influenced by the wonderful cookies that the wife of my Methodist pastor, Rev. James Carlisle, would serve me and my roommate, Owen Watkins, when we would go over to the parsonage for our much needed home life. We spent a lot of time there. Reverend Carlisle, Owen Watkins, and I were sent to the Methodist conference in St. Louis, Mo. when the vote was taken on reuniting the Northern Branch of the Methodist Church and the Southern Branch of the Methodist Church. The District must have sent us as delegates because we were voting members.

Owen Watkins and I were seniors at A&M and wore the only clothes we had, our military uniforms, complete with boots. If you will remember, the rumbling of war was going on in Europe. Religious people did not like war, wanted nothing to do with war, did not want even to be reminded of war. Our being present in this Religious Conference was almost more than some of the delegates could stand and they wanted to throw Owen and me out. They were overruled and the conference went on as scheduled. The vote was to reunite the Methodist Church which had been split since Civil War days. I had not thought about it being such an important event until recently I was talking to Rev. Wayne Williams, and he was amazed that I had been at that conference. We Aggies got around.

Looking for a Job
When I graduated, I needed a job. Having practically no money, I decided to go to Dallas to look around. This country kid was scared

to death and didn't have the least idea of what to do. I was traveling by air, "Air you going my way, and can I have a ride?" We Aggies traveled everywhere that way (hitchhiking). I decided to go back to A&M, that was home, and a place I knew how to get something to eat. On the way, I saw a large manufacturing plant in Corsicana, and as it was late in the afternoon, too late to call, and an excuse to put off an interview as long as possible, I decided to blow my last "$5" on a hotel room at the Navarro Hotel in Corsicana and call on the Chief Engineer early the next morning.

American Well (July 1939)

The American Well and Prospecting Co. manufactured the "Gumbo Buster Line of Oil Field Equipment." Man, I liked that. I met Mr. Carl Anderson, chief engineer, and was thoroughly impressed. He showed me all around the plant, saw the machinery that was in the process of being built, took me up to the engineering office, made me know that there was no other place in the whole world that would be as much fun to work. He told me to leave my application, complete with picture of me and my Aggie boots, and he would let me know if a vacancy came that I could fill. My heart was broken.

I went back to A&M, spent the night, and went to Derby. Hitch-hiking around was a way of existing because the people who picked Aggies up would usually buy them a hamburger when they stopped to eat. Present day airlines were not as good as the way I traveled. I could beat any bus or train schedule and besides most of the time, the meals were free. I always traveled in my Aggie uniform.

Coltexo Gasoline Plant (July 1939)

When I got home, there was a telegram from the student placement board at A&M, with the offer of a job from The Coltexo Gasoline Company in Lefors, Texas. Salary $100 a month. Boy, I accepted and left immediately by air—"Air you going my way?" The job was not doing what I really wanted to do with my life, but an ex-Aggie ran the company, and there were some of the boys there who I had worked with in the pattern shop in school. One of them probably recommended me.

Coltexo was in a big gas field. It was a camp with about a dozen houses. One of the employee's wives cooked meals for the bachelors

154

1960 photo of rooming house where I lived at Lefors, near Coltexo

Coltexo Gasoline Co. in Lefors, Texas

like me. Natural gas that was rich in casinghead gasoline would be collected from the gas wells and sent to the Coltexo plant. (This gas has a low vapor pressure, and when it is cooled a little it becomes a

Oil well near the Coltexo plant in the Texas panhandle

18 gas compressors at Coltexo

John D working on a gas meter
at the carbon black plant

liquid.) There was a tower there, a steel cylinder. They would pump natural gas in the bottom of the tower and spray "lean oil" from the top. The oil would rain down through the gas and absorb the casinghead gas out of it as it fell. Then the oil would be pumped to another tower where it was heated. The casinghead gas would vaporize out of the oil. Then it would be sent to a radiator where it was cooled and turned back into a liquid. The resulting liquid was called "casinghead gasoline." It had a low vapor point. The casinghead gasoline would be sent to a refinery to blend with gasoline which was being made at the refinery from oil. The resulting gasoline blend would vaporize easily so it would make it easier to start your car.

After the natural gas had the casinghead gas absorbed out of it, then the "dry gas" would be sent to a carbon black plant several miles away. A carbon black plant has a metal building with upside down channel iron in it. Below the channel iron was a series of jets where gas was burned in a very limited amount of air. The oxygen-starved fire resulted in incomplete combustion. The flame created lots of soot (carbon) on the bottom of the channel iron. An endless chain scraped off the carbon and took it to the end of the channel iron. The powdered carbon, or "carbon black", was collected to be used in tires and other products.

Dust was everywhere, black dust. You would breathe dust and get it all over your clothes. You could see a carbon black plant for fifty miles. They said it didn't hurt you, but I hated it. The carbon black plant was several miles away, but I used to go over there to work on our gas meters. My job consisted of rebuilding the big compressors in the plant and other routine jobs that were around the gasoline plant. We worked on all the gas wells around us and repaired the gas meters in such plants as the Borger Carbon Black Plant, where the smoke from the burning of the gas to make carbon was so bad you could scarcely see your hands in front of your face.

American Well Again

After 3 months of this, I wrote Mr. Anderson at the American Well and Prospecting Company and told him I was doing something that I did not like, I wanted to design oil field equipment and I wanted to go to work for him. Well, the picture of the boots must have impressed him because he wrote me back and said that his draftsman was quitting to go to A&M and I could have his job, but he couldn't pay me any more than his salary, which was $100 a month. I jumped at the chance, but this time I rode the train. After all, I was now a working man.

Mr. Carl Anderson had been assistant chief engineer for Oil Well Supply Company in Oil City, Pennsylvania before he came to be Chief Engineer for American Well. He had tremendous experience

American Well and Prospecting Company in Corsicana

American Well secretaries, (Wynona Melton second from left)

in the design of oil field equipment. He taught me everything that I knew about the business. He was my Dad away from home. One day several months after I started working for him, I had a severe case of appendicitis and had to be taken to the P & S Hospital. I had a good looking young nurse at the hospital. We decided to do some research. She took my temperature. Then we would hug and kiss, and she would take my temperature again to see if it had changed. Regardless of how much hugging and kissing we did my temperature wouldn't go up. The true nature of a research engineer was coming to light.

Now Mrs. Anderson always went back to Oil City, Pennsylvania every summer and Mr. Anderson was living alone except for the maid that came every day to keep his house and cook his meals. It was summer time and Mr. Anderson was alone so he insisted that I be taken out to his house after I got out of the hospital so his maid could take care of me. When I was well enough to go back to work, I told him I should go back to the YMCA where I had a room, and he acted as if his feelings were hurt that I was leaving. I went anyway.

At the "Y"

Mr. Anderson immediately put me on a job to design a throttle control for a rotary table to control the speed of the engine with a cable. I had more fun on that job. I was making $100 a month. Out of that I sent $30 a month to Betsy so she could go to college. I had purchased a little six inch lathe, which cost me $6.60 a month, and a radio, which cost $2.50 a month. I paid $15 a month to the Sims Boarding House for two meals a day. The "Y" cost $12 a month. Then a durn encyclopedia salesman came along and he took my courting money. I had breakfast at a little café. My schedule was so constant that the woman at the café would have my breakfast cooked when I got there. Things were tight, but I eventually was able to buy some clothes besides my uniform.

Army Reserve
The rumblings of war were going on in Europe, and being a second Lieutenant in the US Army Reserve, I wanted to keep up my studying in the Reserve, so I asked if there were any reserve officer meetings in Corsicana. I was told to go to the Post Office where there was a John Garner who could tell me all I needed to know. The Texas National Guard was the 36th infantry division, and it had units scattered all over the state of Texas. Any town that had any size to it had a National Guard unit stationed in it. To make a long story short, in about six weeks John Garner had me transferred from The Coast Artillery, Anti-Aircraft, U.S. Reserve to the Texas National Guard Artillery. More specifically, Battery D, 132nd Field Artillery of the 36th infantry division. John Garner was a major in the 132nd Field Artillery.

Working man

Andrew, Lynn, and Grace Melton in 1918

Chapter 20
Wynona Melton

William Andrew Melton and Grace Otis Cobb were married on November 1, 1914 in Kerens, Texas. They had a son, Leonard, born in 1915, and another son, Lynn, born in 1917. Leonard lived for just 15 months, and Lynn lived only 13 months. Both were buried in Burkburnet, Texas, where Andrew was working in the oil field. Later they lived in Eastland, Texas where Wayne Andrew Melton was born to them in 1920, followed by Wynona Louise Melton on August 15, 1921. A fifth child, a daughter, was born in Corsicana in 1923, but she lived only a day.

Andrew was a worker in the oil fields a good part of his life, and they moved all over the oilfields. Eventually he went to work for the Post Office in Corsicana, Texas. That is where they became real close friends with John Garner. One time Andrew quit the Post Office and went to Corpus Christi because he thought he could make more money in the oil field again. While they were living there, Andrew was killed in a traffic accident. He died November 1, 1934, when Wynona was 13.

Andrew at the Post Office

Andrew (sitting) at work on a drilling well

Wynona and her mother and her brother had no other place to go but to her father's father's house in Powell, Texas. Powell is a small town in the country near Corsicana. So they moved in with him. It wasn't a very satisfactory arrangement because the grandfather was a kind of a demanding old so and so. He was one of those people who fussed at the chickens because they didn't go to bed early enough and he was always in bed by the time the chickens got up in the tree just outside his bedroom window. He fussed at Wynona a

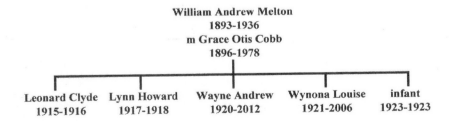

Melton Family Tree

164

whole lot because she ate so slow. She lived there in Powell with them for a while.

Her daddy had a brother named Lloyd Melton who lived in Powell and he was a rural mail carrier. Lloyd had two sons and a daughter named "Bibba". Anyway, Wynona and her cousin Bibba were just like the Gold Dust Twins. They were together everywhere they went in Powell. They really liked each other a whole lot.

Wy, Grace, and Wayne 1923

Wayne and Wynona photographed by a traveling photographer

Wynona's mother put up with her father-in-law as long as she could. Then she finally moved to Corsicana and got a house, and made her living by sewing. She was a wonderful seamstress and made lots and lots of dresses. People used to bring her the labels out of Neiman Marcus dresses and had her sew those labels in the dresses that she was making for them. I think she made a whole dress for about a dollar and a half. I don't know how in the world she supported herself and her two kids on what she made sewing, but she was pretty darn good at it. I really loved Grace Melton, Wynona's mother. In fact, I fell in love with her mother, really, before I fell in love with Wynona. She was such a great person.

Back in the early days when Wynona first moved to Corsicana, her mother did her best to train Wynona and her brother. There was a woman in Corsicana who used to teach Wynona and Wayne dancing. When the woman moved to Waco, they would get on the train with their mother and they would go to Waco for dancing lessons. They were pretty doggone good at it.

Anyway, Wynona grew up there in Corsicana and she had lots of friends. When she got out of high school she went to Navarro

Wynona

Commercial College. I think her mother paid her way through Navarro Commercial College by sewing. She sewed for one of the ladies who was in charge of it and helped pay for Wynona's tuition that way. Wynona was an excellent student. She set the world's record almost on how fast she could type. I think she got up to 140 words a minute. She could take dictation like nobody's business. So, she was a choice student that graduated from Navarro Commercial College. Naturally when the American Well and Prospecting Company needed a secretary to work for them Wynona fit the bill. She went to work for them in the Purchasing Department. She was working in the Purchasing Department,

Wayne and Wy

I believe, by the time I got there. Times were hard and she spent lots of time in the Purchasing Department filing and refiling things to keep busy.

She used to deliver the mail to the Engineering Department and flirt with Jack Anderson when I wanted her to flirt with me. She also dated Olin Taylor, but he had a car.

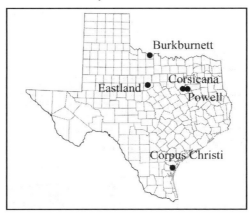

Cousins Bibba, Tinie, and Wy

Wynona riding on a float (center, on fender)

Grace, Wayne, and Wy before Wayne left for the war

170

Chapter 21
Getting Married
1941

Wynona Melton

I got to know Olin Taylor in Battery D and even dated his sister a few times. You see I didn't have much money, so I double dated with him. One night he had a date with Wynona Melton. He made a fatal mistake; he introduced me to Wynona. Since we were all broke and wanted to go buy a coke, Wynona borrowed 15 cents from her mother, Grace Melton. I had always wanted to marry a rich woman. We went out and had our coke and I set my sights on the girl.

Olin Taylor

We used to go to a pavilion at City Lake to dance. There was a nickelodian and a song only cost a nickel. All the kids would go out there to dance. One night I was wearing suspenders and pants with cuffs. Somebody stepped in my cuff and almost pulled my pants off.

I started trying to date Wynona. She didn't like my boots. She said I was too arrogant, I was a stinking Texas Aggie, I thought I knew everything, I was too smart-alecky, and she just really didn't like me. At first I didn't get very many dates with Wynona. I tried to get

171

a date with Olin Taylor's sister, and Wynona said, "You don't want to go with him, he's too cocky." She really ran me down. Olin's sister got the word that I wasn't fitting date material.

I finally got it where Wynona would go with me. Her brother had gotten in the army air force and he was going to a little old college out at the airfield where they were learning to be airmen. There was a boy out there who took a shine to Wynona and he got a date with her every time he could. I had real competition there.

National Guard Federalized

On November 25, 1940 the government decided to federalize the Texas National Guard. That means that they called in all of the troops that were in the unit and they went to their armories. They camped right there at the armories until provisions were made to move them to Camp Bowie, at Brownwood, Texas. We stayed there in Corsicana for some time and drilled the troops. We practiced marching, and this and that and the other. I remember I marched the battery clean out to Powell and back one time, and we marched them all around town. We had quite a deal going there in Corsicana. But then came the day they said, "We're moving to Brownwood."

John D at Camp Bowie

After I got to making more money as an officer, I bought a 1934 Ford V-8, four door car, and started dating Wynona as heavy as she would let me. It was a nice little car, I really did like it. It ran like a million dollars at 62-1/2 miles an hour; at any other speed it would vibrate like the dickens. But, Lord, did it use oil. Couldn't keep enough oil in it. I ran it around the block and it needed more oil. When we were moving to Camp Bowie I was trying to take my car out there. I had a bunch of spare oil and I would drive it a little while and I'd stop and put oil in it. And I'd drive a little while and I'd stop and

172

put oil in it. It was just throwing that oil out like crazy and I didn't think I was going to get there. Well, I did that so many times that I finally lost the oil filler cap where I was pouring that oil in the engine. After I lost that cap miraculously the engine quit using oil. It didn't use any oil at all. What had happened was that the engine was building up pressure in the crankcase, and the pressure forced the oil out through the main bearings and it was spilling on the ground. They

Winter training

didn't have the modern PCV valve, there was a breather on the side of the crankcase that had gotten stopped up. I took the filter out of the breather and cleaned it out and I didn't have any more trouble. I went on out to Camp Bowie at Brownwood.

I had been dating Wynona, and she lived in Corsicana. Progress was pretty good, but I had strong competition. I would drive back and forth from Brownwood to Corsicana. Lord, I would drive back and forth a lot, every weekend that I could. I didn't leave until 2 o'clock on Monday morning to drive back to Camp Bowie. It was 186 miles. If you try to leave Corsicana at 2 o'clock in the morning and you try to be back to Camp

Swabbing out the barrel of a French 75

173

Bowie in time to stand reveille at about 6 o'clock you've got to really hustle. You've got to hustle fast. So Wynona and I would be on a date and the last thing we would do is go to a place that sold sandwiches. I always bought a ham sandwich and I ate it before I started back to Camp Bowie. I would not only have a sandwich, I would have a cigar and a wet towel in my lap, and I'd take off. It was the most dreaded trip in the world because I'd go to sleep and I'd nod off. I believe that I can truly say that I have driven every foot of the way from Corsicana, Texas to Brownwood, Texas in the bar ditch. Every time I'd drop off to sleep and run down in the bar ditch it'd wake me up and I'd pull back on the road and keep on going.

I got out there every time in time to stand reveille. Since I was one of the youngest officers in the 132nd field artillery I was the one that had to exercise the battalion. So we'd get out on the parade ground and I'd have to get on top of that stand where the whole battalion could see me and I'd call out the exercises to them. All of the other officers (most of them were older) would stand back behind the troops and I was up in front of them. I'd roll those shoulders, I'd get even with them rascals that made me get up there. I would hold my arms out there and I'd roll those shoulders, and I'd see that those old officers in the back row were getting tired and their arms were getting lower and lower and lower, and I'd holler, "Get them arms up, let's rotate these things right." I exercised the fool out of them.

But that was quite a deal.

Wynona with John D's car

You know while we had our camp out there at Camp Bowie we had a strange situation. We had one guy who was a state senator, but he was also a National Guard officer from Kerens, Texas. When the state senate would meet he'd have to take off from camp and go to Austin and do his job as a senator. We had little tents, two officers to a tent. I had a tentmate named Larry Hagman. His wife was Mary Martin, a famous movie star. His son was to be JR on the television show "Dallas". He was a pretty good old boy, though.

Finally I got the upper hand. I ordered a 1941 Oldsmobile blue club coupe, (cost $1200 dollars without a radio, the most that I could afford). It was a dilly! I loved that car. I was working hard trying to convince Wynona that I was the man that should be her "Honey Do".

Wynona and Grace visit Louisiana maneuvers

Louisiana Maneuvers

The Division was sent to Louisiana on maneuvers, so I let Wynona keep my new car and in addition to that, I put a radio in my car for her birthday. I thought that would make her marry me to protect her investment.

175

One weekend while we were on maneuvers, Wynona and her mother, Grace Melton, came to Louisiana to see me. That is when I won the battle—her mother told her that she should marry me. I loved that Grace Melton ever since.

Narrow Escape

Wynona and I planned on having the first military wedding to be held at Camp Bowie. Since Wynona's father had been killed in a car wreck, and he was a real close friend of Major Garner, we decided that Major Garner was going to give Wynona away at the wedding. The Garners and the Meltons were real close friends because Mr. Garner and Mr. Melton had both worked in the Post Office at Corsicana and over the years they developed a real close friendship. So I was out there at Camp Bowie and we were going to get married on November 1st. That was the wedding anniversary of Wynona's parents and also of my parents.

Before we were going to get married they decided they were going to have to ship out a regiment of infantry and a battalion of artillery. When we moved out there the 36th infantry division was what they called a square division. It means that there were four battalions of artillery and four regiments of infantry. When you have a regimental combat team it consists of one regiment of infantry and one battalion of artillery. So the division had four regimental combat teams. They decided that they were going to reorganize the division because they didn't want square divisions anymore. They wanted triangular divisions, having three regiments of infantry and three battalions of artillery. They were going take one of the battalions out of the division and the Army was going to send it somewhere else.

They wanted to see that what they sent out was full strength. They were short a first lieutenant in the artillery battalion, and the only two first lieutenants available were Isaac Morgan and me. I was

176

LT. JOHN D. BENNETT
BATTERY "D," 132ND FIELD ARTILLERY
CAMP BOWIE, BROWNWOOD, TEXAS

Dearest Folks;

How is every one at home. I am getting along fine,
can't say that you will have a single son too much
longer though. It is pretty definite that my promotion
is going to come through about the 1st of February, I
hope, and at that time I draw $166.66 salary plus
$60 room plus $18 rashion for my self and in case I
get hitched $18 for my wife. All total $262.66 a month.
Her mother told me last week end when I was back there
that she never thought that she would find a boy that
she would let her daughter marry bedause she didn't think
that there were any good enought for her but she couldn't
find a thing wrong with me. Kind of made me feel pretty
good I should say.

One officer has to stay in camp at all times and the
Captain's folks are kind of sick so I can't go to Corsicana
this week end but next week and either she is comming out
here are I am going there. I think she plans to come out here.
Looks bad doesn't it folks, I fell hard and am in the
position to do something about it with one of the nicest
girls that I have ever meet and from one of the nicest
families that I have ever meet. The girls father got killed
about 6 years ago and her mother has made the living for
them every since. She had to take up sewing and makes
a darn good living at it. Aw well, it may all blow over,
one never knows.

So sister is comming home this week end. I bet that you
will be glad to see the little devil. I would like to
see her myself but I guess that it will be some time
until I get to come home. You can't go very far leaving
here Saturday at noon and having to be back here by
Monday morning at 5;30.AM

At 6 oclock in the morning, I crawl out of bed. At 6.45
I supervise the roll call two blocks away from my tent.
At 7.15 I eat breakfast, at 8.00, I am four blocks away
from where I eat breakfast and on the drill field doing
my exercise. At 10.00 I am in class, four blocks away
from where I did my exercise. At 11.30 I am back up where
I took my exercise and at 12.00 I am back to where I eat
breakfast. At 1215 I eat dinner and at 1.00 I am back
up on the drill field. At 5 oclock, I am back in my tent

and at 5.30 I eat supper. Retreet is at 6.20 in the
evening and having nothing else to do, I usly stay
up at the office until about 10.00 at night. I usely
get to bed about 12.00 that night. That constitas my
week day. On the week end, I go to Corsicana, If I
get off.

Well floks, I must close this bull and tell you good by
for to night.

Write me when you have time to do it.

                    Love to you all

                         John

going to be the groom and Morgan was going to be the best man in our wedding. So the hierarchy had to decide what to do. So they decided to ship Morgan out to fill up the quota of the unit that was transferring out. Since I was going to get married they decided to let me stay with the division. Oh boy, I was

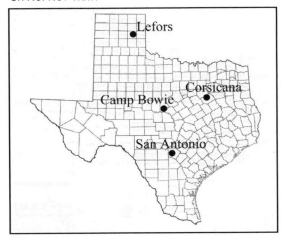

glad about that. Isaac was shipped to Java with the old 2nd Battalion of the 131st Field Artillery, which was captured by the Japanese and became known at the "Lost Battalion." The battalion was used by the Japanese to build the "Burmah Death Railroad" as seen in the movie "Bridge on the River Kwai". Whether Isaac worked on the railroad I don't know, but he is listed as a survivor.

Wedding

Anyway, we were going to have this wedding out there at Camp Bowie on November 1st of 1941. Now, I went up to corps headquarters and asked them for permission to go to Mexico on leave. Then I went back to Corsicana to American Well and Prospecting Company, where I had my old job. I was piddling around up there doing a little work in the office, helping out a little bit, and I got a phone call. It was from Mrs. Garner. She still lived in Corsicana and her husband was out in Camp Bowie. She said, "Johnny, Major Garner called and told me to tell you that if you are going to get married, you better do it today and get out of the country."

That was Oct 28th. I hadn't been paid. I didn't have any money. But I had to get married. So Wynona and I jumped in the car and headed out for San Antonio. We stopped in San Marcos and picked up my sister, Betsy, where she was attending the state teacher's college. We called my parents and they were waiting for us at the Gunter Hotel when we got there. My future mother-in-law and my future brother-in-law and the lady that lived with my mother-in-law drove down to San Antonio. I went in and met Dad and Mother in the Gunter Hotel. Dad was crippled and he couldn't get around too well. He'd do much better in a motel than he could in a big old hotel. The people in the Gunter were so nice, they just brought them water and everything else, just real great to them. So I asked one of the people there, "Listen, I've got to have a good motel for my Dad to go to. Do you have any recommendations?" They said, "Yeah, go out Broadway and there's a good motel out there," and they told me the name. So we all went out there to the Park Motel and were getting ready to have the wedding.

We had decided that we were going to have the wedding in the Travis Park Methodist Church because my Daddy had gotten married there, Sid and Delma had gotten married there, and my great grand-father organized the Travis Park Methodist Church. So there was no place else to get married. So we got ahold of the assistant pastor and he was going to come down and marry us. So we got ready to leave and Mother and my future mother-in-law decided that they had to get some flowers for the wedding. So they took off from the Park Motel and went somewhere and found some flowers. When they were coming back I think they were speeding a little bit, because a policeman pulled them over. My mother gave him a sad story, and told him, "Oh officer, we are so sorry we were speeding. We were trying to get back in time. My son's fixing to get married and we've got to get these flowers up there. Oh, officer, please let us go." So he let them go. They didn't get a ticket.

So we got all ready to go down to the Travis Park Methodist Church. Cars were parked in there pretty tight. I was as nervous as a stuck hog. So Wynona and I got in my car, in my new 1941 Oldsmobile club coupe. We started out and everybody else was going to go there, too. When we backed up my fender hooked on my Daddy's front bumper. Oh, good Lord. I pulled up and there my fender was standing out like a wing on an airplane. You know I drove all the way to Monterey, to Mexico City, 100 miles south of Mexico City, all the way back to Fort Sill, Oklahoma, and that fender was sticking out like an airplane wing. But I was the one who was flying.

We got down to the Travis Park Methodist Church and were married at 10:45 PM. When we got there I said to my Daddy, "Gosh, Daddy, I haven't got any money at all. I haven't been paid. Can you lend me $15 so I can pay the preacher?" So he lent me $15 so I could pay the preacher and everything was fine. We had just a little bit of money, not much. Wynona and I managed to find a motel on our meager funds but we decided that it was not royal enough for the occasion so we found another better one for the same money. If

Honeymoon in Mexico

this was a romance novel, well, I could elaborate, you will just have to imagine to get your kicks. Anyway, we went to that motel and spent the night, and the next day we went down to Derby, down to the farm.

Honeymoon
The next day, we stopped at the Dilley State Bank, where Dad had banked all of his farming years, and without any collateral except the big grin on my face, borrowed $100 for our honeymoon trip to Mexico. I told Mr. Avant I'd start paying him back immediately, as soon as I got paid. So we took off for Mexico. Oh boy. Just me and my bride. Boy, going to Mexico City on my honeymoon. It was some trip. I drove all the way down there with one arm. The other arm was around my sweet bride. We went down those mountain roads and around everywhere. Every once in a while we'd stop and there'd be some Mexicans on the side of the road trying to sell something. 'Course I could speak Mexican as good as the Mexicans

could, but Wynona couldn't speak a word. I'd stop and talk to them and she'd get scared to death. There'd be people come up beside the car wanting to sell us something. That's the Mexican sport. You've got to negotiate with them. We negotiated back and forth, back and forth, where we got things for practically nothing.

I wore my uniform on our honeymoon, I didn't have any other clothes. All of the Mexicans thought I was an officer in the Mexican

Newlyweds crossing the border into Oklahoma

Army, and I got lots of respect. To make a long story short, we went a hundred miles south of Mexico City to Cuernavaca and came all the way back to Laredo. We crossed the border and we had a trunk full of all kinds of gadgets that Wynona had bought. We had serapes, we had mariachi gadgets you shake, we had everything. After all of our expenses for eight days, we still had $8.35 left out of our borrowed money when we crossed the bridge back into Texas. My sweetie got a glimpse of what life with an engineer was going to be like when I got out my slide rule, at the border, to figure the rate of exchange and how much I was supposed to get back on my money. All the rest of it we had spent in Mexico for eating, for gasoline, for tourist courts, and all of the trinkets we brought back. It was amazing. We started out with a hundred dollars and we had $8.35 coming back. That got us back from Laredo clean up to the farm, where Pop and Mom were.

We were broke again. I hadn't been paid again. I had to borrow a little money from Dad to have gasoline, and we drove all the way to Corsicana. That Oldsmobile would go from Derby to Corsicana on one tank of gasoline. You know my Daddy, God bless him, he was a farmer. He had a gasoline tank there on the farm. Gasoline was rationed and was supposed to have been used in the tractors. But he let me fill my car up from that tank and I had gasoline to get to Corsicana. There we saw the telegram that had come ordering all of the troops back to their units. I borrowed another little bit of money from my mother-in-law and we had enough money for gasoline to drive all the way to Lawton, Oklahoma and Fort Sill. I knew that if I ever got to Fort Sill I could get my paycheck. "Cause they paid us at the end of the month and I was already past my paycheck time. And I knew I could get some money.

We found out the reason why all this had to take place was the division was recalling everybody who was on vacation because they were moving part of the division, especially the gun sections, so they could furnish the guns for the battery officers' training school at Fort Sill. They had to have guns to shoot up there and there were very few 105s available at that time, so they sent our battalion up there to serve as fire support.

Shooting Lesson

When we first got in the service we knew Wynona was going to be traveling all around and I wanted her to have some protection. There was a boy by the name of Dennis Moore who used to be a policeman in San Antonio, and he was in my outfit. I said, "I've got to get a pistol for my wife." Dennis said, "I've got one. It was my old service pistol. I'll sell that to you." So he sold that to me for little of nothing. Before I went overseas I gave it to Wynona. One day I said, "Honey, I think we need to go out and get some target practice." So we went to get some target practice. So I put three leaves on the side of a tree trunk that must have been fifty feet away. I said, "Try hitting those leaves." Bam! Bam! Bam! She hit every one of them. I said, "Honey, I think target practice is over. You don't need any more." You may not know it, but a woman is very, very deadly with a gun. They have a natural instinct. They don't aim them, they just point them, pull the trigger, and Bam! That's it. Well, she was good with that gun.

Wynona at target practice. Notice her homemade uniform coat

Target practice at Chambers Creek

Chapter 22
Preparing for War
1941-1943

Fort Sill (November 1941-March 2, 1942)

So we went out to Fort Sill and were looking for a place to stay. But there was no place to stay. They had moved all of these troops up to Lawton and things were kinda crowded up. There was a place north of Fort Sill called Medicine Park. There was a big old mountain up there and a pretty little stream and they had a resort hotel out there with a bunch of little one room cabins. The cabins had little porches covered with screen wire that had been dipped in plastic and all the little holes in the screen wire were plugged up so you had a porch with screen that the wind wouldn't blow through. It was dead cold up there, I'll tell you. See that was about November the 10th and all we could do was rent one of those summer cabins. It had a bedroom and it didn't have a kitchen in it, but it had a little bitty tiny bathroom and you sat on the commode when you took a shower if you had any water and you could stand it. Wynona took her showers in the big lodge where she had some friends. I took my showers on the commode with ice cold water. Oh Lord, it was cold.

We still hadn't gotten any money yet. We had a little bit of stuff to eat. There were rats up there so we emptied our clothes out of our suitcases and put our food in the suitcases and slid them under the bed and that kept the rats out of it. So we had something to nibble on. My battery was already in Fort Sill, all set up. Oh boy! Wynona and I would go to that battery and inspect the mess at least three times a day. We got three good meals, you know, eating the battery mess. We were doing pretty good there. Finally I got paid. Man was that something when I got paid. We were looking around and found a room we could rent in Lawton. It was with a school teacher who had two little girls. She was widowed, or something. We rented that room in her house. We had kitchen privileges. Oh boy, we were all fixed up there, we were living great.

The artillery range at Fort Sill was very difficult to fire on. It was fairly flat with deep ravines that you could not see from a distance. You could never tell whether your round was "short" or "over" when shooting at a target. We got some good practice on that range.

They transferred me to battery officers' school. That's where I learned to shoot artillery. I was an artilleryman, but we didn't know how to shoot artillery, we hadn't learned. In order for the people at the school to learn how to shoot artillery they had to have guns. And that's why I had my guns. Battery officers' training school is where you learn how to be a battery officer, you learn how to shoot artillery, you learn how to do a whole lot of things you were supposed to have known and you didn't. That's what the school was for.

Dinner for Colonel Garner
Wynona decided that she wanted to have a little meal and invite Col. Garner out to eat with us. She really loved Col. Garner and he loved her because they were friends of the family. The school teacher had a refrigerator in the kitchen-breakfast room and the top of the refrigerator was rounded. Wynona baked a cake. Oh, Col. Garner was going to be there and we had a cake. She set it on the top of that round refrigerator. Well that refrigerator would start up and run. Well the first thing you know that cake moved over and over and over and then Flop! It came off of the top of that thing, turned upside down and hit on the floor. Oh! She was mortally wounded. But we got through that dinner just fine, and old Col. Garner was real good and everything was lovely.

We had been up there a month and Wynona told her mother that we had spent $42 that month for groceries. Oh! Her mother raked her over the coals. "What do you mean, wasting money like that? You're not supposed to spend money like that, girl." She just gave Wynona a fit because she'd spent $42 for that whole month. After all, we'd had Col. Garner our there to eat and we'd had Charlie Hearn to come over to eat.

In fact, Charlie Hearn was visiting with us on December 7, 1941. That's the eventful day of Pearl Harbor. Charlie and I were sitting up there in the middle of our bed playing solitaire, cheating. We had a map on the back of the door of the war that was going on in Russia and Germany. We'd stick pins in the map wherever the action was. It's a wonder that lady didn't shoot us all for messing up her door with pins, but we did it anyway. Charlie and I were sitting up there playing sol when Pearl Harbor hit. Boy that was a sad situation. That was on the 7th. I think it was on the 19th that Charlie married his wife, Jo.

As things were going along there pretty good I was in the battery officers' school that was a week ahead of Charlie's school. I all of a sudden caught the mumps. I don't know how I caught the mumps, but I was in the hospital. I was put back a whole week, and I had to finish in the class that Charlie Hearn was in. From then on we were bosom friends. The four of us took off in my car and drove to Camp Blanding, Florida. From then on we were together all the time. He turned out to be one of my battery officers. His wife and my wife were the very closest of friends. And our wives kept in very, very close contact with each other all during the war. Those two girls, bless them, they each one wrote their husbands a letter every day for the entire 26 months that we were overseas. I would always report that I'd seen Charlie and he would report that he'd seen me, and the girls would immediately get together and compare notes, 'cause Wynona was living in Corsicana and Jo was living in Hillsboro, towns that are not too far apart. They spent an awful lot of time together talking about the situation.

In later years, after he got out of the war, Charlie Hearn gave a substantial scholarship to Texas A&M to honor me and my wife Wynona. After Wynona passed away he and Jo, his wife, gave a $25,000 scholarship to the Texas Methodist Foundation so that the proceeds from that could be sent to our Methodist church here in Marble Falls to give college scholarships. Charlie and I were always very, very close, because we were in the National Guard together, he was one of my battery officers, his wife and my wife were real close friends. It was a very, very interesting experience to be with Charlie and Jo all of that time. Being as Charlie was one of my officers I did everything I could to make it whenever we moved I would be in command of the battery and move it and I'd detail him to move our girls.

Camp Blanding (March 8-July 6, 1942)
When we left Fort Sill we were going to Camp Blanding, Florida. Before we reported in to our units we had to find a place for our wives to live. We found a place to live at Glen Cove Springs, but they only had one room. That one room had a big bed and just a twin bed. So Charlie and I drew straws to see who was going to get the big bed. Wynona and I won and got the big bed. That's alright 'cause Charlie hadn't been married very long and he needed a little bed. Anyway, come the next morning we got ready to go to camp and we had to shave. Back in those days we used a brush and lather and a razor. We had to have something to heat some water in. We looked and looked and looked and looked and we couldn't find anything to heat water in. Finally we spied a tin can that had wax shoe polish in it. So we scraped that wax shoe polish out of that tin can, cleaned it up, put our water in it, put it on the stove and got it hot. And that's what we used to shave with, 'cause we didn't have anything else. You've got to be resourceful when you're in a war.

Green Cove Springs was a nice little town on the St. Johns River. To get to Green Cove Springs from Camp Blanding you had to go east, and about ten miles from Camp Blanding was a town called Penney Farms. J C Penney, back in the early days, was very fond of Methodist preachers, so he built a farm there and a whole bunch of houses for retired Methodist preachers to live in. Each one of them had a spot where they could have a garden, and there was a nice chapel there, and they'd take turn-about preaching every Sunday. Wynona and I stopped there a time or two just to go to church.

Then I decided, "You know, maybe I should give Wynona a little training about changing a flat", 'cause girls are not too good on changing flats. And when they are out on their own they've got to be independent. So what happened was I told Wynona she had to learn how to change a tire. The place we were living had a big tree out in the yard, so I parked my car under the tree and I sat under the tree in the shade directing the operation of changing the tire. Bless her heart, she had a hard time getting that jack out and getting that car jacked up. But she finally did it. She got the car jacked up and she had a hard time getting the lug nuts loose on the wheel, but I showed her how to put the lug wrench on it and then kick it. She finally got all of the lug nuts loose on the wheel and she took that wheel off and she put it back on. You know people would drive by and see her out there working on that tire, just a-working up a storm, and there I was sitting under that tree just a-laughing. I guess they thought I was a mean so-and-so, making his wife fix the car while I was sitting in the shade. Anyway, the girls had a pretty decent livelihood there in Camp Blanding. They walked all over town. They did a lot of walking, and they would come to see us at the camp.

36th Division training locations before leaving for Europe

The reason they moved us to camp Blanding, Florida, was because there was a great big lake in the middle of this camp. They wanted us to learn how to do amphibious work on that lake, moving vehicles and things across the lake on rafts, and we did a pretty good job. We also did some other things around there. I had a boy that had been an enlisted man in the National Guard. When we got mobilized he was able to get a commission as an officer in the Army Air Force. He transferred out and became an officer in the AAF. You know enlisted men always have a grudge against their officers. So, one day while he had his little artillery liaison airplane parked there right next to my battery, I told him I wanted to go for a ride in the plane. So he says, "Fine." I got in the back seat. Golly bum! I had a real good pair of sunglasses. I didn't have sense enough to know that you weren't supposed to stick your head out the window of an airplane; the wind might blow your sunglasses off. So I lost my sunglasses. He decided he was going to have some fun with me. He had an officer in there and he was going to teach that officer a lesson to make up for those days when he was an enlisted man. I was in the back seat of that airplane and we were just flying around. Boy, he turned that airplane every way in the world to get me all shook up. And he shook me up to where I got sick as the dickens. We had earp bags in that airplane. I got an earp bag and I filled it full. Finally I reached up and caught ahold of the back of his collar. I said, "If this airplane hits one more bump I'm going to spill every bit of this stuff down your neck." You know, that airplane flew the nicest you ever saw all the way back to the landing field. It was a great ride.

We did quite a few things down there in Camp Blanding. We practiced moving things across the lake. We had to learn how to swim a hundred yards. We did that in the lake. Finally they said they were going to have to send us on maneuvers in North Carolina. They wanted us to get some practice operating in the mountains. So we had to move our artillery battery to North Carolina. Well, since Charlie Hearn was one of my officers, I was the captain. I decided I was going to put him in charge of the details of seeing that our wives got to North Carolina alright. He had gotten a car by then, so he and his wife got in their car and Wynona got in our car and they followed us all the way to North Carolina.

I had built a trailer sometime during my stint at Fort Sill that I could pull behind my car. It was a simple little old trailer. Dad used to have a coupe. He had a little trunk that slid in that coupe that made it kinda like a pickup truck. He had disposed of that trunk so I got that and one weekend I got some wheels and springs and made a little trailer that I could pull behind my car. So we pulled that thing with us. We had the Hearn's and our stuff in that little trailer. We didn't have very much. When it came time to move we loaded our artillery trucks and guns and everything up on the train. We were going to learn how to move our equipment on the railroad. So we loaded the train and got it fixed up. We had a whole bunch of flatcars, and they had some ramps they could put from one flatcar to the next one. You could drive up on the end of the train and keep going until you got to the front of it, with all of that equipment going from car to car to car until you got to the end. Then we got it all tied down and got it ready to roll. I sent Charlie on ahead, he and his wife in their car and Wynona in our car pulling that little trailer. And we went to Wadesboro, North Carolina.

Wadesboro (July 7-August 16, 1942)
Now the girls scouted around and they found a place to live in Wadesboro, North Carolina. 'Course there were other wives that were moving along with us at the same time. We'd all gotten to be pretty good friends. Wynona and I were in one house, and the lady that owned that house was a real nice lady. We were doing a lot of maneuvering out in the country. Way out in the country there was a store that was called White's Store. There was a telephone line that went from Wadesboro to White's Store. It was a one-wire telephone line. We had telephone equipment and we knew how to run telephones and what not. Every night kinda late, almost dark, old Charlie and I would get in the Jeep and we'd drive to where we found that telephone line to White's Store. Well, the store was closed by that time. We'd drive a stake in the ground and the ground would serve as the return wire. We'd hook up to that other wire. We'd dial the telephone and tell the operator to ring the number where our wives were staying. So we'd talk to our wives every night while we were out on maneuvers. Those poor people at White's Store, it like to drove them crazy 'cause somebody was always using their

telephone line. I don't know whether they ever had to pay anything or not, but we took the privilege of using that telephone line to call our wives.

And I can remember one time, a little bit of scandal. I had come in from maneuvers and I was in our room upstairs. Now one of the other soldiers and his wife had a room upstairs, too. There was a bathroom between us. Well, I guess precautions weren't best in the world. One night I went in that bathroom stark naked, and just as I opened my door

John D and Wy at Wadesboro

to go into the bathroom, the lady on the other side opened her door to go into the bathroom, too. Of all the hollering! I sure did get out of there in a hurry. Other than that everything was pretty good. The lady that Wynona was living with had a son in the service in New York State, I think it was New York City, and he was going to graduate. Oh, she tried to get Wynona to go up to New York City with her so she could watch her son graduate. But 'course Wynona wouldn't go and I wouldn't let her go. So that was the end of that.

We did a lot of maneuvering around in the Carolinas. They wanted us to learn how to operate in the mountains. So we went up the mountains. We went up some mountains that were so steep that you couldn't turn the Jeep around. What you had to do was tie a rope on the front bumper and run it around a tree and then tie it to the back bumper. So that as you went backward and forward like a bow on a fiddle trying to get the vehicle turned around that rope would keep you from rolling over and rolling down the mountain. We got pretty good at that kind of stuff, we got where we could do about anything. We would let guns over a cliff on a winch cable. Those gun crews could pick up stuff and move them like nobody's business. So we did pretty good.

Camp Edwards (August 19, 1942-February 25, 1943)
Eventually we went up to Camp Edwards on Cape Cod. We got up there and there was a bunch of other troops there and they were in the barracks. There were no barracks for us, we had to camp out. So we pitched tents. Eventually the other troops moved out and so we moved into their barracks. We had to find a place to live up there. You know those two gals, they got to be real good at finding houses. They'd find a place to live and then they'd come and find us and tell us where they were. They were tough little critters. Boy, they really knew how to take care of themselves and always find us. God I loved that gal, she was so fantastic.

Anyway we moved out to a place that was on Lake Mashpee. It is a pretty sizeable lake on Cape Cod. There was an old man and his wife who owned a farm that bordered the lake. It was called Bessie Farms, their name was Bessie. Charles and his wife got a room in the house with the old man and woman. They had a pretty nice setup there, 'cause it was a pretty good house. The house that I had was a summer cottage. It was right down on the lake. It had a fireplace, but no other kind of heat, no hot water. The water you got was pumped out of the lake and you were always scared to death it would freeze. Oh Lord, and when it came time to take a bath and it was wintertime you had to put a big old washtub in front of the fireplace. Now when you take a bath in a washtub in front of the fireplace the side towards the fireplace gets almost scalding hot. If you touch it it'll burn the dickens out of you. On the opposite side from the fireplace it is just like ice. At times it got to 17 degrees below zero when we were on Lake Mashpee.

We had to warm ourselves with firewood. This summer house was down a real steep bank so we had to throw that firewood down that bank and then carry it into the house. Taking a bath was so difficult I did one of my experimenting things. I decided I was going to make a pump and run the water up a tube and then use it kinda like a shower to wash myself off. I made a bellows. It had two boards and a piece of rubber from an inner tube. As you'd mash on those boards it'd suck water in that bellows and it would run out of that hose up at the top. So you'd sit in that tub working your foot up and

House at West Falmouth, Massachusetts with the trailer

down to pump water to get a shower. Oh boy! Life was terrible at that place. Cold, my gosh, it was a log cabin. Poor little old Wynona spent her entire time while she was there in that cabin caulking the cracks. She caulked and caulked and caulked and caulked, and there I was over on the camp tending my duty and there my poor little old wife was trying to keep from freezing to death in that damn cabin on Lake Mashpee.

Finally, what we decided to do was get with the Joneses. We rented a pretty decent little house with Remus and Winifred Jones at West Falmouth. It had a kerosene stove in the kitchen and a coal-burning stove in the living room and a kerosene hot water heater. The pipe froze one time between the kerosene hot water heater and the bath tub. So we couldn't get any water through. Finally we got it thawed out by using the two electrodes off a welding machine. We hooked one of them up by the hot water heater and one on the pipeline next to the bathtub. We turned the juice on and it heated the pipe up and thawed that pipe up so we could get water. Boy! I'm telling you when it's seventeen below zero it's cold. Every time the snowplow would come by he'd completely block our drive. Poor old Remus Jones and I would have to get out there with a shovel and shovel the driveway out so we could drive to the camp, which was about five miles away. But we made it alright.

Then we had to do gun drill in that extreme cold weather. They wanted us to know how to operate in the cold. Seventeen below zero, and we had to get out there and act like we were shooting artillery pieces. And it was cold and miserable. So I decided I might as well have a little fun when we were suffering so much. So I made me an air rifle that was run by the air compressor. When you hit a valve it would shoot a blast of air down a copper tube which I had put inside the barrel of the 105 and it would shoot that BB out of there with a bang. So we'd get out there and do gun practice. We would move the gun and aim it and see where the BB went just like it was a 105 shell. We did a lot of crazy things.

In October they decided that they were going to have some maneuvers. They were going to have a fake enemy that was going to attack Cape Cod from Martha's Vineyard. Those boys were very resourceful that were in my gun crews, so they rounded up four hooks like those that go on the back of these 2½ ton trucks. They mounted one on the center of each front bumper. On this maneuver they were going to grade us on how fast we could approach an enemy that was invading us and how fast we could get our guns around and get them into position. So my boys got those hooks and put them on the front bumpers, and the first thing you know they were pushing 105 artillery pieces in front of the trucks. They were going down the road 30 mph pushing that gun like it was a wheelbarrow in front of them. So naturally when we had the maneuvers our guns were already in place. The "enemy" was coming and we were advancing toward them and the guns were out in front. We didn't have to stop and take the guns loose, turn them around and line them up and whatnot. We already had it lined up; it was already in front of us.

So we won all the prizes. We had a lot of fun doing that. I was promoted to captain on September 23, 1942.

Fort A. P. Hill (March 1943)

In the last part of February the battalion with some other units of the division left Camp Edwards for the Piney River area in Virginia to take part in mountain maneuvers. The battalion moved to A. P. Hill military reservation near Amherst, Virginia. The girls were moved to Port Royal, Virginia from the end of February to March 6, 1943. After two weeks at A. P. Hill, the battalion moved by train to Fort Dix, our staging area. Here we became prisoners, as the big secret was we were about to ship out. The girls started for home on a long journey, leaving us on March 6, 1943. Boy it was a sad day when Jo and Wynona had to get in their cars and head back to Texas. Thank God, they got home after four days and only one flat on the trailer, and we talked to them before we shipped out. We boarded the *S. S. Argentina* at Staten Island on April 1st of 1943, and we landed in Oran, North Africa on April the 13th.

John D with Charles Hearn

Chapter 23
North Africa
1943

This is a phase of my life that I wish had never happened, except that it did give me a very strong belief in the Almighty, and made me realize that nothing was going to happen to me unless it was His will.

Being color blind to certain colors, I could see camouflage that someone with normal vision could not see. War equipment is always camouflaged for normal eyesight. I could see artillery rounds hit where the normal person could not. I had a God-given gift of being very mechanical and developed the skill of knowing exactly where an artillery shell was going to hit just by the sound of it as it passed over my head. I developed skills that told me exactly the location of a rifle or machine gun location by the sound of its "thud". The distance to the gun was learned by the location of the "crack" over my head.

Oran (April 1943)
Now in Oran, Algeria we camped out on a place where some more troops had previously been camped, at Ossi Ben Oakbar, 15 mi SE of Oran. We got in there at night on April 13th, my 25th birthday. I want you to know that those troops that had lived there previously had not been properly trained in sanitary discipline. They had messed all over the area. They probably did not know how to dig a

This is not a complete history of the 36th Division in World War II. For more information see www.TexasMilitaryForcesMuseum.org/gallery/36div.html

197

latrine. Oh God, it was terrible! Then we stayed there for a few days, and then they loaded us up on a train. Now this train had what they called "40-and-8" cars. That meant that they would haul forty soldiers or eight horses. They loaded us up and shipped us off into the desert south of Oran. I think the name of the town was Magenta, but it had a French Foreign Legion post and French soldiers. So we went down and camped out pretty close to where they were.

What we did down there is learn how to shoot rifles (M-1s). We never had been taught how to shoot an army rifle, or how to find a target. What you'd do is you'd go out there with a buddy. One person would describe a target on the hill, maybe three or four hundred yards over there. You had to figure out a way to describe how to find that target. So you'd say, "Well you see this? Alright, you got that. Now if you just go three fingers wide from that", you'd hold your hand out and you'd use the width of three fingers as a measuring distance. "You see something else?" "Yeah, I see that." "Now you go up so many fingers and you see something else?" "Yeah, I see that." Well then you would identify a target. So that man would then take his rifle and shoot at that target while you used your field glasses to see how good he was at hitting it. So we did a lot of practicing shooting rifles like that and learning how to do it. That's all there was to do. It was hot and dry.

Rabat (May-June 1943)
About that time the military got to worrying about the Strait of Gibraltar. They said, "My gosh! What if the Spaniards cut us off from going through the Strait of Gibraltar? That would mess up the whole war effort." So what they decided to do was to ship our division to the cork forest at Port Lyautey. Now there was a cork forest just outside of Rabat, French Morocco, and it was very close to Spanish Morocco. We had our artillery cub planes. So, every day we'd get in those artillery cub planes and fly up and down and look over into Spanish Morocco to see if we could see any kind of activity that might be going on at all to see if they might cut us off at the cork forest. So we did a lot of flying up and down, up and down.

Now this cork forest was a very peculiar place. They had great big trees in there, and the bark on a tree sometimes would be 3 or 4

Getting a haircut in North Africa

inches thick, and it was nothing in the world but cork. What they'd do is they'd take one of those trees, and they'd go up about eight feet high and cut a ring around the top. Then down at the bottom they'd cut a ring around the tree. They they'd run the knife down the tree all the way, and they'd peel off a great big piece of bark that almost looked like a boat, it was so big. So that was the cork forest. That's where the industry was that made all the stoppers for the wine bottles.

Well, you know when you think about cork you begin to think about ice cream freezers, my goodness. I told you I had some of the most resourceful boys there ever was in the world. So they decided that they wanted to build an ice cream freezer. Well, that's fine; we'll build an ice cream freezer. So they built a big old box almost four feet by four feet by about four feet high out of wood and they lined it with cork. Then they got a big garbage can and put it in the middle of it. That was the container to put the milk in. They made a dasher. Then there comes a problem because the vertical shaft of the dasher sticks up, but you need a horizontal shaft to put a big crank on so you can turn it like a conventional hand-turned ice cream freezer. They needed some spur gears. Like I say, my boys were very resourceful. We weren't the first troops to land in Africa. There was an initial invasion there. When the initial invasion went in the troops scuttled a few boats. My first sergeant and motor sergeant took a couple of mechanics over where those boats were and they found a nice set of beveled gears, just perfect to make an ice cream freezer. So they confiscated those gears. We were just about to have ice cream. About that time the CIA was trying to find out what happened to those beveled gears from the steering mechanism of the French ship that had been scuttled. Oh boy! The boys didn't know what to do. I told them, "Boys you'd better get rid of those gears. You better take them out there and bury them or do something with them. But you better get rid of them." They got rid of those gears, I'll tell you. We never did get to make any ice cream.

When we first landed at Oran I told you we were at a filthy spot where the troops had been camped before and the troops were really messy. There was sort of a notch in the beach, a cove. The boys decided that they wanted fish for supper. They were going to go fishing. I said, "OK, Go fishing if you want to." Well, they took some hand grenades and they went fishing. They threw those hand

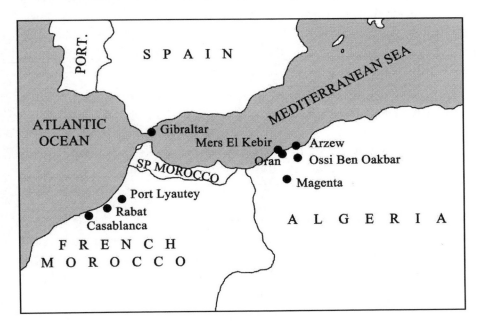

grenades in that water, and boy the fish came bubbling to the top and we had the biggest mess of fish you ever saw. We fed our whole battery with fish that those guys had killed with just two or three hand grenades. We had lots of fish.

We got ahold of a pretty good car engine and an airplane propeller. We bolted the propeller to the engine and built a frame to hold it. We pulled that around with us, planning to make a snowmobile for use in Italy.

John D and Charles Hearn in North Africa

As we were going on that road to Rabat from where we were around Oran you would see these natives lie down on the side of the road. You know, the wind would be blowing and that sand would be drifting like crazy because the roads weren't paved, they were just dirt roads. That sand would be drifting and drifting, and they didn't have sense enough to get up and move on the other side of the road so they would be upwind and wouldn't be getting all that sand and dirt on them. They just lie down on the ground and just pull those sheet clothes up over them and just sleep like nothing had happened, just like another little sand storm. They didn't worry at all. Oh Lord!

Eventually we stayed in the cork forest for a while and patrolled that thing up and down and we finally decided that everything was pretty secure around the Straits of Gibraltar. So they moved us back to Arzew, near Oran (July 4) in preparation for the attack on Italy. Now we did pretty good there, got lined up in the ships. We sailed on September 5, 1943 from Mers El Kebir, headed for the invasion of Italy.

Chapter 24
Camp Life

Artillery Shells

We shot 105 mm howitzers, or simply "one-oh-fives". Artillery rounds, or "shells", came with a separate projectile and shell case. The shell case was brass with a side less than 1/16 of an inch thick. The base had a flange that prevented the shell from going into the breech of the gun too far. There was no seal to prevent the gas from escaping when you fired the shell, but the thin casing wall expanded to the diameter of the wellbore. The base of the shell case was thicker and had a primer about 3/4 of an inch in diameter and recessed about 1/16 of an inch. You hit that baby and that's what set it off.

The projectile was a separate piece, weighing 33 pounds, and fitting loosely into the top of the shell case. They were mostly hollow steel with explosives (TNT) inside, and a fuse in the nose. They came in different styles. A regular shell exploded when it hit the ground. If it hit a tree limb and exploded in the air it was called a "tree burst". An "armor piercing" shell was what we used to shoot at tanks. Later in the war they invented "proximity shells", which had "proximity fuses", and exploded about thirty feet in the air. They would rain shrapnel down on soldiers in slit trenches. After they came out that is mostly what we shot.

Each brass shell case came with about six charges inside it. Each charge was in a bag connected to the next one with a string. They were as big around as the shell, and the height depended on the charge. If you were going to shoot charge "five" you pulled out the top charge and yanked it to cut off the string on the top of the shell.

Then you threw the excess charge away. A charge "six" had a trajectory that was almost flat. It you were going to shoot over a mountain you needed a less flat trajectory so you used a smaller charge than a "six." At Mt. Castellone our target was down in a ravine, so we had to use a smaller charge.

Heat

We accumulated quite a bit of powder bags if we did a lot of shooting. We put the extra powder bags in a pile. The gunpowder itself was not actually powder, but it was kinda like short pieces of spaghetti about 1/16 of an inch in diameter and 3/16 of an inch long. It didn't explode if it wasn't under pressure, but would burn. Then on a cold day we would start a small fire (not too big so the enemy wouldn't see it). We would sit around the fire, and every guy would have a handful of gunpowder. Every now and then someone would throw a little into the fire. It would flare up briefly and give us some heat.

When we were out of the line we would sleep in pyramid tents. When we were in the line we slept in pup tents. We used our little one burner stoves in the pup tents, but we had homemade heaters in the pyramid tents. We would take a 105 shell case and drill about eight or ten holes about 1-1/2 inches above the base. Then we took a copper tubing with a valve on it, and put the end into one of the holes in the casing. We hooked the other end to a can of gas. The men would liberate a downspout from a house and make a chimney for the stove. We pulled back the fly that covered the hole in the top of the tent and stuck our stovepipe out there. We would set the gasoline on fire, and it would get red hot about 3 feet above the ground.

White Gasoline

When the National Guard were on maneuvers in Louisiana we knew we would need something for light. I bought some gasoline lanterns. Lead in gasoline would plug up the lanterns, so we made our own "white gasoline", and continued to do so all through the war. Our gasoline would come in 5-gallon cans with a screw cap. We would get a 50 foot coil of copper tubing. Then we would drill a hole the same diameter as the tubing in the cap of the gas can and insert the end of the tubing. We would set the gas can three or four feet from a fire. The gas vapor would go through the tubing and condense into a liquid. The lead would remain in the 5-gallon can, and the liquid coming out of the tubing would be lead-free white gasoline suitable for our lanterns.

Eating

We had one-burner stoves that burned gasoline. We carried white gasoline in canteens to burn in our stoves. The stoves were about 3-1/2 or 4 inches in diameter and sat inside a container about 10 inches high. The bottom container was about 8 inches high. The top container came down on top of the lower one, and was a good 3-1/2 or 3-3/4 inches high. It made a nice little compact unit. The stove was inside it. It had a little thing that came out that looked like a wire. When you turned it around it would poke open the gas jet. It has a screw valve that you opened to control the height of the flame. It had a fill cap, and maybe an air pump. The top had some little fingers. If the fingers were flipped in they made a grill, but if they were flipped out they made a top that would hold a pan. It was a wonderful piece of equipment and kept me alive. I would sit down in that hole when it was raining every day and freezing every night, and I would sit there with that stove between my legs. The cap had a wire handle that you could fold open and it gave you something to hold on to while it was hot.

The battery had a cook, and sometimes we could eat in the kitchen. But most of the time we had to eat "K" rations or "C" rations. Everybody liberated a baby spoon and carried it in his pocket. The only washing they ever got was a good licking. A "C" ration came in one can. It was ready-to-eat stew or hash. They were awkward to carry, so we never carried enough. Then we would share with our buddies. Maybe each man would eat a third of a can. It was a miserable meal, but a can of stew and a can of hash mixed together with some water in a one-burner stove would make a pretty good meal. A "K" ration came in a cardboard box coated with wax. It contained chocolate, pretty good canned cheese, some crackers, dry sausages, and some hard candy. A "ten-in-one" ration was food for ten men in one box. They included cans of milk and some bacon.

Showers

About every six weeks they would send us to a place near a stream where they had a pump set up and a shower. The time would be more or less than six weeks, depending on the fighting situation. We would leave our clothes as we went in and get some others when we came out.

Drinking water came up from the rear in five-gallon cans—sometimes on a mule or horse, sometimes on a truck. We always carried about half a roll of toilet paper with us and we went wherever we were.

Mail

When I was at the battery I got mail every day that it came. When I was on the front-line someone would bring the mail up from the battery every few days. It was always V-mail, or occasionally a package. Wy would send me canned lemon pies.

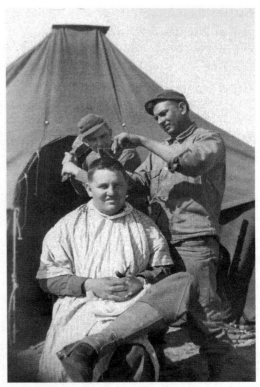

Trucks

My artillery battery had about 12 or 14 trucks (four trucks pulling guns, four ammunition trucks, several trucks for the cooks, one command car, and a jeep for every officer). Every truck that didn't pull a gun pulled a trailer.

When I was with my battery I had an orderly, Alford Bilski, from Brenham. He made my bed and took care of every need I had. He had other jobs, too.

Alford Bilski with frying pan

He was really a good boy. I had a driver, Joseph Starman, from Carroll, Iowa. He was of German descent, and could speak German, so we called him Kraut. We travelled at night with no lights, but Starman was never lost. He was always where he was supposed to be. When I was on the front line Starman and the jeep would go with me. Every night Starman would come and find me. I don't know how he did it.

I had my jeep and carried "C" rations in it. My air mattress stayed in my trailer. Most nights I slept on it. One of my biggest worries was that the Germans would shoot a hole in my air mattress, but they never did. My driver, Joseph Starman, always had it near where I was.

Joseph Starman on left

Chapter 25
Italy
1943-1944

Salerno (September 9, 1943)

When we were going to make the landing at Paestum, I was on the attack transport *USS Joseph T. Dickman*, and for some reason or another I had grown a silly damn mustache. Well, everybody's gotta grow a mustache in his lifetime just to see how stupid he looks. Anyway, I had this mustache. We loaded on that boat and were fixing to make the landing in Southern Italy. I was sleeping on the top bunk. It had one of those oscillating fans, and every time that fan would oscillate it would blow the hairs up my nose. I had to get up and shave that dang mustache off before I could ever make the landing in Paestum.

USS *Joseph T. Dickman*, APA-13

As we landed we came into Paestum. I came in in the second wave. We thought that the Italians had surrendered and it was going to be a breeze to go in there. There wouldn't be nothing. We didn't know those Germans were sitting there waiting for us. We went in there and made the landing, and gosh it was bloody. Things were really popping there on that beach. I went in on the second wave because I was looking for a place to put my gun battery. As the guns come in on the DUKWs ("ducks"), we had uncased the ammunition out in the ocean because we didn't know if we might have to shoot the guns out of those ducks. We could do that if we had to, but we sure didn't want to. We uncased a bunch of ammunition, took them out of the paper fiber containers. You know the 105 shell case, the back end part where the powder is, is a thin brass shell. You can hit those and dent them real easy. Coming in on those boats the shells rolled around a little bit 'cause we had them all ready to use. We came in and unloaded the guns. I was already there lining the guns up so they would be parallel. At the time there wasn't any other battery

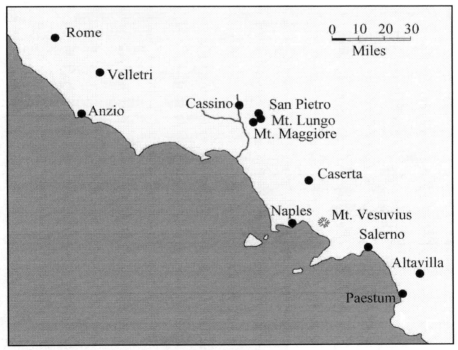

Important places from Salerno to Rome

commander there. So I was lining up all of the guns that came in, all 12 of them, lining them up so they could shoot parallel like one gun battery. (During the Civil War, at Shiloh, Ruggles had an artillery battery that had 62 artillery pieces lined up hub to hub. When they fired they shot out a blanket fire and killed everything in front of them.)

We had these 12 guns all ready. The Germans finally found out that we were coming there and they were throwing in a tank attack. Boy, they were on the road quick getting there with that tank attack. Our gun crews grabbed ahold of that ammunition, tried to put it in the gun, and it wouldn't go. They couldn't push it in because it was dented and wouldn't go. And you don't bump around on the back end of the shell cases too much because that's where the primer is, right in the middle of the case. If you hit that primer that thing's going to explode and it's going to kill anything that's around. When the guns wouldn't work something had to be done. That's one of the unfortunate parts about being a battery commander. You've got to do the unthinkable.

I told my gun crew to get out of the pit and hand me an ax. So they got out of the pit, handed me the ax, and I hammered that first shell in the breech of that gun. I knew it wasn't going to go off 'cause the Lord took care of me. That primer was just a little bit recessed below the surface of the back of the shell case. I knew that our axes had been used so many times, driving stakes and what not, that the heads were kinda concave. If I was very careful how I hit that shell case with that ax so that it would be flat and straddle that primer then I could drive it in. So I drove it in. There was Col. Garner, the man who was going to give Wynona away when we had that first military wedding at Camp Bowie. He said, "My God! What am I going to tell Wynona when Bennett blows himself up hammering those shells in?" But as soon as I got through hammering a shell and we fired that first round off, the explosion rounded that shell case up and it came out just as easy and pretty as you ever saw. So those other crews grabbed their axes and started hammering those shell cases in. They were just in time because those tanks weren't over two or three hundred yards in front of us, just a coming at us. We stopped the tank attack. Boy, it was something!

The first man I lost died in my arms at Paestum as he bled to death. Both of his jugular veins in his neck were cut by shrapnel and there was nothing that we could do but let him die. Things like that will drive you crazy and it is the reason I have war nerves disability (PTSD) today. I have fought some form of the war nearly every night since then. It has only been about the last ten years that the military has decided to give me a disability pension. It has been only about three years since I found out that they would pay me to go to the VA and get my medical needs taken care of. Nobody tells you these things and you have to find out for yourself. If you are a veteran get one of the books from the VA and find out what your rights are.

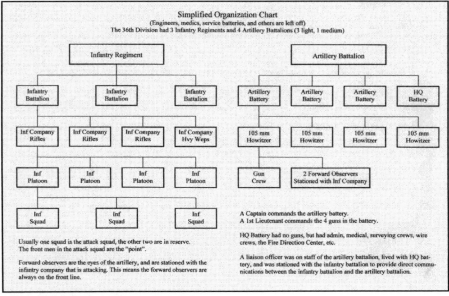

Simplified Organization Chart

I found some things to take my mind off the gruesome aspects of the war. The BBC put out a good news program, but you had to have something you could pick it up with, and when you were traveling on foot you couldn't be carrying a radio and power plant. The military put out an article telling how someone had found that you could touch a wire to the side of a safety razor blade and it would make a diode. Now if you had ever played with a crystal set radio when you were a kid you were able to build a radio. I had a walking cane that I mounted the razor blade on the side of and I had a radio earphone. I wrapped some wire around the cane that I could throw up in a tree for an antenna, and a piece of wire that went in the ground when I pushed the cane in the ground. It made a radio that needed no tuning, and anywhere we stopped I could pick up BBC and listen to the world news.

Power Plant

We hit one of those German "kübelwagens." A kübelwagen is a command car, kinda like a four door open-air sedan. It's a "thing", a VW jeep. We hit one of those right about the back wheels with one or our artillery pieces. We hit it so hard that it broke the housing that held the engine up on the back of this little thing, and it fell on the ground. As soon as there was a lull in the fighting I told my boys, "Boys, let's save that engine and see if we could make us a power plant."

Well, boy they got to work as soon as they got a little chance and a breather. They built a frame and set that jeep engine on it. When I got a little breather I got up inside one of those German tanks and I took out the DC electric motor that traversed the big gun back and forth from one side to the other. I mounted it on the wooden frame to use as a 220 volt DC generator. We bolted some 2 x 4s on the back of the flywheel of that jeep and sawed them out to where they were about the right length. We got an old file and sharpened it and used it as a wood turning tool and turned us a nice V pulley on the back of that engine. We put a belt on it, slapped the belt on that generator, and made the sweetest little light plant you ever saw. When we were relieved from duty on the front-line we already had an electric generator. We had the first electric generating plant before any arrived from overseas. It was months before anybody else had one. Lt. Col. John "Pete" Green was my battalion commander. Any time we got out of the line for a day or two, he'd be sure that the Headquarters Battery was real close to "B" Battery (my battery). He had the wire crews run two telephone lines over to my battery: one for the telephone and the other so I could send 220 volts back to his tent so he could have electric lights. We would rob light bulbs out of the Italian houses. I liberated a radio that worked on the standard 220 volts AC. It took me a while to learn how to convert it to run on

220 volts DC from my power plant. The power plant worked like a charm, but it had to run real slow, and the spark plugs would get fouled. Every night before supper the four battery officers would each clean a spark plug from the engine.

On about the second day they sent me up with the infantry as a forward observer. I went up to establish an observation post. After about 15 days they shifted officers around and I became a liaison officer. A liaison officer is the go-between who keeps up communications between the infantry and the artillery. The liaison officer is part of the infantry battalion commander's staff and stays with him all of the time. Whenever we were out of the line I was part of the headquarters battery. But I didn't spend much time with the artillery because when we were out of the line the infantry battalion commander, James Minor, had me spend my time training his officers and non-commissioned officers how to shoot artillery. From then on I was rotated between jobs, usually a liaison officer, but sometimes a battery commander.

We were out of the line right after this terrible, terrible battle that lasted for two or three weeks, when we were almost kicked back into the ocean. We were camped there; we hadn't gone in very far.

Altavilla
We had bad casualties when we landed and they had to have a replacement that could go up and direct artillery fire. (This was before we had that break where we made the light plant.) Artillery was no good unless it had eyes on the front line to tell you where to shoot. Col. Green sent a bunch of us officers that were not normally doing that kind of work. I was a battery commander and I was supposed to be with my battery. I had junior officers that they sent up as forward observers and things like that. Well, some of them got mixed up and were captured. So you do what you have to do with what you got. So the first thing Col. Green did was send me up to the front to a place called Altavilla.

Altavilla was a very, very interesting place. There was the most beautiful grape orchard up there. You could walk under the grapes, which were on trellises. I drove up in the town of Altavilla and parked my jeep, which had a radio in it (Sepember 12). I couldn't go any farther with my jeep. That was at the infantry command post. So I borrowed a couple of walkie-talkie radios from the infantry. We were going to post one of them right there at the jeep, so that when I radioed back on the other one to the one at the jeep they could relay the information through the radio in my jeep back to the artillery battery to get fire support. Charlie Hearn had been up there and radioed back, "I've been hit." I said, "What's the matter Charlie?" He said, "A tree burst came in and I've been hit in the back." I said, "Charlie, is there any infantry around you there?" He said, "Nope. I don't see a soul." I said, "Charlie, crawl out of there if you can, and come on back, 'cause you can't stay up there by yourself without infantry protection."

Well, I went on up to Altavilla, and I went through this grape orchard. Oh boy, you could reach up and get some grapes off and eat them as you were going up there to the front. I got up there and there was nothing but Germans up there, and no infantry at all. And, God, I had to come back in a hurry. So I came back in a hurry and went to where the infantry was supposed to have a command post, and they were all gone. They had been run out. And there was my jeep sitting

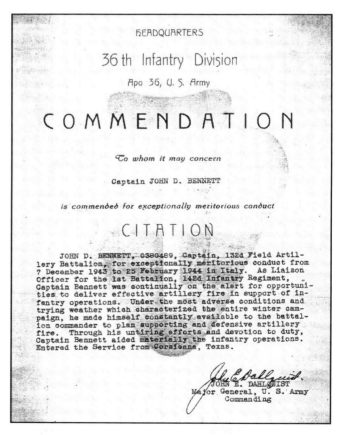

HEADQUARTERS

36th Infantry Division

Apo 36, U. S. Army

C O M M E N D A T I O N

To whom it may concern

Captain JOHN D. BENNETT

is commended for exceptionally meritorious conduct

CITATION

JOHN D. BENNETT, 0380489, Captain, 132d Field Artillery Battalion, for exceptionally meritorious conduct from 7 December 1943 to 25 February 1944 in Italy. As Liaison Officer for the 1st Battalion, 142d Infantry Regiment, Captain Bennett was continually on the alert for opportunities to deliver effective artillery fire in support of infantry operations. Under the most adverse conditions and trying weather which characterized the entire winter campaign, he made himself constantly available to the battalion commander to plan supporting and defensive artillery fire. Through his untiring efforts and devotion to duty, Captain Bennett aided materially the infantry operations. Entered the Service from Corsicana, Texas.

JOHN E. DAHLQUIST
Major General, U. S. Army
Commanding

215

there. I had Pvt. Lloyd with me, and he said, "Captain, I'll drive the jeep down if you'll go with me." And I said, "Let's go." So we cranked up that jeep and started down that road from Altavilla, and we got down there, oh, two or three blocks and got between two buildings. An 88 round come in and hit the building above us and knocked a big chunk of it over in the road. It blocked the road where we couldn't go any further.

I jumped out of the jeep and went over a wall that was about eight feet high. I had that little infantry radio with me. When I hit the bottom I was holding that thing by its strap. I hit the bottom so hard that the guts of that radio went right out the bottom of its case and fell on the ground. So I pulled out my pistol and I fired the only small arms fire that I fired during the entire war through that infantry radio. 'Cause I didn't want the Germans to be able to pick it up and know what we were doing.

I'm not sure exactly whether Pvt. Lloyd went straight ahead, or what happened to him. I think he did show up at the artillery battery later on, but I don't know how. But I went over that wall and down through a ravine, and finally wound up back where my artillery battery was. From then on I was doomed to the front. I was color-blind and they knew that I could see German camouflage and they wouldn't let me off the front. I had to do an awful lot of shooting of artillery. I can truthfully say that I believe that I have shot more artillery than any man that has ever lived or ever will live because I had 420 days of combat. I had over 360 on the front lines with the infantry. They had 300% casualties. That means every man in that infantry outfit was replaced three times. I was up there with them most of that time. During the time that I was on the front with the infantry during the war the Lord had me by the hand and I never was touched by a piece of shrapnel or a bullet or nothing. But I had people standing as close as an arm's length away, standing right in front of me who were shot in the head with a rifle bullet. Col. Minor was shot in the helmet with a rifle bullet, but it went just a little bit above his head, just kinda creased his scalp and didn't hurt him. After that we removed our officers' insignias from our helmets and collars.

In Charlie Hearn's incident when he thought he was hit in the back, it was a tree limb that hit him. A little while later I saw Charlie sitting up on the back of a jeep, just as well looking as you ever saw. He scared me so bad I could have killed him. But, thank God nothing happened to him. Well Col. Green got real worried about Charlie, and he needed somebody to run the fire direction center. Now that is where the artillery battalion commander hangs out. They are the ones that have the maps and they plot where the guns are and where the enemy is and figure out how far it is to the enemy, and all that kind of stuff. The forward observer or the liaison officer is up on the front line with the infantry, and he tells the fire direction center where the last shell that was fired landed. He tells him where the target is. So the fire direction center figures out how much to shift the guns and how much to increase the range in order to hit the target. It's a very, very important job. Charlie Hearn had had a lot of experience in surveying, and he was absolutely perfect at it. Charlie was a captain. Before it was over with, Col. Green told me, "John, Charlie's been doing this job for quite a while and it's supposed to be the rank of a major and I think I've got to pass him over you in order that he can have the rank he deserves. Besides that, you've got to stay on the front." So I was locked on the front, they wouldn't let me off. So I got passed over. I got teed off at Col. Green because I thought he did me a real injustice. But I couldn't feel too bad because he had my best buddy in my life doing the job that I really should have been doing, and I couldn't complain about that.

Million Dollar Mountain (December 2, 1943)
We had rested about six weeks near Altavilla and Naples after that terrible fighting we had when we first landed. Eventually we were put back in the line about 40 miles north of Naples. There was a mountain called Mt. Maggiore; we called it 1205 or the "Million Dollar Mountain". (1205 was the elevation of the mountain printed on all of our maps.) The reason we called it Million Dollar Mountain is because we had spent so much in human lives and ammunition trying to capture it. It was captured before I went up there, I think by the Rangers. I went up there and spent at least a couple of weeks. Cold, it was so cold, it was terrible. There were dead Germans all

over the top of that mountain. I can remember where I had my forward observation post there was a dead German that had all the back of his head blown off, and he was lying up there leaning against a rock. Thank gosh he never did get to stinking. You finally learn to live with that kind of stuff around you. It was very difficult.

Mt. Lungo (December 16, 1943)

The Italians had surrendered; they weren't going to fight us. Well eventually, after the Allies were up on 1205, the Million Dollar Mountain, the Italians had gotten together an army to help us. They were going to take Mt. Lungo. North of Million Dollar Mountain was a big mountain. In between was a smaller mountain, Mt. Lungo, with a north-south valley on each side of it. Up one of those valleys was the Appian Way into Rome. Up that valley was the way into Cassino, and eventually to Velletri and Rome.

The Italians decided that they were going to take Mt. Lungo. Bless their hearts, they were not soldiers. They lined up like the British did during our Revolutionary War, shoulder to shoulder, while the Americans were back there scattered out, hidden behind trees. They mowed the British down. Well the Germans were on Mt. Lungo and they were dug in real good, and you could just see those Italians fall over like dominoes when the Germans would mow them down with the machine guns. Well, that was bad, very bad. Especially when we got word that we were going to have to take Mt. Lungo the next night. I was up on 1205. It took eight hours to carry a wounded man from the top of that place down to the aid station on a stretcher. It was very, very difficult terrain. And we had to take Mt. Lungo the next day. Well, the infantry decided they were going to take it that night (December 15, 1943). So we slipped down the mountain, 1205, and came across the little valley and came up on the side of Mt. Lungo about halfway of its length from one end to the other. We slipped up on that mountain, came up behind the Germans, where they had dug in protecting the forward slopes of that mountain, and where they had massacred all of those poor Italian soldiers. Well, our boys slipped up there at night and they captured a German, and they made that German tell them where those dugouts were. He went around with them and pointed out the dugouts to them. Our infantry would tell the German troops to either come out or they'd

218

get a hand grenade thrown in. Most of them came out, but some of them got a hand grenade thrown in. Anyway, we took the mountain that night without losing a casualty. The next day the boys were going to go back and get supplies. They naturally fell into the natural trails that led off that mountain back to the rear, and they

HEADQUARTERS 152nd FIELD ARTILLERY BATTALION
A.P.O. #36, U. S. ARMY

21 May 1945

SUBJECT: Recommendation for Award

TO : Commanding General, 1st French Army
(Through Commanding General, 36th Infantry Division)

1. It is recommended that JOHN D. BENNETT, O-380489, Captain, Field Artillery, 152nd Field Artillery Battalion, be awarded the Croix de Guerre.

2. Throughout the month of February 1944, infantry elements of the 36th Division occupied and held Mount Castellone through Hill 706 to Hill 593, in the Cassino Sector, Italy. The latter part of February the infantry elements of the Division on Castellone Ridge were relieved by elements of the French Expeditionary Corps, and the 152nd Field Artillery Battalion was given a general support mission reinforcing the fires of the 1st Battalion, 67th Group, D.I.A., French Forces. Captain John D. Bennett, Liaison Officer with the 1st Battalion, 142nd Infantry Regiment, remained on Castellone Ridge to act as liaison and observer for the French Forces. The only observation in the sector was from the ridge line, which in many instances was also the outpost line, so his observation post was established in a cave along the crest of Mt. Castellone near Hill 706. Snow, sleet, rain, and the bitter Italian Winter made observation difficult, but many good targets were observed from this post and taken under fire, successful and damaging fires being adjusted on German mule trains, infantry and installations. The slightest movement of any kind on the ridge promptly brought forth heavy German mortar and artillery concentrations. The Germans also promptly shelled or mortored the ridge whenever they thought that observed fire was being conducted from that point, and many times when only unobserved fires were being delivered. In one instance a 105mm round crashed through the roof of the cave, coming to a stop next to Captain Bennett. Fortunately it was a dud. However, regardless of the intensity of the German shelling or his sensitive reaction to our own artillery fire, all targets observed were promptly engaged. In one afternoon three mule trains and an infantry column on one mountain trail were taken under fire and dispersed with casualties. No further activity was observed along that trail. Until he was relieved on 15 March when the battalion returned to a rest area, the effective and damaging artillery fire directed by Captain Bennett was of inestimable value to the infantry elements of the French Expeditionary Corps on Mt. Castellone.

3. The undersigned has personal knowledge of the information stated in this recommendation.

JOHN H. GREEN
Lt. Col., Field Artillery
Commanding

1 Incl
Proposed Citation

stepped on a bunch of "S" mines. Quite a few of them were hurt by these "S" mines. (When you stepped on them they jumped up about three or four feet and exploded. They caused a lot of trouble.) Anyway, we captured that mountain.

Mt. Castellone

The French were on our right, and they had already crossed the Rapido River up river from where we were operating. The Appian Way that went towards Cassino was to the left of the Rapido River crossing that the 36th division was ordered to cross under Gen. Mark Clark. (He ought to have been shot because of doing what he did, because he annihilated so many 36th Division troops.) Anyway, the French managed to cross that Rapido River. They had done a pretty good job of getting across, but they had a lot of casualties. So they decided to send the battalion I was with, which was the First Battalion of the 142nd infantry, to cross the river (right where the French had crossed, right beside a mountain called Mt. Cairo). We were to go up the side of Mt. Cairo, and then get on that hogback, called Mt. Castellone. (The rest of the 36th Division remained behind.) The Mt. Castellone ridge went from Mt. Cairo on the east to the Abbey on the west.

I was going up there and Lt. Col. Amick was the infantry battalion commander at that time. He and I were travelling along the edge of Mt. Cairo when he got shot and wounded. They had to evacuate him. Immediately they put Major James Minor in command of the first battalion of the 142nd. Oh, Lord, that was my doomsday. Minor knew I could shoot artillery, he knew I was colorblind, and he knew that he wasn't going to have anybody else up there but me to help take care of his troops with artillery. I spent much, much time with him until the end of the war. I was his liaison officer, and every time Lt. Col. Green would let me rotate back to command an artillery battery so I could get some rest, Minor would call Col. Green, "Send Bennett back up here." Minor thought that just because he was doomed to die as an infantry man, I ought to be there with him. He was wounded on two different occasions when we were talking. By the grace of God, I was never even touched.

Col. Green knew that he was not doing right by me. His desire to

John R. Gabbert

win the war at any cost was greater than his sense of fair play and I deeply resented his actions. I never even wanted to keep up with him after the war, and I never saw him again after I was rotated home.

There was another captain by the name of John Gabbert who had a very similar operation as mine. He commanded "A" battery of the 132nd Field Artillery battalion when we went overseas, and I commanded "B" Battery of the 132nd, and a guy by the name of Mark Hodges commanded "C" Battery of the 132nd. Well, Mark Hodges got wounded on the beach at Paestum, and of course he had to be evacuated and sent home.

We got up on Mt. Castellone during January 30-31, and it was freezing cold. We were so high that they took supplies up on the backs of mules so far, and then they had to load them on the backs of soldiers to carry them the rest of the way. Looking over the top of that mountain you could see in the Liri Valley up towards Rome, and we really wanted to go that way. But the valley right in front of us was a real, real steep ravine. For the Germans to get to us they had to come up that ravine, up the side of that mountain. Well, we fortified ourselves, but our boys had not built foxholes 'cause you couldn't dig foxholes, it was too rocky. They had stacked up rocks and they were inside of these pens of rocks. When the Germans threw in a counterattack (February 12, 1944), it was so severe that our infantry was shooting the Germans and they were falling over in the same rock pens that our soldiers were in. There were tremendous casualties on both sides. It was so bad, in fact, the Germans asked for a truce. So we gave them a truce (February 14, 1944), and I don't remember how long it was. Anyway their medics came up and picked up their dead and wounded and our medics went down and picked up our dead and wounded. After the truce was over the battle started up again just like it had never stopped.

One day the Germans hit my radio...Bam!... and knocked it about 50 feet. I had been down in a hole for protection. But that wasn't a close round. The close one was the one that came from the front side and hit a ledge up above where I was. If it had been six inches further over, it would have been down in the hole with us. But, as it was, it hit on the ogive of the shell and broke off the fuse. We found the fuse between me and my buddy. That didn't get us. So, after that I decided that, you know these Germans can't do anything to hurt me until the Lord's ready, and so I got out of that hole and pitched a pup tent on top of the mountain. Every day I got new holes through my pup tent where bullets or shrapnel would go through it.

Gasoline
After that I decided I better go down and check up on one of my forward observers, who was down toward the abbey, oh two or three hundred yards, maybe further than that. When I got down there, why there was Col. Pete Green. I said, "Col. Green, what are you doing up here?" He said, "John, I had to come up here, because if I didn't some of these young boys would think I was a mean old bastard that just sent them up here to get killed, and I had to show 'em I was not scared." I said, "Col. Pete, you belong in the rear. You go on back where you belong. I'll take care of things up here. You don't have to be up here, at all. Now go." So he left. After I'd checked out my forward observer I decided that it was time for me to go back over to my command post where I was set up. So I started running back over there, and the Germans started trying to hit me with what I called a 50mm mortar, they called it a "knee mortar". It was a small mortar and they could fire it pretty doggone fast. They were just popping right on my tail as I was running back.

When I finally got to where I was going I told my boys there at my liaison place, "Hand me that canteen of water, I've got to have drink." I was really exhausted. He handed me a canteen, I took the top off of it. I said, "Oh, no. This one has got gasoline in it, hand me the other one." I knew we just had one canteen of gasoline. Well, it so happened we had two. (We had the little one-burner gasoline stove that we heated our food on. At night we'd put them between our legs. We'd put the blanket over the top of it and burn that thing beneath that blanket between our legs and you'd see the blanket just steaming because it would rain every day and freeze every night. Oh Lord! It was miserable.)

Anyway, I told that boy, "Give me that other canteen." I took the lid off and gulp, gulp gulp. I drank half of that canteen before I realized I was drinking gasoline. Oh! I stuck my finger in my throat. Gasoline came out of my mouth just like it was coming out of a spigot at a gasoline pump. It was really coming out. Old Col. Minor was standing there, and he called up Capt. Mintzer, who was our medic, down at the foot of the mountain. He said, "My God, Mintzer! Bennett's drunk gasoline. What are we going to do?" He said, "Well, take up some of the milk out of the 10-in-1 rations we were eating, and have him drink that milk." I was already earping and earping and earping. So

```
                    HEADQUARTERS 36TH INFANTRY DIVISION
                         APO #36, U. S. Army

AG 200.6                                              4 September 1945

SUBJECT:   Award of Oak Leaf Cluster.

TO     :   Captain JOHN D. BENNETT, 0380489,
           132d Field Artillery Battalion,
           APO #36, U. S. Army.

        Under the provisions of Army Regulations 600-45, as amended, you
are awarded an Oak Leaf Cluster in lieu of a second Bronze Star Medal
for heroic achievement in combat.

CITATION

        JOHN D. BENNETT, 0380489, Captain, 132d Field Artillery Battalion,
for heroic achievement in combat from 26 February to 13 March 1944 in
the vicinity of Mt. Castellone, Italy. During this period Captain
Bennett, as artillery liaison officer and observer, worked under bitter
winter conditions of rain, sleet, and snow in an open observation post
that was almost constantly subjected to enemy shellfire. He effectively
directed artillery fire against all enemy targets, and his courageous
and tireless efforts resulted in the destruction of German mule trains,
infantry installations and personnel. Entered the Service from Corsicana,
Texas.

                                     R. I. STACK
                             Brigadier General, U. S. Army
                                     Commanding
```

223

when I got through I drank that milk. You know I never even had a belly ache. Nothing. Nothing at all! So old Minor was standing there. "I said, "Minor, what in the hell has a man got to do to get off this damn mountain?" He came up to me and took his index finger, and he'd pull it back. He says, "Can you do this, John?" I said, "Yeah, I can do it. Why?" He says, "Oh, that's your trigger finger, and as long as it's not frozen you can't get off this mountain." While he was telling me that, he was standing there with his feet frozen. It was so miserable up there. God, it was miserable!

We used to dig "slit trenches". They were as long and as wide as your body, and just deep enough that you could lie in them to avoid being hit by any shrapnel that came along at ground level. Of course, if a shell fell into your slit trench it was all over. When the Germans started shelling I could take a nap in my slit trench. When the shelling was over sometimes I could reach out and put my hand in a new shell hole. One time the fighting was getting pretty intense, and I said to Col. Minor, "Let's get in those slit trenches over there." He said, "John, I can't do that. I've got to be out there with my men."

While we were on Mt. Castellone I saw 1200 guns fire a T.O.T. ("time on target") at the Abbey at Monte Casino (which was at the west end of Mt. Castellone.) A T.O.T. is when different guns firing from different ranges are timed so that their shells all arrive on the target at the same time. The abbey was bombed from the air, too, and we would bet on which dive bomber would hit the abbey when they dropped their bombs. We shot the abbey at Cassino all to pieces because we thought the Germans were using it to observe us. Years after the war I met the German general who was in charge there. He said that the Germans were observing us from a mountain way off to our right. We had no idea they were observing us from there.

Rapido River (January 20-21, 1944)
While the First Battalion of the 142nd Infantry was on Mt. Castellone, north of the Rapido River, the rest of the 36th Division was still south of the Rapido River. We couldn't go to the north from Mt. Castellone, so we were recalled to the south side of the

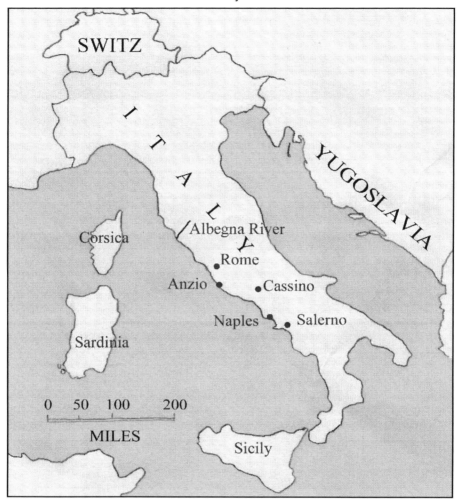

Rapido River to rejoin the rest of the Division. Gen. Mark Clark was the Fifth Army commander (who everybody in the 36th Division hated with a passion), and Gen. Walker was our division commander (who everybody in the 36th Division loved greatly because he was just a great general). Gen. Clark ordered a regiment to try to cross the Rapido River near the town of Cassino. Oh! That was a manslaughter. I'm telling you the soldiers were just slaughtered. They tried to carry bridges down there to cross the river. When they'd try to set them down, the mines would blow up and ruin the pontoons of the bridges. It was absolutely slaughter! And then that

225

damn Clark ordered Gen. Walker to commit the second regiment of infantry. They got shot up just like the first regiment. There just was no way you could get across that river because the Germans were so fortified and ready for us, and there just was no way to cross it. So then Gen. Clark ordered Walker to commit the third regiment, of which I was a member of the first battalion. Gen. Walker refused to do it. He said, "I will not slaughter any more of these troops." He refused to do it. Well, 'course old Clark had him relieved. Eventually he was sent back to Fort Benning to be head of the infantry training school, getting troops ready to go to the war. We all thought that Gen. Walker was one of the finest generals there ever was. He was a real practical practitioner. And we thought Clark was the low-downest, meanest SOB that ever lived. In fact, after the war the 36th Division tried to get Mark Clark court-martialed before Congress. But Clark was a West Pointer, and he had too much West Point influence going for him. Boy you mention Clark before the 36th Division and it was an immediate cuss word. Out of 6000 men of the 36th Division committed at the Rapido River, 2100 were lost.

Mount Vesuvius
We were in the vicinity of Mt. Vesuvius. During the war our airplanes would come out of North Africa and go into Europe on bombing runs. If they couldn't drop their bombs, they didn't want to go back and land with a load of bombs. When they flew back over Mt. Vesuvius they would drop their bombs in the crater. Bam! A big explosion. Bam! They were just dropping bombs in that thing all the time. The first thing you know Mt. Vesuvius erupted (March 18, 1944). So this young fellow that gave me that joyful ride in Florida, was camped next to my battery, 'cause we had a little landing strip there. He was eating with us. I told him, "Let's go look at Mt. Vesuvius." We got in that airplane...it takes young people to fight a war because they are certainly idiots. We got in that airplane and flew around Mt. Vesuvius while it was erupting. Raised that old baby up on the wing and looked down in that crater just to watch it erupt and it was just kicking up stuff coming and going, and there he and I were just flying around that thing looking at it. When it was all over with we flew back and landed. But it sure takes crazy people to fight a war.

Anzio

We didn't have any luck trying to cross the Rapido River, so they decided to try a run-around invasion and land at Anzio. While we had the Germans distracted at the Rapido River we sent a bunch of troops up to Anzio, and they went in almost without resistance, and got a pretty good beachhead. But they didn't exploit the beachhead. They went in and stopped and dug in. If they'd kept on going they would have been right behind those Germans that were causing so much trouble blocking that line that we were trying to get through. For some reason they did not exploit it. They dug in, and then it became a booby trap and had a lot of people slaughtered. The Germans eventually moved troops around to contain them and they couldn't get out. They even had a gun up there they called the Anzio Express. It was a great big, high-powered, long range rifle on a special railroad car. The way you aimed that gun is that you had a curved railroad track. As you moved up and down the curve of that railroad track it would swing the muzzle from one side to the other. Boy when that thing fired it sounded like a freight train.

After months of stalemate and tens of thousands of casualties they decided they had to break out of Anzio. They took the 36th Division, what was left of it, which was practically nothing but that one regiment....they took it and moved it around to Anzio by sea. They left the artillery in position opposing the Gustav Line (at the Rapido River) in order to support a new attack which was being started by some more troops. They really did a lot of firing (May 11, 1944). As soon as that was done they pulled us back real fast, put us on boats, and sent us up to Anzio. So we had to break out of Anzio.

The Germans had time to mine Anzio and you couldn't get out of there without going through mines. So the Americans did a very ingenious thing. They fixed up some tanks that had whipping chains on front of them. They had a shaft out six or eight feet in front of the tank that had big chains on it. They could rotate that shaft and cause those chains to beat the ground in front of the tank, especially in front of where the tracks were going to run. That way they would explode any mines that the tank was going to run over. So they got several of those things fixed up ready for the breakout. They knew they had to go through this minefield. So they took a bunch of 55

227

gallon barrels and cut them from top to bottom in two pieces, which made it kinda like a little bathtub. Then they'd take one "bathtub" and chain it to the back of another "bathtub". A soldier could squat down in each one of them. They tied a whole bunch of those things like a pig-tail train, and they pulled them behind the tracks of our tanks. As that tank was going along beating the ground in front of it exploding any mines and dragging these barrels with soldiers in them across the ruts that the tracks had just gone over, they crossed through that minefield and broke through it (May 23, 1944). So we headed for the town of Velletri.

The Battleship *Texas* was floating around out there in the Mediterranean. I told you we were rationed on ammunition. We only had so much ammunition we could shoot. The Battleship *Texas* was sitting out there with those big guns, so we called on that thing. By gosh we directed the fire of the Battleship *Texas* against those Germans. Boy, when that big old 12 inch shell hit it made a hell of an explosion. It made me real proud to think that we were firing the Battleship *Texas* and telling them where the shells were landing.

Velletri
Velletri was a very interesting place. There was a road that came from the south that went up towards Velletri. Right before you got to Velletri it turned off to the left down towards the ocean. It was part of the Appian Way on the road to Rome. When we got there the Germans had Velletri; we couldn't get in there. So we slipped past Velletri from the south side of town and passed east of town and got into an apple orchard (May 30, 1944). We tied all of our equipment down real carefully so it wouldn't rattle. At night we each put our hands on the shoulder of the soldier in front of us and we slipped through that orchard at night on the east side of town. We got up on Mount Artemisio Ridge, which was up behind the town, and we were up there come daylight.

First time in my life I ever shot artillery when the target was between me and my guns. My guns were way down in the valley, then there was the target, and then farther north was me up on top of the mountain. I was just shooting artillery like crazy and the Germans were trying to get out of there. They had a bunch of horse-drawn artillery that was coming up that road from the south. They'd get to that bend in the road and turn towards the ocean. Then it went through a whole bunch of trees. Now we were rationed on ammunition and we weren't supposed to shoot any ammunition we didn't have to shoot, and the general was very specific about that. Well, old James Minor and I were the biggest liars in the world. We'd try to shoot artillery and they wouldn't give it to us, so we'd tell them a tank attack was coming. Boy! A tank attack! You'd think they'd opened the floodgate. We had all the ammunition that we could shoot. So we shot everything. One time Col. Minor told me, "John, there's not any amount of artillery that's worth one of my soldiers."

The Damn Horse
So I was up there on the mountain north of town. I saw some horse-drawn artillery coming up that road, and boy I was shooting at that horse-drawn artillery. I shot and I shot and I shot, and the artillery turned the bend of the road and went off down in those trees. The horses were running, and that makes a very difficult thing to hit. It is not just aiming a gun and firing, you have to figure out where the target will probably be by the time the orders are given and the firing battery executes the command, and the shell gets there. Well I just covered those trees good with that artillery. But I said on the radio, "The damn horse got away!" Well, it just so happened that the general of the artillery was listening on my radio frequency when I said, "The damn horse got away." Boy, he called Col. Green up and chewed him out unmercifully. "Why was Bennett wasting all that ammunition shooting at a horse?" Well, I wasn't shooting at a horse, I was shooting at horse-drawn artillery, and there was a whole bunch of it.

You know, back in 1991 I went back to Europe with a bunch of 36th Division people. When I was over there in a town in France there was a soldier that came up to me and said, "Captain, do you remember when you were shooting at that horse-drawn artillery in Velletri?" I said, "Yeah. That's when the general chewed me out." He said, "Captain, I want you to know I went through that forest there, where that horse disappeared, and there were hundreds of dead horses in there that you had killed." I wish that damn general could have heard that, but he didn't. You know I got to where I

John D (left), Gaines Boyle, Charles Hearn,
Lt. Seward (foreground)

didn't respect the higher rank and all. They didn't amount to poodle-do to me.

Gaines Boyle
One of our favorite captains, whose name was Gaines Boyle, was a tall, tall guy. When we were back in Camp Bowie he loved to dance with my wife better than anything in the world. He had size 15-E shoes. We called him "Littlefoot." Our infantry was advancing up there one night, and they were single-file. When you have a single-file of infantry at night you don't have any support. The Germans hit them in the flank on that single file and killed poor old Gaines Boyle. Oh, I tell you we loved Gaines Boyle. In fact after the war Charlie Hearn gave the 36th Division Museum $12,500 in honor of Gaines Boyle. He also made me a life member, as well as himself. Charlie did a whole lot for a lot of people.

Rome
As we finally went on I didn't know that there was such a comedy going on about what troops were going to get to go into Rome first. Was it going to be the French or the Americans or the British?

There was a real interesting story. What a person needs to do is read some of those military books that talk about the hierarchy and the squabbles they had about which troops were going to get to go into Rome first. Anyway, we went into Rome without too much trouble. After we'd captured Rome the Pope reviewed gobs of soldiers.

The Pope was really on the Allies' side. He did the best he could. When we went into Rome they decided to have a huge open house for the soldiers. They got a great big old room with rope barriers down the middle and stools on each side. A bunch of the troops were there, and the Pope went down the aisle shaking hands with the soldiers. I was with the infantry. A bunch of Italians wanted to break through the line to get close to the Pope, but we wouldn't let them through. When he came along I said, "Hi Pope," but there were so many people there he didn't hear me.

Albegna River (Late June 1944)

After that we advanced to 100 miles north of Rome. The last shooting that I did in Italy, there was a river up there with a bridge about a thousand yards in front of us. James Minor said, "John, I want you to see if you can hold that bridge until my infantry can get there and capture the bridge." I said, "OK. I'll put a round on the left side of the bridge. I'll move it over 50 yards and put it on the right side of the bridge. I'll just rotate it back and forth like that, and that way the Germans can't come up to blow it." So we did that for quite awhile, and finally Col. Minor said, "John, my infantry is ready to take the bridge. Lift your artillery fire." So I lifted my artillery fire. Well, those damn Germans were sitting over there in one of those Volkswagen "things", those four-door command station wagons. They came running out from behind that hill, and came up to the end of that bridge and blew it before our infantry had a chance to capture it.

I was still there when a German Tiger tank started firing at me. He was out there in the middle of the field, about a thousand yards beyond the bridge. I was in a two-story rock house on the south side of the river. The walls were all rock; the partitions between the two rooms were rock. There were two rooms upstairs with a door between them, and there was a window in each room in the north side of that building, which faced toward the bridge. That tank was out there piddling around, shooting here, shooting there. I was in there trying to make a "precision adjustment" on that tank to see if I could hit it. My guns were back to the south four or five thousand yards from the tank, which is way back there. It takes awhile for that artillery round to get up there. Shooting that far is difficult because the shell can be affected by a head wind or a side wind. Anyway, I was trying to make a precision adjustment on it. That means you try to get a round short of the tank, raise your round a hundred yards and try to get a round over the tank, and then you cut the range back 50 yards. That means you ought to be almost on the tank. Well, I'd get a precision adjustment going, and I'd get a "short" and I'd get an "over", and I'd go in to "fire for effect." It would take two or three minutes between rounds, and he'd wiggle out, and move to the side. He knew exactly what I was doing. He was a good artilleryman. So I'd make another adjustment. I thought if I could ever make the precision adjustment, being as we were rationed on ammunition, I'd do it with one gun. As soon as I got the adjustment, then we'd bring in the whole battalion, and all twelve guns could shoot at it at one time. So I made the adjustment, and I made the adjustment, and Sgt. Wachter, who was one of my radio operators, said, "Captain, we hit him." I said, "Like hell we did! He fired!"

Well, you know I was in the house looking out the window. I was looking out of the window on the left side and there was a window on the right side. I was in that room back from the window, so they couldn't see me. I was looking right down his barrel with my binoculars when he fired. I saw that projectile come out of that gun, rise up just a little bit, move a little bit over, and I knew it wasn't going to hit me. It came in that other window. Boy, he almost got me. It was just by the grace of God that it didn't hit my window. He thought I was in the other window. I kept firing at him until I finally chased him off. But I never did get him.

That's the last firing that I did in Italy. After that firing they moved us down towards Naples. We were getting ready to make the invasion of Southern France. The infantry was already near Naples. We went back and got in boats and headed for Southern France.

Chapter 26
The Home Front

The war was going on in Europe, but there was also a lot going on back home.

Derby was a place of activity. Mother and Dad lived there on the farm, Betsy was home, and Harry was still home. I gave Wynona instructions that she was not to work during the war. Her job was to go and be with my mother and daddy and keep them company at least every other month. She was very good about that. She would go down there and visit with them. And all of the time she was writing me a letter every day. I couldn't have made it without all of that good support.

Wynona's daddy had been killed in a car accident when she was very young. She had to live with her mother, and they had no other place to go except to her daddy's father's house at his farm in Powell. That was a very unsatisfactory living arrangement, and as soon as they could they moved to Corsicana.

When we got married Wynona missed her daddy very much. When she'd go down to Derby to visit my parents you would always find her standing behind my daddy in every picture that we took. She took a liking to my daddy and he took a terrific liking to her. She always sat next to him at the dinner table. He'd get a cup of coffee and stick his spoon in that cup of coffee and swing that wet spoon over the top of Wynona's hand like he didn't know he was doing it. A drop of hot coffee would fall off the spoon and land on Wynona's hand, and he'd say, "Heh, heh, I'm a mean old devil." They really liked each other, and I was grateful for that.

Now Betsy was down there, and she was the authority on what was going on in Derby. What I know was mostly hearsay and what Wynona would write me in her letters. But Betsy was there all of the time, so I'm going to let her fill you in on some of the activity that went on around there. I know that they had a victory garden, and we had some cousins that came down and they used to go to Sid and Delma's.

Betsy's Recollections

<u>Betsy</u>: Daddy had a nickname for Wynona. He always called her

Lionel plowing the victory garden

"Skeeter". My husband George was overseas with the Eighth Air Force flying the P-51. I was pregnant, and went home and stayed a lot with my parents and stayed a lot with George's parents in Pearsall while we were waiting for him to come back home. Wynona would come down and visit and we were real good buddies, in fact we were good buddies always. We used to write our daily letters to our husbands and we loved to go to the post office every day. We even tried to get the postmistress to give us our letters on Sunday after we went to church at the little country church we all went to. Sometimes she was in a good mood and she would let us have them, and other times she wouldn't. That was a bright spot in our day, every day, to go to the Post Office.

We had a cousin named Tookie who lived in Derby, which was about a mile away from Mother's house. My brother and his wife, Sid and Delma, had a house about, oh, half a block I guess if you

Grace Melton and Martha Bennett in the victory garden at Derby

want to call it that, down the hill from Mother and Daddy's. We'd go down there and play games with my brother while my sister-in-law went to the Baptist church. She didn't like us playing cards. In fact, she got real upset with us, so we had to quit doing that.

Wynona, Betsy, and Harry at Betsy's Lake

There was a natural lake on the farm. When Grandma and Grampa came in the 1870s they camped out. It rained all night and the water got up to the axles on the wagon because they were camped in the bottom of that natural lake. During the war the lake was enlarged and called Betsy's Lake. The reason we had the lake was the highway department was building a new bridge over the Frio River and they had to have caliche to build the embankment. They dug a 16 acre hole, it was huge. My Daddy had an artesian well, and he turned that into the lake. That helped fill it up, and then what rains we got (which weren't too many) ran into the lake. We filled that lake up, it was a beautiful lake. The state stocked it with fish. My mother loved to fish, and she would go up there by herself and fish. She didn't care whether she caught anything or not. It was her way of getting away from everything and all of the worry. That was a beautiful lake for years and years. We had a sign on the gate, "Betsy's Lake, Swimming 10¢."

Eventually they dug some more caliche out of the lake, and dug down through the caliche and got down into the gravel. When they did it was like putting a hole in the bottom of the lake, and the water would drain out.

In 1939 I graduated from high school. John D had a girlfriend who went to Mary Hardin-Baylor College. He arranged for me to go there and be Zelia Belle's roommate. I got a job as a waitress in the dining hall and John D sent me $30 a month to go to college. The next year I transferred to San Marcos. I had a job there in the children's library. John D sent me $30 a month until he met Wynona. Then I moved into a co-op. When I graduated I went to Richmond and taught school that spring semester, and that was all of the teaching I wanted to do. So, Wy invited me to come up to Corsicana and stay with her and her mother. I stayed about four months. Then I decided I was going back to Derby. In October, 1943 my old boyfriend George Kemper came to town and we started dating again. Grandma Bennett unlocked her parlor one day and called George and me in. She told George, "There's never been a Bennett to be an old maid." (I was already 21.) We got married in December.

I [Betsy] was staying down in Derby [in 1945]. I had a little baby boy named Butch, and his dad didn't get home 'til he was eight months old. When he did get home the service gave us a trip to Miami, Florida to relax and enjoy life for a little while. Mother and Boney [Wynona's mother] kept Butch for me while we went down there. We were there about two weeks. It was a rest and recuperation deal. [George had been a POW at the end of the war.]

Wynona and I would do everything together. In fact we would help mother get lunch together. Mother had a little Mexican girl who helped her. After we would eat, immediately everybody had to jump up, that's the way Mother did, she didn't let anybody sit at the table long. We had to get up and get the dishes cleaned up. Wynona and I would dry the dishes for Mary while she was washing them. When we got to the pots and pans we'd have to do something else, and we always sneaked out on the pots and pans. When I think about it now, that was not a very nice thing to do. Harry was off in the war by then.

We had ration cards, a lot of things were rationed: sugar, coffee, shoes, gasoline, tires, bacon, candy. My father-in-law had a grocery store in Pearsall. He used to get some extra candy, and he'd sneak it

War ration book

out from under the counter and give it to Wynona and me. The first fight I ever had with my husband was over one of those shoe stamps. I had one after we married and I figured I had to spend that stamp. I bought the prettiest pair of shoes, they just cost six dollars. I guess we didn't have that six dollars, because George wasn't very happy about that.

I got married while John was overseas [in 1943]. We got married in the Methodist Church in Pearsall. Times were really hard. We had a very simple wedding at the church. My best friend was supposed to stand up with me, but she had gotten into the poison ivy when she was getting autumn leaves to decorate the house when they gave me a bridal shower. So Wynona wore my friend's clothes and she stood up with me instead of Neva. Wynona stayed down there at least six weeks that time.

John D: Pop was a farmer, and farmers were given

Jo Hearn and Wy posing for their husbands

gasoline to run their tractors. They had to be very careful how they used that gasoline. Wynona would come down in our 1941 Oldsmobile club coupe. We were very fortunate that we bought that car just before they quit making them. It was a wonderful car. I paid

Wy and Betsy sewing, 1944

$1200 for that car. She had that all of the time. She would fill it up in Corsicana and a full tank of gasoline would take her all the way to Derby. Whenever she got ready to go back home, Pop would tell her, "Skeeter, I'm going out to the farm. You go fill your car up. I don't want to see you doing it." So she'd go out to the tank on the farm and fill her car up so she could drive all the way back to Corsicana nonstop.

Betsy: She didn't always come in the car. When she came by herself she would take the train. I can remember we'd all go to Pearsall and meet the train. Wynona was loved by everybody in Derby. Derby consisted of our relatives. That's my Dad's family. All of them lived in Derby, and all of Mother's family lived in Pearsall, which was just 10 miles away. We had lots of cousins and we were a very close bunch of people and we had a real good time. Wynona was down there one Christmas and I remember we decided we would draw names—the cousins, and everybody. We had our tree in my grandmother's parlor. Usually the parlor

Betsy, Harry, Clara, Martha, Wynona

239

was locked unless it was a very special occasion. Grandma opened up the room for Christmas and I can still see all those red tissue paper and green tissue paper presents wrapped up on my grandmother's dining room table. We couldn't pay over 35 cents for a gift. I still have my little dish I got for Christmas, I think Wynona gave me that dish. You know it's not what the gift is, it was the spirit it was given in. It was so much fun.

Every time we were at Grandma Bennett's house at Christmas the grownups always ate first. The grownups got through eating and then we could eat. The DeVilbiss side of the family was in Pearsall.

They always let the children eat at the same time. I had an aunt named Aunt Dime and she said when she got married she wasn't going to ever make the children wait to eat. She wasn't ever going to invite the preacher for dinner, ever, on Sunday, because they always ate up the best part of the chicken before she got any. And she kept to that. She never did have the preacher over for dinner.

Dad listening to the war news

Mother had a beautiful orchard in the backyard. She had huge lemon trees that had great big lemons on them. They were at least six inches in diameter. She had tangerines, satsumas, oranges, grapefruit, pink grapefruit, pomegranates (but in those days we never ate pomegranates). Finally Mother and Daddy cut those trees down after they froze several years in a row in the late 60s.

John D: it was hard to get the trees through the winter. Dad's men would haul dirt up there and stack it way up high on the tree trunks

240

In the front yard at home

so they wouldn't freeze in the winter time. It was a lot of work to keep the orchard, but boy it was nice.

Betsy: I think the weather changed because nobody down in that part of the country has fruit orchards anymore. Lots of people had orchards, they were beautiful. I know when my boys had an accident and were in Wilford Hall Hospital in San Antonio at Lackland, Mother used to send fruit up there to them and they'd put it underneath their bed and all the nurses would go in there and get it when they wanted some.

We had a county agent lady named Bird Boswell, and she taught everybody how to can. Everybody canned during the war. Up in Pearsall they used to have a canning plant. My other sister-in-law Janice Lee canned everything in the wide world that we could get our hands on.

John D: Wynona learned how to can those little lemon pies that she sent overseas all the time. They came over there in perfect shape. She canned them in Derby.

Betsy: In those days we didn't have a telephone at our house. We had a party line for years and years. They got tired of keeping it up. All during my teenage years we didn't have a phone. We didn't have a phone during the war. If we got a phone call from anybody we'd have to go to Derby. They'd come down and tell us we had a

Wynona and Betsy

phone call and we'd have to go to Derby and talk on the long distance pay phone. I remember John D says that Mother used to call him, and talk to him for a little bit [even after she had her own phone] and say, "Well, our time's up". And she'd hang up.

I guess I can say this about Wynona, I never had a sister, but she was just like to sister to me. That's how I thought of her. I don't' remember Wynona and I ever having a cross word. We didn't always agree on everything, but we were real good friends.

<u>John D</u>: Wynona and I have a cemetery lot in Pearsall, and she's buried right at the foot of Mother, and I'll be buried right at the foot of Dad.

242

Wynona and Lionel making ice cream

Martha

V-mail

Wynona in 1944

Chapter 27
France
1944-1945

Southern France (August 14, 1944)

We got into big ships, and then off the coast of France we got into those little landing boats. We were going to go into a place called St. Raphael. It was kind of a resort area, with a beautiful beach. But the Germans had put a whole bunch of underwater obstacles in there, so that you couldn't come in in boats and land. You would hit those obstacles. So the Navy decided they were going to send in a bunch of radio-controlled drone boats loaded with high explosives to blow up the obstacles. Well, there was only one hitch to that. As we got those boats going in there and headed towards the beach, the Germans found out how to turn them around. They turned the boats around and they were headed back towards our Navy. Well, we were floating out there in those landing craft between the Navy and the beach, and those guns on those ships were not a whole lot higher than we were. Oh Lord, the Navy lit in shooting. They fired and fired and fired, and they sank every one of them. That was something to make you remember!

Well, we couldn't get in at St. Raphael. But somebody had been doing some snooping around, and they found that there was a beach (Yellow Beach) maybe two miles east of where we were. There was a little stream that came down and hit the beach, and the beach there wasn't very wide, maybe a couple of hundred yards wide. There was a road that came down to it. By gosh, we landed there and started slipping down that road without any Germans attacking us at all. They were all over at St. Raphael, where we had thought we were going in. We started up that road, and we got up there a way, and the first thing you know we were in there a mile or so, and I looked up on the mountains on each side, and there were just hundreds of people up there.

FFE

Well, I have to back up a little and tell you that before this war started Germany decided they wanted to try out their war machine. So they instigated a revolution in Spain. They took their armament into Spain and defeated the Spanish government. The defeated Spaniards jumped in boats, went to sea, and came back around the border between Spain and France, and came into France behind the Germans. And they got up in the mountains, and they became what is known as the FFE, the Free French Forces of the Interior. They were working in cahoots with the British, who were making what they call the "rat gun". Now the rat gun was a little old gun that wasn't over 12 or 14 inches long, when it was folded up. And it had a stock that was made out of a heavy gauge rod about a quarter of an inch or 3/8 of an inch in diameter. When you folded it back it made a stock that would go against your shoulder, so you had kinda like a rifle. When you were through you'd fold it up. It wasn't very big and you could even carry it around under your clothes. Anyway, they had these rat guns, and they fired captured German 9mm ammunition. So the British made the guns, German soldiers furnished the ammunition for it, and the Spaniards were the FFE.

Jose Garcia

When we got to this bunch of people blocking the road I was right there in front and my artillery battery was behind me. There was a guy that came down, and his name was Jose Garcia. Now, I was raised on a farm in South Texas, and the first kids I played with were Mexicans, so I could speak Spanish as good as most Mexicans could. When I saw Jose I started speaking to him in Spanish. He said, "I want to go with you." I said, "Jose, you know the Germans are going to be up here in just a little bit. Why don't you have your men (he was a captain in the FFE), get on my trucks back there and ride up with us so that when we meet these Germans we'll have some more support." He said, "No, I'm not talking about them. I'm talking about me. I want to go with you." I said, "OK, if you want to go with me, get in my jeep." So he got in my jeep. You know what, that man decided that he was my personal bodyguard. I could not go to the bathroom that he didn't go with me! That beat anything that I'd ever seen in my life. He took to me like a leech, and 'course I could speak Mexican, he could speak Castilian Spanish. We never missed a word. We talked just like we'd been talking all our lives. He stayed with me all the way up through France, over into Germany. I'll tell you more about him later.

Rhône River Valley

As we went into France (I had Jose with me) the Germans were retreating pretty doggone fast. They were afraid they were going to get cut off, going up the Rhône River Valley. We went on a side road, and we got where we could shoot a round of artillery on the main road in front of that column of tanks and vehicles that was trying to evacuate north. We'd shoot a round of artillery up there and stop them. We'd take the rest of the battalion and eat them up from the rear. We just butchered hundreds and hundreds and hundreds of vehicles. In the daylight the air force came and saw all those German vehicles all gathered up, hemmed up, and boy they just literally blew them all to pieces. It was really a mass slaughter. It was almost bumper to bumper junk all the way up and down the Rhône River. I remember as we went on, after that was over, we ran into a bunch of German troops that were on bicycles. Boy, they were pedaling those bicycles like crazy when we caught them. Some of them got away, but some of them didn't.

I am an avid piddler, and war or no war I had to piddle. Now when I made my power plant in Italy I liberated an Italian radio. It had a little wooden case. A little later I liberated an Italian phonograph player. I converted those to where they would run off my 220 volt DC light plant, and I had them with me all the time. We ran into some of those "donut girls", as we called them, they were special service girls. They gave me some records. Now I had a radio, a phonograph, and some records. Anyway, as we were advancing up the Rhône River Valley we'd go into a town, and Jose would get some of those little French boys and say, "Tell your sisters there's going to be a dance in the square tonight." We'd post a roadblock on the north side of town. Then we'd take my radio and phonograph and set it on a second story window down on the city square and we had it fixed where we could run this thing now off a converter that I had fixed up that would run off a jeep battery. So we'd get those records going and those infantry boys would have more fun dancing with those French gals. They really loved that. The next night we'd advance a little further. We'd put out another roadblock in case the Germans tried to come back on us (which they never did), and we'd have another dance. We had several dances. I'm telling you, they were having a lot of fun. Then one night we looked up and the whole blooming roadblock was back at the dance. They had left their post and come back there to dance with those French gals. So we had to quit having those dances, I'll tell you. We couldn't take a chance on being overrun.

We almost had fun going up that Rhône River. Those people were so glad to see us. People were lined up on the side of the road, and as we'd drive along all of these women, young ones and old ones, had bread and eggs and wine and they'd hand it to us. We'd take the eggs and the wine and the bread from the pretty ones and give them a kiss on the cheek. The old ones, we'd just take the bread and wine and eggs and reach for the next pretty one. That's the only fun we had in the war, going forward.

Going up that Rhône River, every now and then you'd see a bald-headed woman. They were collaborators. Those people knew who they were and they'd shave those women's heads.

Another Power Plant
The light plant that I made in Altavilla stayed with the artillery battery, but I spent a lot of time up front with the infantry. We needed a light plant on the front. Would you believe that while we were doing that advancing, going forward, I was sitting in my seat wrapping an armature off a shot-up American command car radio converter? I had taken the wire off the armature, very carefully saved it, and rewrapped it to get the correct voltage. Artillery shells bursting all around and what not, going forward, and I was counting turns wrapping that armature to make a converter to run my radio and stuff with. I soldered the wires with a liberated German gasoline-powered soldering iron, which I kept in a toolbox under the seat of

my jeep. I finally had the neatest little light plant you ever saw. I liberated a German air compressor engine. It ran my little 220 volt AC generator. Whenever we'd go into a town at night we would pull up to a house we wanted to make the command post. We'd pull the main circuit breaker, take our telephone wire, and run our electricity right up to the house circuit. Then we had lights all over the house, one room at a time, mostly in the basement. We couldn't burn but one room 'cause that's all my generator would put out. Two Dog Smith told me after the war that whenever he went up to the front he could tell where I was because he could hear the little generator running. We used that thing until the end of the war. Every battle we fought we had electric lights at our command post.

Jeep

One night when I was a battery commander in France the French army was in line right next to us. My jeep disappeared in the middle of the night—the French stole it. The artillery general was going to make me pay for it. He said it was my fault, I should have been guarding it. Col. Green went to bat for me. He told the general, "I can tell you that I can steal your jeep any time I want it. I can even tell you the night I'm going to steal it." So the general decided he didn't have to make me pay for the jeep because he knew he might lose his.

One day my driver, Joseph Starman, and I decided to put an armored plate on the windshield of our jeep. We got a piece of quarter inch steel and had a slot cut in it that we could look through. We mounted it on the

John D in a national guard jeep before the war

249

windshield, and then decided we should test it. So we took a rifle and fired a round at it. It went right through, so we decided the armor was useless. We took it off.

When we drove on rough or muddy roads the mufflers would be dragged off. So all of our jeeps were modified so that the muffler was mounted across the front bumper above the chassis and in front of the radiator. Another problem was that the Germans would stretch piano wire across the road in an attempt to cut off the heads of unprotected drivers. So we mounted a vertical pole with a hook on the top on the front bumper of all of our vehicles that would break the piano wires.

Metz Forest
Finally we got on up the country further and we came to the Metz Forest. The Metz Forest was very thick and we could hardly see our way through it. And we didn't know exactly where we were going. So I made an arrangement with Charlie Hearn that he'd fire a round of white phosphorous out ahead of us up in the air so we could see where it was. He would fire that on the route that we were supposed to be taking. So we'd go towards that round of white phosphorous, and when we'd get there he'd fire another one, and he led us right on through that forest.

One day we were in that forest and I had Jose with me. The infantry came back and said that they'd captured an SS trooper and wanted to know if we'd guard him. I said, "Yeah. We'll take care of him." I said, "Jose, would you take care of this German prisoner for us?" He said, "Oh yeah, I'll take care of him." I thought he was going to take care of him. Problem was, he did. I saw him a few minutes later and I said, "Jose, where's the prisoner?" He says, "I shot him." I said, "What do you mean you shot him?" He says, "Certainly I shot him. You think that's the first one I ever shot?" I said, "Jose, you can't do things like that. If we shoot our prisoners and the Germans find out about it it'll make it that much harder on their prisoners. You can't do that." But Jose was a soldier of fortune and he believed in shooting those Germans.

One day when I first got him I said, "Jose, The boys want to take up a little money for you so you won't be broke, you'll have a little

HEADQUARTERS 36TH INFANTRY DIVISION
APO #36, U. S. Army

AG 200.6   27 Oct 1944

SUBJECT: Award of Bronze Star Medal

TO   :   Captain JOHN D. BENNETT, 0380489,
           132d Field Artillery Battalion,
           APO #36, U. S. Army

     Under the provisions of Army Regulations 600-45, as
amended, you are awarded a Bronze Star Medal for heroic
achievement in combat.

CITATION

     JOHN D. BENNETT, 0380489, Captain, 132d Field Artil-
lery Battalion, for heroic achievement in combat on 28
September 1944 in France. When the assault of the 1st
Battalion, 142d Infantry Regiment, was delayed by direct
fire from four hostile machine guns, Captain Bennett,
field artillery liaison officer, moved to a small knoll
abreast of the leading rifle platoon to observe the enemy. Finding the knoll occupied by hostile soldiers, he
called for three riflemen and directed them in repelling
the enemy force. Then, ignoring the heavy small arms
fire directed at his position, he set up his radio and
calmly directed artillery fire on the machine guns which
were only 150 yards to his front. As a result of his
bravery and skill, the machine guns were forced to with-
draw and the battalion continued its advance. Entered
the Service from Corsicana, Texas.

                         JOHN E. DAHLQUIST
                    Major General, U. S. Army
                         Commanding

something to buy something with." He said, "I don't need any money. The Germans pay me." I said, "What do you mean the Germans pay you?" He pulled out a roll of bills about three inches in diameter. He said, "The Germans will pay me." He would shoot one of them and loot the money they had. He was strictly a soldier of fortune.

Ring of Fire

We finally broke out of the Metz Forest, and were advancing and began to go over some rolling hills. We came to the top of a hill with about two platoons, and we went down that hill just lickety split. Down at the bottom of the hill was a ravine. We drove three or four jeeps and trailers with us right down to the bottom, and we hid them in the trees at the bottom of the ravine. It was getting pretty close to dark, and we had moved to the right a way. You see what had happened, we had advanced so fast that we got ahead of the units on each side of us. We always tried to keep abreast of the units on each side so that when we went forward we weren't out there by ourselves.

Well, gosh, we got out there by ourselves. The only communications we had were through my artillery radio. So we got out there to a point, and it was getting dark, and the Germans began to close in on us, and by gosh we got into a hand grenade battle with them and we began to run out of hand grenades. They were all the way around us. So old Minor says, "Let's shoot some artillery." So I said, "Ok, I'll put a ring of artillery fire all the way around us." So I adjusted a round of artillery fire so that the fire was falling in a circle all around the infantry that I was with. Then we gradually started moving that circle, the whole circle, back towards where our jeeps were. I guess it was a good half a mile back there. We kept moving the ring of fire back and we kept retreating in that ring of fire. That ring of fire was keeping those Germans from getting up there close enough to throw those hand grenades at us, and we were out of hand grenades. So we kept on and kept on, and finally we got to where our jeeps were. We decided that we had to get back up that mountain that we'd come down. It was so slick and rainy that those jeeps wouldn't climb that hill. So the infantry got around the jeeps and the trailers and they literally lifted those jeeps and trailers up that hill. It was dark at the time. Boy, we got to the top and just broke over the top of the hill when daylight came and the Germans saw us and they cut loose shooting at us like crazy, but we were over the top of the hill and they couldn't see us after that.

Sainte-Marie

Wynona used to cook little lemon pies (according to Grandma

252

Bennett's recipe) and can them and mail them to me in Europe. They got there in perfect shape. She also sent cookies to Jose. He was so appreciative that when we got to Sainte-Marie in November of 1944 that he searched all through the town and found a cloth factory where he liberated two bolts of cloth to send to Wynona. He also found a bust of Hitler about 3 feet high. I sent it to Carl Anderson and he put it in a service club in Corsicana!

Koenigsbourg Castle
After the third battalion of the 142nd infantry captured the

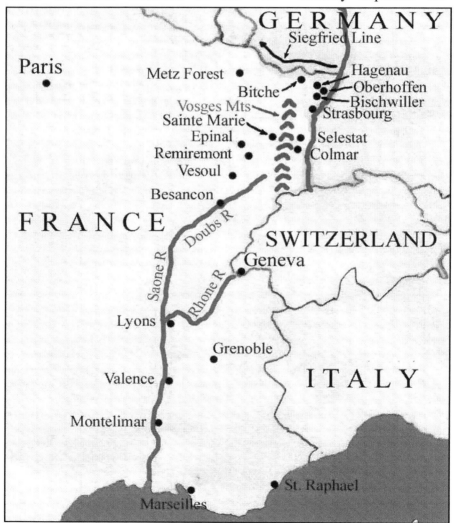

253

Koenigsbourg Castle, just west of Selestat. I was sent there as an observer for my battalion for about two or three weeks. The castle had two drawbridges and several moats. There were 300 steps to the top of the tower. It was amazing what you could see from there. I could look across the Rhine River and see trains on the other side of the river, but they were too far away to shoot. While I was there, fortunately, I missed out on the terrible fighting at Selestat.

Oberhoffen (February 1-11, 1945)
There were some woods north of Oberhoffen with German tanks in them. By then I was a liaison officer again. We had a terrible artillery duel and we shot down every building in town before we could capture it, but the cellars were still there. When you go into a town like that you just take over houses to live in. We found a shot-up house, but it had a good cellar, and that cellar had a whole bunch of potatoes, and had hams hanging up off the rafters. So, we moved in that cellar and we were eating potatoes and ham. I slept in a potato bin. Wynona and I went back to Oberhoffen in 1990 with a veterans' tour, and we were welcomed as heroes for liberating their town. They had a big banquet for us, but I didn't tell them that I had shot their town down.

George
In mid-February we were relieved for a few days. They gave me R & R so I took that to go to England. When I went to England, I went by London and had a picture made and I mailed it to Wynona. Then I went on to look up my brother - in - law, George

On R&R in England

Kemper, who was flying P-51s out of Steeple Morden Airfield, Cambridgeshire, England. He'd fly from there into Germany.

It so happened that I got to George Kemper's room on February 22, 1945, exactly at the time that his flight came back from strafing a train over in Germany. When they strafed trains they liked to strafe the engines because they would blow up. As soon as they would strafe a train they would fly over each other and check each other's airplane out. They told George that he had been hit by

George Kemper

machine gun fire in the airscoop underneath his P-51 and the oil was coming out, they had better head back to England. Well, they headed back toward England as fast as they could, and they didn't get too far before George's engine froze up. So he had to go down and make a belly landing. The other pilots flew around until they saw George get out of the airplane and run over towards some trees. So we knew that George had made a forced landing and got out of the airplane. We didn't know what had happened to him.

Well, I was in his room when his flight crew came back and they told me exactly what had happened. You know, during the war the officers censored the enlisted men's mail. Nobody censored the officers' mail. So I decided, by gosh, I was going to write my sister a letter immediately and tell her about George being shot down. So, I did. I also wrote my wife, who was normally in Corsicana. I had told her I wanted her to spend at least every other month in Derby with my family. Well, she had gone to Derby, and was down there. They both got their letters at the same time, telling about George being shot down.

George's P-51 "Betsy K" (He was shot down in a different plane.)

That is truly one of the miracles of the war that the Lord gave me R & R time to go to England and look up George exactly at the time that his flight came back, and also that Wynona was with Betsy at the time the letters arrived. It was six weeks before the War Department ever told Betsy that George had been shot down.

George was taken prisoner and he had to walk from northern Germany down to southern Germany. After the war Betsy went over to Germany with George while he flew the Berlin Airlift. George took Betsy and showed her exactly where he was shot down and the route that he walked as a prisoner. They even met some of the priests that operated some churches that befriended the prisoners on the route to southern Germany. That was quite an experience.

Haguenau (March 1945)
Well, as we went on through there finally we came into the town of Haguenau. (I'm leaving out an awful lot of stuff, but I'm giving you a little highlight, so that you'll know what was going on.) The

weather had been terrible. It was cold and nasty. Haguenau looked real good to us. We came to an apartment building that was several stories high. The infantry said, "We're going to hole up in this apartment building tonight and get some rest. Go find you an apartment." So I went up on the second floor and found me an apartment. That apartment had a bedroom in it, and a living room and a little kitchen. In that bedroom were two twin beds. I told my boys, "Now listen, fellas. I'm the senior ranking officer here and I'm going to sleep in one of those beds tonight." I said, "I don't care who sleeps in the other one."

About that time there was a knock on the door, and it was the gal who owned the apartment. She had been hiding out in the basement. She came up, and she said, "Are y'all going to stay up here in the apartment?" I said, "Yeah, we're going to stay up here in the apartment, and I'm sleeping in that bed tonight." She says, "If you're sleeping in that bed tonight, I'm sleeping in that other bed tonight." I said, "Alright, if that's what you want to do, you can sleep over there, I don't care. I'm sleeping in this bed."

Well those places have big pillows on the bed. They're just half of a bed long. You're supposed to know how to sleep under that pillow to stay warm, and I didn't know how. So this old gal got her gown on, and she saw me trying to get under that pillow. She came over there, "I'm going to tuck you in." So she started to tuck me in. Her old tits were slapping me in the face as she was tucking me in. Finally she got me tucked in and she went in her bed and we went to sleep. My boys told me the next morning, "Captain, you remind us of a man in the middle of the Sahara Desert. Just because you weren't thirsty, you didn't want a drink and you didn't want anybody else to get a drink." We knew what she had been up to because she had stacks of cigarettes on her dresser. She had probably been entertaining the German troops. Those people did anything they had to to live. That was the end of that story.

Hoerdt

I'm not sure when it was, but it wasn't too long after that we were in the town of Hoerdt. Hoerdt is about 20 miles north of Strasbourg. We stayed in a house that belonged to a family that had a daughter.

She was a real pretty French gal, a student at the University of Strasbourg. One of my forward observers was named John Welles Smith. His code name on the radio was "Two Dog". If I ever talk to John Welles Smith, to this day, he'll say, "This is Two Dog speaking." Anyway, John Smith and this gal got pretty familiar. Well, that lasted for a day or two. We had to send John Smith a little bit closer to the Rhine River as a forward observer. We had a wire line going from him back to our battery so we could talk to him. This gal would get on that phone and she'd say, "Smiiiitty, come see me, please, come see me." You know, they worked up quite an affair there.

Back in the 90s Wynona and I went over there, and John Welles Smith went along. We went to Hoerdt and decided to see if we could find that gal. Smith and her got to be real good friends; I think they communicated after the war. Smith wasn't married then. After we went over there we found out she'd died. We found her husband and talked to him some. We sure would have loved to have seen her because she was a real nice person. We had stayed in her house there, and that was our command post for our artillery battery while we were there.

Silver Star (March 18, 1945)
It wasn't too long after that that the Battle of the Bulge showed up all of a sudden, and we had to move our artillery battery 100 miles one night in the blackout. We got up there and set up forward observers and got into the Battle of the Bulge. After that was over we came back and were trying to get through the Siegfried Line (a line of fortifications) northeast of Oberotterbach a way. The roads in that country were like ditches. They were real deep. You could travel on a road and you might be in a ditch 10 feet deep. We were advancing toward the Siegfried Line. We passed a wagon on the road that had all of the worldly possessions of some family on top of it. It had a moped scooter up on top of it. I saw that moped as we went up.

We went up there and we bounced off that Siegfried Line like a rubber ball. We ran into a whole bunch of machine guns up there, and we were down in that road going towards that Siegfried Line. They say that we had 13 tanks that were up on top, they weren't down in that rut like we were. The machine gun fire was so thick that night that it shot the antennas off all those tanks. Well, I was down in there and that machine gun fire was terrible, and I decided I had to do something about it.

You know when a rifle bullet goes over your head you hear a "crack" and a "thud". The bullet makes the "crack" over your head and it tells you how far it is to the gun. Then when you heard the "thud", that was the sound the gun made when it was fired. That tells the direction to the gun. So you get a crack and a thud, and boy they might as well tell you where that machine gun is. And then I

HEADQUARTERS 36TH INFANTRY DIVISION
APO #36, U. S. Army

AG 200.6   25 April 1945

SUBJECT: Award of Silver Star

TO   : Captain JOHN D. BENNETT, 0380489,
           132d Field Artillery Battalion,
           APO #36, U. S. Army

       Under the provisions of Army Regulations 600-45, you are awarded a
Silver Star for gallantry in action.

CITATION

       JOHN D. BENNETT, 0380489, Captain, 132d Field Artillery Battalion,
for gallantry in action on 18 March 1945 in France. Captain Bennett
was accompanying the forward elements as artillery observer during an
infantry attack on a town. When enemy machine gun fire halted the advance, he set up his radio in an exposed position, and proceeded to
adjust artillery fire on the hostile positions. Although the enemy
directed heavy machine gun fire into the area, and at times shells
burst within 15 yards of him, he steadfastly remained in his exposed
position for over an hour, until his accurately directed fire had
silenced the enemy machine guns. Captain Bennett's courageous and determined devotion to duty enabled the infantry to continue on its mission. Entered the Service from Corsicana, Texas.

                                          JOHN E. DAHLQUIST
                                     Major General, U. S. Army
                                              Commanding

had shot so much artillery that I could tell by the way it went, "tsch, tsch, tsch" over my head, exactly where it was passing over my head, and how far it was to where it was going to hit.

You know, I directed artillery fire to knock out all of those machine guns that night from the very bottom of that ditch, strictly by sound. I never saw one of them. All I ever did was hear them, and I knocked them all out. There was a little infantry guy that was so impressed that I knocked all those guns out, he thought I was up on top of that bank with those tanks. But I was right down in the very bottom of that ditch. He put in for the Silver Star for me, and I got the Silver Star.

When daylight came we had to retreat out of there in a hurry. I went back by that wagon that had that moped on it. I reached up and yanked that moped off that wagon and started pedaling back to the rear. I pedaled and I pedaled and I pedaled for two or three miles back to the town of Oberotterbach. I was in a hurry to get back. The whole town was afire. When I almost got there I wondered if that moped would have started. I turned the switch on and it started right up. I could have been back a whole lot faster with a whole lot less effort if I'd had sense enough to turn it on and let it run. You could turn the gas off and lay it on the side. I put it on top of my trailer and hauled it with me to the end of the war. I hated to leave it behind when the war was over.

Pillbox (March 21, 1945)
Well, there's another little story that I need to tell you. We left the other side of Oberotterbach and went northwest up a steep hill. The Germans had cut down a bunch of trees so they fell towards us, improving their field of fire and creating an obstacle for us. We were west of a well-known archway on the Siegfried Line. When we got up that hill there was a big pillbox 20 feet in diameter in the Siegfried Line. (A pillbox is a concrete enclosure with gunports.) They had those pillboxes where machine gun fire from one pillbox covered the approach to the next pillbox. Well, you know after you've been walking and marching and climbing you get awful tired. When I got up there I had to go to the bathroom. There is nobody going to go to the bathroom in a pillbox that has about 20

soldiers in it. You're going to go outside and be a gentleman. So I went outside to be a gentleman. I had my pants down and all of a sudden I heard a round come. I whipped out my compass to get the direction of that round so I could counter-fire a battery on it. That damn round had hit right in front of me, not 6 six feet in front of me, maybe eight feet. It went all the way under me and then came out behind me. It ricocheted. It never touched me. That round must have been an armor-piercing round, because they were probably firing at that pillbox (they knew that we had it). They were trying to penetrate that pillbox with that round, and that's the reason it didn't go off—it was armor-piercing and it just went under me.

Anyway, after we were on that mountain a guy come up there named Capt. Hundley, just a panting and a blowing. I said, "Capt. Hundley, what are you doing up here?" He said, "Oh, I had to bring Col. So and so's instructions up here." I said, "Why? Why didn't he bring them up here?" He said, "Oh, he sent me up here." So when I got back down I saw Col. So and so. I said, "Colonel, why did you send Capt. Hundley up there with your instructions, up on top of the Siegfried Line, instead of coming up there and issuing those instructions yourself?" He said, "Oh. That would have been too dangerous. I might've gotten killed." I said, "You are a yellow bastard, aren't you?" Well, that was the end of that conversation. He never said anything else. He never tried to court-martial me or anything. He knew he was a yellow bastard.

Jose Again
There's another thing I wanted to tell you about that happened right near the Seigfreid Line. I can't remember if it was before or after. One day Jose came in and said, "Captain, I've got to kill your sergeant." I said, "What do you mean you've got to kill my sergeant?" He said, "Well, I've just got to kill him." I said, "Now Jose, you're drunk. We'll talk about this tomorrow. You promise you won't try to do nothing tonight." "OK, I'll promise I won't do nothing tonight." Well, the next morning he and that sergeant was walking through the chow line, arm in arm, like they were bosom buddies, like nobody else. What had happened was, they had been drinking schnapps that they had found. Well schnapps is pure liquid dynamite, I'll tell you. They had found that schnapps and were drinking

it and was fighting over a French gal. So, that was the problem. After that everything was lovely.

It wasn't long after that they began to have some trouble on the Spanish border. I said, "Jose, you know that Spain is your country and you ought to be over there helping take care of that trouble they're having on the border." He said, "I ought to be over there." So we liberated another one of those German "things". We put a bunch of cans of gasoline in the back seat and sent him on his way. The last we heard of him he was going through Paris. The "Stars and Stripes" had heard about him and were writing him up. I never heard from him since. I just wonder whatever happened to him.

Chapter 28
Germany and Austria
1945

Rhine River (April 24, 1945)

After we broke through the Siegfried Line, we went on up and crossed the Rhine River at a bridge some of our troops had liberated and swung back down towards Austria. About that time my artillery battalion commander came to me and said, "John, I want you to go into this town and get some billets for us. We need some places to house our troops." Most of the infantry and artillery were miles behind. Well, I had my jeep driver with me, Joseph Starman, from Carroll, Iowa. He was the most fantastic person there ever was. He was of German descent and spoke perfect German. (I called him Kraut). There was no way that you could lose Joseph Starman. At night he could drive anywhere without any lights and never get lost.

So we drove into that town and went around a corner into the town square. To our surprise it was filled with hundreds of German SS troops. Oh, Lord! It liked to scared me to death. I said, "Kraut, ask them where their commanding officer is." So he asked them where their commanding officer was. A guy stepped up and said, "I'm the commanding officer." I want you to know I was scared to death. So I bluffed, and said, "Where have you stacked your arms?" He said, "They're stacked right over here." They were waiting to surrender and had already stacked their arms. There was a pile of rifles and pistols and machine guns 20 feet in diameter and 10 feet high. Man! Was I glad to see that. Well, I liberated a 22 Walthers pistol out of that stack, and a good German rifle.

End of the War

We went on down towards Austria and got down there almost to the place where Hitler had his hideout up in the top of the mountains, Eagle's Nest, near Munich. We met the Germans up on a hill some-where east of Innsbruck, Austria, on May 9th, and they surrendered, and the war was over as far as I was concerned. Col. Pete Green kept his word that I wouldn't have anything to do when the war was over because I had stayed on the front so long. So when the war was over I got my jeep driver and a sergeant who was a friend of mine and we headed north. The sergeant had a brother who was killed and was buried in Luxembourg.

I had decided I was going to go up and find my little brother, Harry. He was up in the northern part of Germany and had recently come over with an ordinance company. We went by Luxembourg and found the grave of my sergeant's brother. Then we went on up and found my kid brother. I told him that I was expecting to take him back down to a town named Meinengen for about a week. We were living in a great big castle down there. Y'see what happened on that castle, when we went into that town as occupational troops we had cleared out some real nice houses in the town and everything was real comfortable. Then the division artillery commander came around and says, "You can't stay in these houses. It doesn't have enough prestige. You gotta move up in that castle up on top of that hill." So we moved up in the castle on top of the hill. I was going to

take Harry down to the castle on top of the hill. Up on the second floor is where my artillery battalion officers were staying. So I took Harry up there. They treated him just like he was my brother. There was no show of rank or anything like that. Harry couldn't get over it. After he left he said, "You know, Johnny, I believe officers are human beings, after all." They treated him so nice, and I was so appreciative.

But when I went up there to get Harry, I told him I wanted to talk to his company commander about getting him a pass to go down there. We talked to the company commander, and he said, "Oh, no! We can't let him have a pass to go down there. That's unheard of!" I

30 May 1945

Dear Pokka,

Right now I am sitting here with my old bud, believe it or not. Old Johnny showed up at the company last night around 10 o'clock and believe me that was one of the greatest surprises that I have ever had. It took me about two hours to fully recover and I guess that was because I finally got used to seeing the old rascal. I saw the old rascal open the door and I knew that the face was familiar but it was hard to believe that it could actually be old Johnny. I had been expecting him for so long and he hadn't shown up so I finally decided that he was probably on the boat for the states.

He really looks good and still the same old Johnny with strut and all. The first thing he wanted to do when he got there was to make certain that he was going to be able to get me off and come down here to be with him for a few days. Well, we headed up to see the Captain and found him in his room all ready to relax for the afternoon. I know I felt just about so high walking into the captains room with old Johnny—boy, what a comparison, captain and T/5. Anyway I felt might proud of my bud. The Capt. said he could only give me three days and Johnny wanted right them to go to group and proposition them for at least five days but my CO talked him into waiting until the next morning for it was already getting to be nearly midnight.

We went back to my house and I found a cot and got the old boy to bed for the night and next morning when I went in to awaken him, he was already up. His Jeep had a flat on it so we walked down to breakfast, about a mile, the furtherest that I have seen a captain walk in years. We went to Group to see if they would give me the five days but they said it was over them so we went to 15th Army Hdq. and since they weren't allowed to give passes in Germany, they assigned me temporary duty with old Johnny's outfit and they gave me seven days. I probably won't be able to get away from that company again for years but it is really worth it to be with Johnny. He is all excited about being nearly ready to go home and I hope that before I go back to my outfit that he is all packed and ready to head for home.

Well, I guess I will give this thing to Johnny. He says he has to write his squaw so I guess he out-ranks me a little. If I don't write for a few days it will be because I am busy doing a little nothing.

So-long for tonight and love,
Harry.

Harry and John D

said, "What do you mean it's unheard of?" I've been fighting this damn war from the beginning. I am tired and I want to take my brother to south Germany with me and I want a pass for him." "You can't have it." I said, "Alright, I'll go see the corps commander." "Oh, you can't see the corps commander." I said, "Like hell, I can't." So I went to see the corps commander. And the corps commander said, "Well, I can't give him a pass. But I'll just transfer him to you." So he transferred Harry to me and the artillery. So he was an artilleryman for a week. I took him down there to the place and all the officers just treated him just great. I was so proud of them. We had a nice time, and finally I took him back to his unit.

Going Home (approx. August 27, 1945)
After a while it was about time to send troops home. I had quite a few points, so I was one of the first people to get ready to go home. They transferred me to the 66th Division, which was organized especially to take troops home. I was to catch a train over in France. So I got in a vehicle and drove from Meiningen all the way over to where I was supposed to catch this train to go down to southern France. The only trouble was I was in such a hurry to leave I forgot

to take my discharge papers or anything with me. So I had to get ahold of Col. Green on the telephone and tell him that I had left my papers, would he please send them to me. So he got our pilot in the little artillery liaison plane and cranked it up and the pilot delivered my papers to me just in time for me to get on that train and ride it down to Marseille, France. Why, I wasn't in Marseille hardly any time.

From Marseille I got in the bubble on the front end of a B-25 bomber. (We didn't have any passenger planes.) Boy! When I took off down that runway I thought my butt was going to drag the ground, 'cause I was way out in that bubble out in front of everything. We flew down the Mediterranean, we didn't cut across Spain at all, because Spain was neutral. We flew down the Mediterranean to Casablanca. When we landed at Casablanca I got sick. That was the first place they had ice cream. They had so much ice cream and I ate so much of it I got sick at my stomach. Boy, I was sick. After failing to build the ice cream freezer in the cork forest at the beginning of the war, I finally had Moroccan ice cream.

Then came time to get on that plane and head for the states. I forget what kind of a plane it was, but I can tell you it only had seats down the sides, the middle of it was open because it was a cargo plane. They had set a jug of water in the middle of that plane, wasn't tied down or anything. We took off and landed at the Azores and that jug of water never moved on that entire flight. It stayed sittin' right there where it was put. The weather was beautiful. We flew just great. From the Azores we went to Bermuda, and we gassed up at Bermuda. From Bermuda we flew into Miami, arriving August 28, 1945. For miles before we got to Miami we could see the lights. The blackout was over, and they had turned the lights on, and boy they were beautiful! When we got to Miami I got on a train. Lord, that was the slowest train there ever was in this world. It went all the way from Miami clean to Fort Sam Houston in San Antonio. They were doing their best to get me to sign up to stay in. They said, "We'll promote you to a major immediately if you'll sign up." I said, "No way! I've had all of it I want. I'm an engineer and I'm going back to my engineering profession. I don't want nothing else to do with the Army." So I wouldn't sign up. Oh, Lord! I thought

I'd never get there. And when I got down there my little old sweet wife was down there waiting for me! Boy, What a reunion! God, that was the happiest day of my life. I'll tell you, that was something else.

At the end of the war my main goal was to get out and not have to go to the Pacific. I just wanted to come home. I had the sweetest girl in the world waiting for me and I had a job. That's what I wanted to do. I didn't receive a scratch in the war, but I was wounded. I was wounded in the mind, but they didn't recognize that. I still fight the war nearly every night.

John D and Wy in San Antonio after the war

Chapter 29
Homecoming
1945

After the war I came home and went to work for IDECO. Now, I can't remember the exact date when I came home, but I was discharged at Fort Sam Houston, in San Antonio. Then I got a job working for IDECO, and I was working there when my terminal leave expired on December 15, 1945. Now some time that summer before I went to work for IDECO we had a big picnic down on the river at Frio River State Park. (The park is no longer there.) I'm not sure who got that up. It may have been my brother-in-law George Kemper, because George was a great one for always wanting to

Extended Bennett and Kemper families

O. H. Cook and George Kemper cooking

have barbeques. In fact, he liked barbeque so much he even built a nice barbeque pit down at the old farm house on the farm at Derby.

Anyway, we had this family picnic. Everybody I know who was associated with my family in one way or another was at that picnic. Everybody except poor old Uncle Harry, who was at his house lying on his deathbed. All of my aunts and uncles except Uncle Harry were there, and all of my cousins, and some of the extended family. We were all celebrating because the war in Europe was over and George was home and I was home, and this was our celebration. It was fantastic.

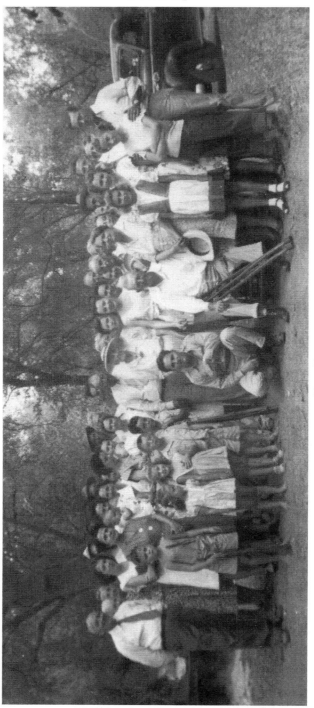

1945 Reunion

At the reunion

Chapter 30
IDECO
1945-1956

The war was over for me even though it was still going on in the Pacific. The boys that took the recruiter's bait, got their promotions on the way to being shipped to the Pacific. I took my terminal leave to find a job; I had a wife to support.

First, I went to see Carl Anderson, who was chief engineer at the American Well and Prospecting Company in Corsicana. I was hoping to go back to work for him. He told me that he had taken a job with Dresser Industries. He was going to be engineering coordinator for Dresser between three  plants they had, all of which made oil field equipment. He told me that he was certain I could stay on with American Well as chief engineer. I told him that I didn't know enough to be chief engineer of anything and that I would like to go with him. His first assignment was to go to International Derrick & Equipment Company (IDECO) in Beaumont. He told me he would take me with him.

Two Bosses
This was the first act that rocked the boat. When he told Mr. Richard Bloss, the general manager of IDECO, that he had brought me with

him, Mr. Bloss didn't like that. He had always been boss and had run everything the way he wanted to and he didn't like any Engineering Coordinator coming in telling him what he was going to do.

Mr. Bloss's habit was that when a young engineer came to see him for an interview, he gave the guy a shoe box with an alarm clock completely disassembled and told him to come back to see him the next day with the clock running. He didn't get to pull that trick on me because Mr. Anderson had already hired me. Mr. Bloss was trying to find out what I knew of an engineering nature so he would call me into his office for a conference. He would ask me a question and if I said that black was black, he would ask, "How do you know that?" I would tell him that Mr. Anderson had taught me that. Oh, he would blow his top, and then Mr. Anderson would say, "Dick, you are just an amateur at this business."

Both men were among the best manufacturing executives in the oil industry. Mr. Bloss already had over 100 patents. He was quite an inventor and a real go-getter. Mr. Anderson had been in the business about six months longer than Mr. Bloss. They were real competitors. Mr. Bloss had me down to his office so many times, chewing me out, because he couldn't get at Mr. Anderson, he began to see that I did have a little sense.

One day, IDECO had a company party out behind the office building. Wynona was at the party and she was talking to Mr. Bloss. She said, "Mr. Bloss, you know why you and John are always fussing?" He said, "No. Why?" She said, "It is because you and he are just alike. You do things alike, think alike, you are like two peas in a pod." From that day on, I could do no wrong. I was made his development engineer, and I did most of my development in his office with him.

Mr. Bloss didn't get to the office until about 10 o'clock in the morning. He had a late breakfast and was ready to work. My call came almost immediately after he got there and we went into conference. Dinner time came, and we were still in conference. I always went home to eat dinner and Wynona would have it ready at 12 o'clock. Most of the time, I didn't get home until about 2 o'clock

274

Mrs. Bloss, Mr. Bloss, John D, Wayne, and Wy at a company party

to eat dinner. After supper he would call me at home and we were in conference for at least another hour. He was a great guy and I loved Mr. Bloss. He taught me an awful lot. Mr. Bloss taught me about patents. He instilled in me the real desire to get patents. Before my retirement, I had obtained seven patents for IDECO and the rest of my 65 patents belong to Sun Oil Company.

Rolling Mill

Mr. Bloss called me in the office one day, and he said, "John, I want you to go up to Columbus, Ohio. We've got a plant up there that we closed and there's a machine up there that I want you to look at and see if you think we could use that down here." So, I went up there to see that, just like he told me. I saw the machine and I saw what they did with it. What they used to do back in the old days, when they had an oilfield they'd make a great big band wheel, and that band wheel would be laying horizontal, and it would be run by an engine. Off the bottom of that band wheel would be a whole bunch of eccentrics, and they would attach pull rods on to those eccentrics, and they'd go out across the land, and they'd pump oil wells with those pull rods. They'd pull it and the mechanism would make the oil string go up and down. Maybe one engine might be pumping a dozen oil wells. So they used this machine to form these great big band wheels.

Mr. Bloss said, "You know, I think we need to make a sheave (pronounced "shiv") for our crown blocks and our traveling blocks." You see, a sheave was a giant wheel with a groove on the outside edge that carried a cable like a pulley, and they used to be made out of steel castings. When you make a great big old steel casting it's awful hard to make something four feet in diameter and spin it say 600 revolutions a minute and expect it not to shake everything in the world down. It needs to be balanced, and there was no way you could balance those big old cast sheaves. Every derrick had about six of them up on top of it, all turning at different speeds, and they'd just shake the dickens out of the derrick.

So, Mr. Bloss said, "We need to make a sheave that is balanced." And he thought about that machine up in Columbus, and he sent me

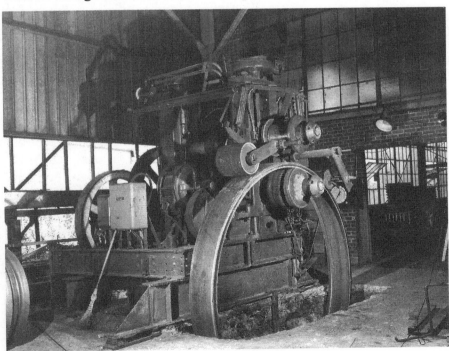

The rolling mill at Columbus

276

up there to look at it. I said, "You know, I believe we can do it." So we made some special dies. Mr. Bloss had a brother named Dick Bloss, who was head of the tool room at IDECO, and a real good machinist. So we designed a sheave that was to API specifications for the cable. I went up to A&M and hired professor Wingram to make a mathematical analysis of the strength of the sheaves. That paid him back for spraying wax all over his coat while I was in school. The old machine from Ohio rolled the rims on the sheaves.

Another Rolling Mill

I built another rolling machine to use in fabricating rotary tables. (You know, it's hard to build things if you don't have good heavy machinery, and sometimes you have to build your own machinery.) So I designed a rolling mill, and it would take a piece of steel about two or three inches thick and maybe twenty inches wide, and roll it up into a circle that wasn't over about twelve inches in diameter. Boy, that was a fantastic rolling mill. The side arms of that rolling

New rolling mill with safety cover removed

mill were cut out of six inch solid steel. I built the machine and it worked like a million dollars.

There was a man by the name of Howard Hughes, who had a business in Houston where he made drill bits. Mr. Hughes was a pretty damn independent man. He had a fantastic pattern shop and foundry. He made the patterns for my IDECO Shorty Block, and he made the castings in the foundry. Boy, we were doing great. Then the union decided that they wanted more money, and they told Howard Hughes. Howard Hughes said, "There'll be no more money. If you insist I'll close the plant." They kept bothering him, so he closed the foundry and dispensed with the pattern shop, so we were left with no castings to make these traveling blocks.

We had a man there at IDECO by the name of Jeff Caldwell. Jeff was one of the most fantastic welding men that I ever met in my life. So Jeff and I got together and we started fabricating stuff with that big heavy rolling mill that I made. We would cast things and make weldments and build them up. We even built the rotary table, which is a very, very complicated piece of equipment. We learned how to fabricate that thing, and we fabricated all kinds of stuff. Then we rolled a band of steel that was maybe eight inches wide and maybe four feet in diameter. We wanted to put it on this rolling mill that Mr. Bloss sent me to see in Columbus. This special machine had two big shafts on it. You'd put dies on each shaft, and as the shafts were adjusted closer together these dies worked on that piece of steel that was hanging in there. I would form it into a shape, but you had to have it real hot to do that.

Furnace

So I made a furnace. This furnace was back in our welding shop. It

Rotary table

had four gas blasts on it, and a floor that would rotate. So you'd take that band of steel and put it in that furnace, light that furnace, and in about ten minutes that baby would be red hot. You'd take that band of steel out, put it on this rolling mill, and roll it, and it'd make the most beautiful groove you ever saw. It was to API standards for a steel cable. Then we would cut a solid web of steel out and fit it to the inside of that band and weld it in there. We would forge a steel hub and put that web on that thing and make the most beautiful sheaves you ever laid your eyes on.

You know Dresser Industries belonged to the Bush dynasty. Back in those early days, when I was designing all that stuff George H. W. Bush was living out there in Midland and Odessa selling some of the stuff that I had designed. In his presidential library in College Station there is a picture of an IDECO warehouse that has one of these IDECO sheaves on the porch that goes around that warehouse. I was real proud when I saw that. Anyway, all of our traveling

Sheave (right) with stages of fabrication

blocks and crown blocks had these special sheaves in them. And everybody wanted them because they wouldn't shake the derrick to pieces and because you had more headroom to pull the pipe out of the hole. So it became the standard of the oil industry. I was real proud of that.

Shorty Block

One day, Mr. Bloss said, "John, I want to get into the drilling hook business. There is a patent by a Mr. Smith that belongs to Byron Jackson Company on the triplex hook. I want you to break the patent." I said, "Mr. Bloss, I don't know anything about breaking patents." He said, "I'm going to teach you." So he taught me how it was done. After I worked for a while I said, "Mr. Bloss, I think I've gotten around that Smith patent." He said, "OK, let's design a hook." And so I started designing a hook. 'Course Mr. Anderson was there all the time, and he was watching all of this. He came by my desk one day, and he said, "What are you doing?" I said, "I'm designing a hook, and I'm designing a traveling block. I'm hooking the two together so they'll be short coupled." He looked at that, and he said, "You know, that really is short isn't it? Why don't you call that an IDECO Shorty?" I said, "OK, we'll call it the IDECO Shorty." So that name was cast in steel, "IDECO Shorty" on that traveling block.

The hook was very unique. The conventional type of drilling hook that Mr. Smith had used in the Smith patent, which Bryon Jackson had built and sold, was really long and had no shock absorbing capability. Incidentally, they told Mr. Bloss, "You can't sell that hook because we've got a million and a half dollars we've set aside to protect that Smith patent, and we're going to sue you." Mr. Bloss, said, "That's alright. You just go right ahead and sue. Won't bother us a bit." Well, they pulled their horns down and we got in the hook business a couple of years before their patent expired.

Anyway, in the drilling business you have a traveling block that goes up and down with steel cables that pull it up—it's a pulley block arrangement. It pulls the pipe up out of the hole. And you keep pulling it up and pulling it up, but the thing that is a mortal sin is to run that traveling block into that crown block, 'cause if it ever hits that crown block something is going to fall to the derrick floor and somebody's going to get killed. So you want as much room as possible from the top to the drill pipe to the crown block. Now, with my setup you had an extra ten feet, at least, over the Byron Jackson hook and the conventional traveling block the way they were hooked together.

When I designed that traveling block and the hook, I didn't like the way the hook was built that Byron Jackson had. It was a triplex hook—that meant there's three hooks on the bottom. One hook is for the bale of the swivel. And the other two hooks are for the elevator links that go down and fasten to the elevator, and that's what snaps around the pipe when you go to pull it up out of the hole. Now when you pull a piece of pipe up out of the hole and you spin it and turn it loose, what you're doing is you're unscrewing it. If you don't lift that piece of pipe up as soon as you unscrew it

Assembly foreman with Shorty Block

then it'll drop down the length of a thread and it'll mess up the threads. So you want to keep that thing pulled up and never let it drop down. But, you've got to have a spring in there to pull that thing up. Boy, you've got to have a spring that's strong enough to pull it up pretty rapidly, 'cause you're wasting time otherwise. And when it gets pulled up you'd like to slow it down so it doesn't hit an internal stop and make it drop the pipe. On the Byron Jackson hook what happened is right above the hook they'd wrap a whole bunch of rope around the hook shank and that rope served as a cushion, so that when the pipe was unscrewed and the hook jumped up it would hit that rope and serve as a cushion and it wouldn't drop anything.

While I was at A&M I was very interested in the guns that they had there. One gun in particular was called the "French 75". Now the French 75 had a very special type recoil mechanism. You know when a gun shoots the barrel goes back. When the barrel goes back then there's hydraulic pressure that pulls it forward into the "battery position". Now if it just went right back into battery you would beat things to death. So they had a real tricky mechanism in there that would let it go back real fast. When it started going forward it'd start going forward real fast, but before it got all the way forward it'd slow down to just a crawl. What happened was, they had an orifice in there that had a tapered plug in it. As long as that tapered plug was down the orifice was wide open and that oil that served as a damper in there could go through that orifice real fast. But when that plug got almost to the top the tapered plug almost completely filled the orifice, so the oil couldn't get out very fast. It slowed it down to a crawl. So I built that mechanism into my hydraulic hook. It worked like a dream. Got a patent on it. You know the patent department doesn't ever know when you pull a fast one, and I pulled a fast one. That should have been classified as un-patentable "old art", but they did-n't have any idea that a French artil-lery piece was built into the trav-eling block of an oilfield drilling rig. So I got the patent on it. Boy, it was a dilly of a

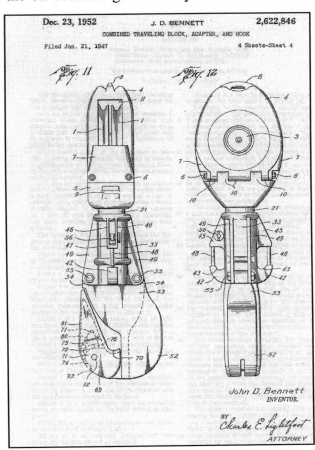

A page from Shorty Block patent

IDECO Rambler

VOL. 1, No. 11   DRESSER EQUIPMENT COMPANY, BEAUMONT AND DALLAS   MARCH, 1953

NEW 400 TON BLOCK IS BIG!

BUT, "BIG SHORTY" IS EASY TO HANDLE

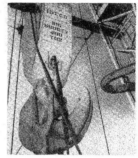

Works Manager Bob LaFleur is the real "Shorty" as he stands alongside a new block in photo at left. Above, the hook is locked into position, opened, and made ready to pick up the swivel.

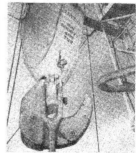

Altho' the block weighs 16,700 pounds, it is easy to handle. It is in position to pick up the swivel from the rathole in the above picture—on the left, one man has positioned the hook under the swivel bail.

hook. You know, that thing was built in about 1947 and to this day nearly any drilling rig you find in Texas will have an IDECO Shorty traveling block on it. I'm prouder of that than any of the accomplishments I ever made. Dresser Industries got a patent on it, and boy did they ever collect on it. They sold gobs of those hooks, and I'm real proud of that. That block was very successful.

Mr. Bloss

Eventually, Mr. Bloss had a heart attack. He decided that if he was going to have heart troubles, he was going to know everything that he could about hearts as pumps, and arteries and veins as hydraulic systems. He got to where he knew his stuff, so he began to interview doctors, and if they couldn't answer his questions about the hydraulics of the blood system, he got another doctor. After interviewing a few doctors, he found one that he decided knew what he was doing, and had him for his doctor. Dr. Quick pulled Mr. Bloss through his heart attack and later we used him to pull my mother in law, Grace Melton, through her attack.

Manufacturing Facility

Then after Mr. Bloss got old and sick and had to resign, they decided that they were going to put me out in the shop. I was in charge of all of the maintenance of the shop. IDECO had a plant in Torrence, California where they built drilling masts. They said, "We're going to start building drilling masts at IDECO in Beaumont instead. And we want you to fix up a manufacturing facility for it."

Well, the first thing I had to do was to fix up a big acetylene gas plant, 1200 pounds of carbide at one time. I built it way down on the end of the property, so in case it blew up it wouldn't damage anything. There was a two inch pipe to carry acetylene from the carbide generating plant up to the welding shop. We put a welding outlet on every post in the welding shop. Every post had acetylene and oxygen and electric welding. Then in another place we had to put all the facilities for building these drilling masts. It meant we had to have a welding machine on every post in that building. It took a tremendous amount of electrical power. So what did we do? We built a substation inside our building. Ran in real high voltage electricity to that substation. We installed traveling cranes and all the other things required for manufacturing masts. I'll tell you what, that crew I had there could do anything.

But, you see they worked the normal shift, and then they helped me do all this building on their overtime. Well, they got paid for their

Drilling rig being manufactured at IDECO

overtime, but I was a salaried employee, and in addition to my regular work I had to do all that work on available overtime, and I didn't get paid for it. So one day I decided that I was going to look for another job. Mr. Bloss was gone, who I loved so much. I was having to work for a guy that you couldn't speak to, his name was Bob LeFleur. I'd speak to Bob and he wouldn't wave, he wouldn't talk to me, or anything. So every time I'd walk by him I'd say, "Hello, Bob." And he wouldn't say nothing. So next time I'd say it louder and louder. Finally I got it where I was screaming in his ear, and he finally broke down and started speaking to me. He turned out to be one of my best friends. But he was in charge of the plant, and I was working for him.

Back when Mr. Bloss and I would come up with a new piece of equipment he would send me down to Sun Oil Company to talk to the drilling superintendent. They would test the equipment and tell us what was wrong with it. I got to know Sun Oil Company pretty well, and really liked what I saw.

An IDECO "Rambler" drilling rig

Finally I told IDECO that I had to have a $50 a month raise. The answer was, "No way." They could give me $25 and that was it. I told them I would look for a new job, and they didn't believe it. When I got the new job, they tried to give me $100 a month to stay. I said, "No way".

Rambler rig at night

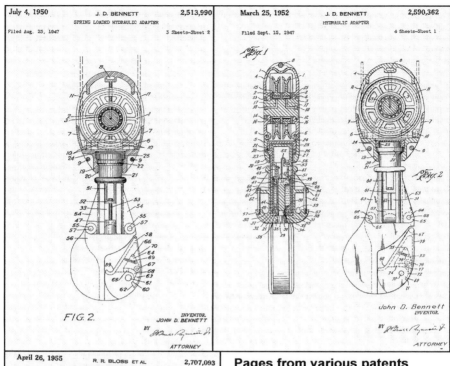

July 4, 1950   J. D. BENNETT   2,513,990
SPRING LOADED HYDRAULIC ADAPTER
Filed Aug. 25, 1947   3 Sheets-Sheet 2

FIG. 2.

INVENTOR.
JOHN D. BENNETT
BY
ATTORNEY

March 25, 1952   J. D. BENNETT   2,590,362
HYDRAULIC ADAPTER
Filed Sept. 15, 1947   4 Sheets-Sheet 1

Fig. 1

Fig. 2

John D. Bennett
INVENTOR.
BY
ATTORNEY

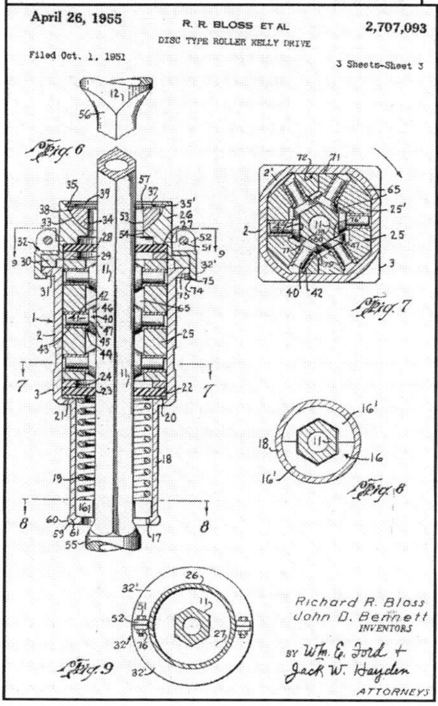

April 26, 1955   R. R. BLOSS ET AL   2,707,093
DISC TYPE ROLLER KELLY DRIVE
Filed Oct. 1, 1951   3 Sheets-Sheet 3

Fig. 6

Fig. 7

Fig. 8

Fig. 9

Richard R. Bloss
John D. Bennett
INVENTORS
BY Wm. E. Ford +
Jack W. Hayden
ATTORNEYS

Pages from various patents

287

Chapter 31
Home Life in Beaumont
1945-1956

When we moved to Beaumont, we got a bedroom in the private home of some school teachers. Wynona had some kitchen privileges, we shared the bathroom with them. Soon our son Wayne came knocking at the door.

We moved to a converted "chicken coop" that was a very small apartment on the back of a garage. It had one room that was just big enough for a couch that you could make into a bed. There was another room with an end that was just big enough for a stove, and there was a little spot on the back that was a bathroom. We would hear noises at night under the floor and it turned out that there was an infestation of large rats six or seven inches long in the vicinity, mainly under the floor. Places were very hard to find in Beaumont right after the war. Wynona just didn't like rats, so we had to move.

We found a duplex which suited us just fine. Here is where I sprouted my wings into the blessed event of starting to collect tools. I had seen advertised a small portable welding machine in the *Popular Mechanics* magazine for just $39.50. Now that we were assured that we could eat, because I had a job and Wynona hadn't yet learned to say, "Oh no, not that!" I bought the welder.

My college roommate's parents, the Reeds, lived in Beaumont. They were real lovely people. Their daughter and her husband became some of our best friends. I had even escorted the daughter around a time or two when the Reeds came to College Station. Like all good parents, they dispensed some very good advice to their young and very inexperienced friends: "Don't buy any property in Beaumont until you see where the high water marks are." Boy, what sound advice that was. Beaumont had not yet addressed the flooding situation in the city and when a real flood came, homes and streets were flooded all over town.

Our First House

In about 1946 we bought property on Lucas Drive and had our first house built on high and dry ground. One of the engineers at IDECO had been a house builder. He was just itching to start building houses after the war. Ours was one of the first houses he built. It was small, only 860 square feet, two bedrooms, a living room, a kitchen, and a one car garage that was about 8 feet deeper than needed for the car.

2461 Lucas Drive

Back on this section, I had a door on which I immediately put a sign that said, "Dog House". I had a work bench and a small shop that was behind the tumbling washing machine. After all, Wayne was on his way and that would call for tons of diapers. We had been placed on waiting lists several places around town for the washer, stove, and refrigerator.

Wayne

Our first son, Wayne, was born on August 24, 1946. You have heard about cutting your teeth on something. Well, when Wayne was barely home from the hospital, I was putting a thermostat on the wall in his bedroom, and I got out the electric drill to drill into the wall. Just kind of figured that the son of an engineering piddler should store in his brain the sound of an electric drill instead of the sound of a crying doll.

Young babies require a lot of attention, especially when it is time for the bottle. Piddling Pop developed a bottle holder for the crib with an adjustable arm that had a clamp on the end for holding the bottle. Worked just fine for me, but Mama preferred the hand held method.

Our house was on Lucas Drive in Beaumont. I installed a post made out of four inch pipe for a lamp post. We had a regular yard light on top of the post, and I drilled 1/4 inch holes into the post to spell out the house number "2461." The holes had 1/4 inch Plexiglas pushed into them and a florescent light was installed in the pipe that burned all the time. At night the little dots of light shone lighting up the

Wayne, Wynona, John D, and Barry about 1954

291

letters. At IDECO we had an artist draftsman that I had write the name "Bennett" out in letters about three inches high. In my Dog House shop, and with 1/8 by 1 inch iron, I formed the letters over the draftsman's script. It was all secured on a pretty formed piece of iron with scrolls on each end and a scroll type bracket to support it. The whole thing was welded together with my new Dynamic Welding machine, and welded on the lamp post above the house number.

There were two of my A&M classmates working at IDECO with me. One was named "Mac" McLerran. His wife we called Shorty, and their little daughter was named Marilyn. She was 6 weeks older than Wayne. They only lived about five blocks down Lucas Drive from us. I built a special holder to hold corn tortillas in a U shape. You would put the tortilla in the holder, hold it in boiling oil and cook it crisp. That would be filled with ground meat that had been scrambled, cut up tomatoes, lettuce, picante hot sauce, and we made tacos. I could hardly ever eat over a dozen of them when we got together with the McLerrans, which we did at least once a week. Wayne and Marilyn would play together, Wayne riding his tricycle and Marilyn standing on the back axle holding on to Wayne's ears. She said she was "kooking his ears." By the way, for dessert, we usually had fresh frozen peaches. Television had not been invented for us poor people yet. This was about 1948. Life was simple.

Water Well
I wanted water to water my yard. I had always heard how mother's dad, Grampa DeVilbiss, had made a bit that was turned to drill a well, and how the casing would follow the hole drilled by the bit because the bit drilled a bigger hole than the diameter of the casing. To retract the bit after drilling, the bit collapsed and would come out through the casing. This was a very ingenious device. Too bad he didn't know about patents.

I found that you could take a water hose with the water running, stick the hose in the ground and it would go right in. It would make a crooked hole because the hose was flexible. Put a straight piece of pipe on the end of the hose and you could drill a straight hole in soft formations. Put one of Grampa's bits on the end of the pipe and turn the pipe, it would really go down, but to prevent the hose from wrapping up, you needed a swivel joint between the hose and the pipe. Of course you could turn the pipe with a Stillson wrench and go round and round, and down the hole would go.

Now in this modern age of machinery, all one had to do was to put a gear reduction on top of the swivel arrangement and turn the pipe with a motor, using a tree for the derrick and you had all the essence of a drilling machine. The running hose replaced the mud pump. The tree, rope and pulley replaced the derrick, crown block and hook, pulling on the rope replaced the draw works. The gear reduction, the rotary table and the electric motor or lawn mower engine replaced the drilling engine.

John D and Wy at a party

After all, I designed drilling equipment. The drill pipe you drilled the well with became the production pipe for the water. This process was very easy and it was less expensive. If you need water in a different part of the yard, just drill another well.

Trinity Methodist Church
About that time Wayne was getting a little bit bigger. We didn't go to church much at all, but we decided it was time to put him in church. We joined the First Methodist Church in Beaumont and started attending. We attended for three or four years. They would have dances in the basement, and the Baptists would send some of their people over to stand at the door to keep the Baptist kids out.

The church sent out a hundred people to start a new church. It met at the Harvest Club, a building at the fair grounds in Beaumont. There would be a dance on Saturday night, and there'd be balloons floating all around when we met the next morning. We got a pretty good collection of people out there. That thing grew like crazy. The first thing you know we built a big building called the Trinity Methodist Church, and we were charter members of that congregation. We really enjoyed going there. We had a wonderful preacher, Charles Williams. He was a guy who preached at the dance hall at the county fair and looked everyone in the eye. He didn't use any notes. The following Sunday he would tell you whether you were in church or not. He called roll mentally in his mind. He was a fantastic preacher and really made the church grow.

Elevator

Babies generate a lot of dirty diapers. Back before the days of dryers, those diapers had to be hung out on the line to dry. This was well and good unless it was raining, and it did an awful lot of that in Beaumont. There were clothes drying racks that opened up, but they took up almost all of the living space in the house. Something had to be done.

We had a pull-down stairway to the attic but it was very difficult for Wynona to use. I decided to floor the attic, as there was a lot of space that we could use, and by stringing two clothes lines, there would be plenty of room to hang that mountain of diapers. The only trouble was that the best part of the attic to use was right where the pull-down stairs was.

We had a hall closet that was offset from where this most desirable location was, so I decided that I needed an elevator to the attic in the closet. I had seen how elevators worked in the real old buildings and decided to copy the idea. There would be a pulley up at the top and a pulley down at the bottom. A rope was put on the pulleys and fixed kind of like the drawstring on a curtain rod. Pull one side of the rope down and the rope would go up on the other side like the drawstring works. The rope was attached to the reversing switch on an electric motor. I built a track guide for the elevator to ride on. There was a stabilizing cage attached to the floor of the elevator with roller guides on the cage at the top and on the platform at the bottom. A simple electric winch with two cables, one for each side of the cage, was attached to the hoisting drum. There was a reduction between the drum and the motor with a magnetically released brake on the motor shaft. Power to the motor released the brake. When the power to the motor was cut, the brake set.

When the elevator got to the top of its travel, a stop on the rope switch cable would turn the motor off. There would be only one way the rope could be moved at the top of the travel and that was to start the motor for the "down" operation. When the elevator got to the down location, a stop on the switch rope turned the motor off, and the only way that the rope could be moved was to the "up" position.

It was all a fool-proof system, but unfortunately we had not heard of Ralph Nader. This elevator did not have a door that would close before it would work. There were no signs that said, "Don't operate the elevator if any of the load overhangs the platform. "One day Wynona put a folding cot on the elevator with the intention of carrying it up to the attic. Wayne was a little kid in his crib. She had her load of clothes with her, not thinking about the cot. When the elevator got up to the top of the closet door, the cot struck the door and the elevator hung. Boy, if there ever was an "Oh no, not that," this was it. She didn't know what to do. The neighbors couldn't hear her hollering, Wayne was in his crib, and she was frantic. She was afraid that if she crawled out between the elevator floor and the top of the door frame and the cot slipped, it might cut her in two. Finally, she decided that she had to chance it and she crawled through and then dropped about 5 feet to the floor. Immediately I rushed home, as soon as she got her breath and called me. That was when we decided that the elevator had to go and we built stairs to the attic in the kitchen.

Barry and the Pie Machine
It was about time for Barry to show up on the scene and that was going to be about $200 extra we were going to have to raise. We never had any spare money, and $200 was a lot. The Lord always provides. Mr. Joe Register was in the pie business. He made small pies about 3-1/2 inches in diameter. Making the crust was very time consuming. A piece of dough was made into a ball and then it was pressed out in the pan by hand to the right thickness, the top

trimmed and then it was ready to be filled. For $225 I made him a machine that would do all that for him, press the dough to the correct thickness everywhere, cut and trim the top. It paid for Barry, who arrived on June 21, 1950.

Electric Cars

Time was moving along, and Wayne was at least four years old and needed a car of his own in order to make the neighborhood kids jealous. His first car (about 1950) was an electric car he could get in and drive all around the yard. He was very popular. He eventually had several cars, finally one with a windshield, gasoline engine, forward and reverse gear, seat for two in front with the steering wheel, and a rumble seat over the engine in the rear. It had a trailer hitch and a trailer. There was a neighborhood mother's association, as mothers didn't go out to work in those days—they baby sat, ironed, cooked, kept house and made their husbands happy when they came home from a hard day at the office. They had birthday parties for the kids, at least one a week in the neighborhood. Wayne's car was in great use at that time.

Lawn Mower

Mr. Pete Wiggins was a next door neighbor. He was also the purchasing agent for IDECO. We found that in lots of six, we could get some little gasoline engines for about $20 each. Several of us made up an order. In about 1948 I took my push-type reel lawn mower and modified it to where the little engine would work on top and made a self-propelled lawn mower that worked great. I must have made a dozen of them. Only trouble was you had to follow it. We tried putting a stake in the yard and let the lawn mower go round and round gradually making a smaller circle but that was too much trouble. I just had to have a riding lawn mower. You have got to realize that this was all before the days of such things as riding lawn mowers. I made one of them later.

Ben-Lee-Whirlaway

My kids were getting bigger. Wayne loved to go out to Entertainment Parks and ride the rides. Any self-respecting engineering, piddling father could handle that. I made Wayne and the neighborhood kids a motor driven "merry-go-round." (Barry was too little to do anything but watch). There was a horizontal beam on top about 20 feet long, mounted on a tower about eight feet high. It had two modified strollers hung by chains from the ends of the beam. There was a pull switch string that hung over the pilot's seat. Wayne would get in one stroller that barely cleared the ground and one of the neighbors would get in the other. With one of the neighborhood mothers as watch committee, Wayne would pull the string and away they would go. The mechanism had a slip drive in case some aspiring pilot ran over to get in, it would not do much more than knock them over and put mother in the state of shock.

All this went very well until my dear friend, the manufacturing tycoon (Harold Lee), decided that we should put these on the market. For his part, he was going to buy the steel (less than $20 worth each), the motor (1/4 horse power from Sears), and I was to make them. The goal was ten in all. We were going to sell them for $150 each. We built them in my yard.

One weekend I had to go to Derby to repair a piece of machinery that I shall discuss later. My good buddy, Harold, decided that he would surprise me while I was gone and he was going to spray paint the merry-go-rounds that we had dubbed "Ben-Lee-Whirlaway." The color was to be aluminum. The wind was blowing and unknown to anyone, the neighbor's car was out in his driveway. Harold painted as good a job on the neighbor's car as he did on the merry-go-rounds.

Never in our lives have Harold Lee and John Bennett worked as hard as we did for about a week trying to clean my neighbor's car. On top of all that, we never sold a single merry-go-round. I think we gave a couple away, Mac McLerran getting one for Marilyn.

Addition To The House
In about 1953 my mother-in-law had a heart attack while she was living in Corsicana. We decided there was nothing to do but build her an apartment on the back of the house so she could live with us and Wynona could take care of her. We built a room almost across the back of the house to serve as a den, took my Dog House part of the garage and made her a kitchen and built her a large bedroom, a bath, and carport. She was fixed up pretty good with all the room

she needed. There could never have been another person as easy to live with. She was an OK mother-in-law.

Wheelbarrow
The kids were getting bigger and they really liked having Grandma living with us. I decided that I should build a little swimming pool. A person has to have help digging a swimming pool even if it is not very big. I needed a motorized wheelbarrow.

I made a three wheel job with half of a barrel as a body. It pivoted on the back axle for dumping, and the third wheel was motorized and steered. The steering handle was also the clutch handle. Pull the handle down and the wheelbarrow went forward. The wheels were little airplane wheels about 12 inches tall and 6 inches wide. The engine must have come off one of my other projects.

One day, I told Wynona that I wished I had a $1000 worth of steel that had been used only one time. On the farm at Derby I had had a big pile of scrap iron that had been used over and over.

Swimming Pool
I dug a kidney-shaped swimming pool in our backyard. The pool had two depths to it and was supplied by one of my water wells. There was about a two foot wall all around the pool to make it safer. In the winter we added a temporary top to turn the pool into a hot-house.

IDECO used to have a large redwood cooling tower that was used with the office air conditioner, until I talked Mr. Bloss into drilling a shallow well to be used as a cooling source for the air conditioner. It worked great, and I got the redwood tower.

The base of the tower was two inch thick redwood. That turned into a picnic table with built-on benches. We used that on our porch, which was glassed in with jalousie windows. The slats of the tower turned into a redwood fence around the pool and a slatted roof over the brick patio by the pool. You could wet the bricks and it made it nice and cool.

This pool caused a problem with the neighborhood kids until I told them they could swim anytime that one of their parents was there to

Cover of company magazine showing pool and redwood fence

watch them. It was amazing how that cut down on the swimming traffic. Our yard was the neighborhood playground and park.

Wynona had a cousin who lived in Galveston. He was the king of the road with his Cushman scooter. It had tires at least six inches wide and a back seat. He must have ridden it a million miles before it fell into disrepair. I gave him $50 for it and fixed it up. Then I rode it another million miles back and forth to work, and home for dinner whenever Mr. Bloss would let me go. I sold that scooter to the Chief Engineer of IDECO when I left IDECO and he rode it another million miles. I understand he still has it put up as a museum piece.

Garage Door Opener
All these stories are not being told in exactly the order in which they occurred, but what does that matter? That brings me to the story about the garage door opener. Nobody had ever heard of a garage door opener when I built mine. Laziness and inconvenience are the mother of invention. My garage door was a one-piece door that swung up and in when it was opened. It was heavy for Wynona to

299

open, so I decided to try and build an opener. First, I mounted a 2x4 lying flat in the top of the garage above the middle of the door. I mounted two 3/8" pitch chain sprockets, one on each end of the 2x4, each with one face exposed. They were connected by an end-less chain. A rod was fastened to the top of the door so it could pivot when the door opened. The other end of the rod was attached to a pin on the chain that extended on one side. When the chain was rotated it would open and close the door. Limit switches were used at each end to stop the door open or closed. No reversing mecha-nism, just a push button switch to make it operate.

Shop
I decided that I needed a shop in the backyard. There was enough room in yard width to have a second driveway that could go to the backyard. A nice slab 30 feet long and 20 feet wide was poured. I built the building like a Quonset hut. I fabricated arched ribs to the laid out design drawn on the slab floor. There was a straight flat wall on the front of the building that was divided into three sections. Two were doors that would swing up to make an awning and extend the area where a person could work when it rained, which was real often in Beaumont. On one end was a small office that was 10x10 feet. There was a large glass window in the front wall and a door that opened into the rest of the building. This was my office.

I had read some information about the wonders of radiant heat. This really did intrigue me. An engineer must experiment. I papered the office walls with aluminum foil. One could work in his shirt sleeves in the dead of a Beaumont winter and be warm strictly from his own body heat that was reflected back to him by the foil.

Geothermal Heat
My Daddy called me one day and said that he was going to lower the house on the farm down to ground level so he could get in the house better. Dad was crippled and couldn't climb the four foot stairs very well. He was going to set the house on a concrete slab. I told Dad that I thought he should put pipe in the floor so he could flow that 98° well water through the slab to warm it up in the winter. His well was 1700 feet deep, flowed 1000 gallons of water a minute and was 98° F the year around. By putting a four inch pipe header

MONDAY, JUNE 16, 1952

The Beaumont PARADE

EDITED BY BOB ALDRIDGE

HE MAKES THINGS . . .

We've discovered one of the handiest fellows to have around the house that you could imagine. He's John D. Bennett of 2461 Lucas drive. John is an inventor and a builder of gadgets to make home life easier and happier. For instance, he doesn't have to get out of his car to open his garage door. As he drives in the driveway he pushes a button on his dashboard . . . and as the car rolls over a buried magnet, the garage door opens . . . particularly nice when it's raining.

Somebody gave John an old monitor-top GE refrigerator. He cut the legs off and put them on the side of the box, so the door would open upward. He installed some tubing on the inside of the box, got a new freezing unit . . . and presto he had himself a deep freezer at a very small cost.

YOUNGSTERS BENEFIT . . .

John has a fine workshop in his backyard which contains lathes, drills, saws and the like for working with wood, iron and steel. There he makes all manner of things for his youngsters, Wayne and Barry. Among these are a little motor-driven back- yard automobile . . . a foot-pro- pelled adjustable "road grader" . . . a hand-pumped merry-go- round . . . a tower and Tarzan- swinging device on which the kid- dies can ride to the ground down a wire stretched across the yard, and afterward the handle is auto- matically pulled to the top of the tower again for the next Tarzan.

Too, John has installed a big, comfortable tractor seat on his power mower . . . a man after our own heart.

PROJECT ABANDONED . . .

An interesting experiment that works . . . John lined the walls and ceiling of the office in his workshop with aluminum foil in- stead of wallpaper. The office now needs no heat in wintertime . . .

J.S.

the heat from one's body hits the wall and bounces back to warm the room! John says it's comfortable in really cold weather.

A backfire . . . the elevator to the attic which he installed in his home. It stuck about half-way up one day with Mrs. Bennett in it! Not because of mechanical failure . . . an object being transported to the attic jammed against the door facing. With nobody at home but her and a small crying baby, she had a trying few minutes. She finally squeezed through the small opening between the bottom of the elevator and the top of the door. Whew!

John converted the elevator back into a closet with shelves!

REAL INVENTOR . . .

John Bennett is a valued en- gineer for Ideco . . . and really is an inventor. He has several patents for drilling machinery inventions which Ideco uses, and has about 10 more inventions now in the patent mill.

PARADE's fanciest camellia to a young man who uses his noggin for something more than just to hang his hat on.

* * *

Beaumont Journal article

301

on opposite sides of the slab, pipes could be put in the slab between the headers and water would flow through the slab.

I told Dad that I would talk to Wayne Long, head of the air-conditioning department at A&M, and ask for his recommendations. Wayne said, sure, he would make a class project out of it and let me know. In the meantime, I bought 1000 feet of used pipe from a dealer in Beaumont and shipped it to Dad.

Now, my Daddy was an impatient man. He called one day and said he could wait no longer for a decision from Wayne Long for how far apart the pipes should be. I told him to put them 18 inches apart. After the house was up and running, Wayne Long said they figured that the pipes should be 12 inches apart. Anyway, Dad had the most perfect heating system in the country and it didn't cost one cent to run.

Dad

Television Antenna

Television became popular sometime after World War II. My next door neighbor in Beaumont bought a television set. I remember all the neighbors would go over to the Lindow's house and watch it. There was a TV broadcasting antenna that was put up between Beaumont and Orange, Texas. I remember it was channel 6. You could get a fairly good picture. It was several miles over to where that antenna was.

My Daddy was one of these people who wanted to be the first person in the community to have anything that was new. After so long a time he wanted a television. When he wanted a television, he wanted a television now! The only problem was that the station that broadcast television in his area, WOAI, was north of San Antonio. And he was way south of San Antonio. It was probably 75 miles away. And the problem was that there were hills around Moore, between San Antonio and the farm. It even gave the railroad trouble when they were trying to lay the railroad through those hills. They were kinda high, and the elevation caused problems. You see television is a line of sight proposition. Whenever the signal is broadcast it will go a long way if there is nothing in its way to stop it, but it doesn't want to bend around anything or over anything. If you've got hills like there are at Moore, you've got to get high enough to pick up that signal.

I said, "Dad, we're going to have to build a real tall antenna." "Well, let's build it." You know, if I suggested something and Dad wanted it, we did it. Beside the northeast corner of the house there on the farm, we dug a hole about three feet by three feet and about four or five feet deep to make a base for this television antenna we were going to build. We put some pieces of steel in the concrete (December 24, 1949) that we could put some big bolts on and bolt to two of the legs of the antenna tower that we were going to make, so that when we stood it up they served as a hinge. When we finally stood it up then the third leg would come down and it would line up with another piece of steel that we could bolt onto. Essentially you could say that the three legs of the antenna tower were bolted to steel that went way down into that concrete base. It was quite a concrete base. I think, as it wound up, we made a tower that was 89 feet tall. That's a long time ago, and I'm depending on my memory.

It seems like the legs of that tower were made of ¾" concrete reinforcing steel. There were three legs about 18 inches apart, and there was a lattice work between the legs that went up and braced it. We built the thing there on the ground, leveled it up the best that I could. I welded, and I welded, and I welded. I thought I never was going to get through welding. We even had a mechanism on top with a couple of wires that went up to the top so you could pull these wires and it would turn some gears up at the top, and rotate the antenna from down below.

Well, the next question was how we were going to stand it up. It was heavy! And it was big and tall! So I think we got some 2x6s

303

about 20 feet long, and stood then up as an X over the top of the antenna that was laid out on the ground. We lifted the antenna up as high as we could and set it up on some barrels to hold the top end of off the ground as high as possible. Then we had these 2x6s that straddled this antenna and were tied together at the top to make a two legged tripod. Then we took a guy wire from almost to the top of the antenna and strung it over the top of these 2x6s and went out there and tied it on to a tractor. We had guy wires all laid out so that as it went up we could have the wires about where we wanted them We had it all stretched out and started pulling on it with that tractor and gradually we got that thing up in the air. Boy it was tall!

You know that thing picked up that blooming station in San Antonio. We had pretty good reception down there on the farm—the best of anybody in the country. My daddy was always the first to do anything in the country. If you wanted to see what was new, you didn't go to the big city, you went to Sidney Bennett's farm and saw what he had just bought. He had the first carbide lights. He had the first electric lights. He had the first monitor-top electric refrigerator. He had the first geothermally heated house. He just had the first of everything all right there on the farm. He was a very progressive farmer, and he really liked to get things done. He got good television, and that thing stood up there for years and years. Finally a storm came along and took the top of the antenna down. Then they used it many years later as a sawed off thing, you might say.

Mail Order Plans for Sale
With all the hard work that I had been doing in Beaumont, I began to see if there wasn't some way that a person could make some extra money. I had built all kind of things. All these projects were simple to build, so I bought a mimeograph machine and turned out instructions on how to make each of the items, such as "Motorized Wheel Barrow", "The Redwood Table With Attached Benches", "The Automatic Garage Door Opener", "How to Drill Your Own Water Well By Hand", "How To Build A Deep Freeze Out Of An Old Ice Box", "How To Build A Three Hundred Watt AC Light Plant From An Old Car Generator." I advertised in the *Popular Mechanics* and the *Popular Science* magazines starting about 1948 or 1949.

At a dollar a word, one did not get too gabby. It took three months after placing the ads before we saw any results. That was a big gamble for someone without much money. The plans sold for one dollar. The postage was three cents and the paper for mimeographing another three cents. People would write and ask all kind of questions about the plans. I had a stamp that said, "These are the plans, if you like them, send me one dollar, if you don't, return the plans". I never lost a dollar, and I sold plans all over the world.

It was so much fun to go to the mailbox and have a bunch of mail with dollars in them. The thing was getting to go pretty good and I was almost breaking even when we moved from Beaumont. Ten years after we moved, I was still getting mail. It was amazing how those old magazines must have been kept and read after that long. Mail-order business is fun.

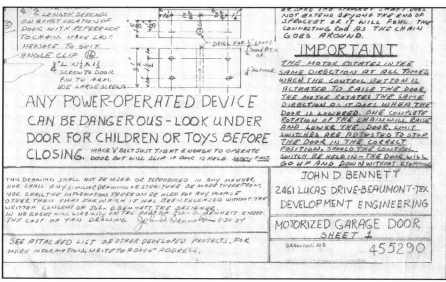

A page from mail order plans

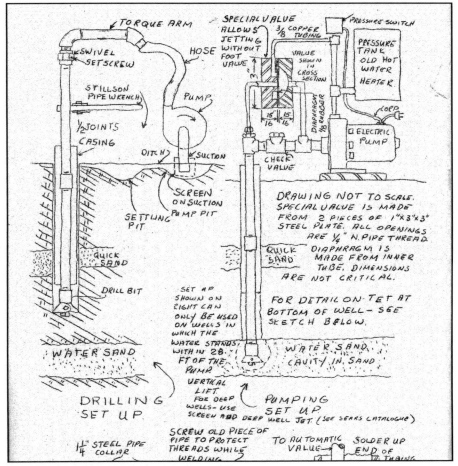

A page from the water well drilling plans

Changing Jobs

For a time Wynona was assistant den mother for the Cub Scouts. Barbara Schroeder was the den mother. We got to know Barbara and her husband King Schroeder real well. My next door neighbor, Gober Lindow, was his chief draftsman. King Schroeder was Vice President of Geology and went frequently to Sun Oil Company's home office in Philadelphia.

When I decided to change jobs, I talked to King Schroder. It is amazing what a VP can do to further your cause. I got the job as Mechanical Engineer for the Sun Oil Company Production

306

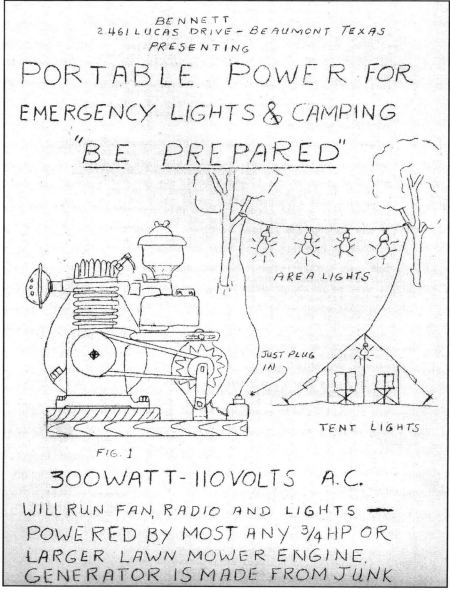

A page from the power plant plans

Research Laboratory in Richardson, Texas. I gave IDECO two weeks notice.

I had to get things in high gear. I immediately found a house in Richardson, Texas to rent and started building a two axle totally enclosed trailer that I used to move all my shop tools up to Richardson. The household stuff was moved by moving van.

Our life of 10 years had changed for the better even if we did have to leave some very dear friends behind.

Chapter 32
Charcot-Marie-Tooth Disease

There is an inherited problem in my family known as Charcot-Marie-Tooth disease. It is a withering of the coating on the nerve, and in time the muscles that are affected loose part of their strength. Most members of our family don't have it, but my Dad did, as well as my brother Sid, and many of his descendants.

We do not know where the problem developed, but I understand there is a considerable amount of the ailment in France, and it probably went to England with William the Conqueror. There is very little of it in the United States. My grandfather and grandmother on my father's side both came from England. I am almost positive that my grandfather didn't have the problem, as he was a very active man surveying the International & Great Northern Railroad from south Texas into Torreon and Tampico, Mexico. I can remember him well, and had he been crippled, he wouldn't have been able to dance so good when I put the Model "T" coil wires in his shoes while he made out like he was asleep. I can remember Grandma real well, too, when I was a kid. She was the best thing to me there ever was. I do remember that I pumped a zillion buckets of water out of the old cistern to water her flowers. I could remember her saying, "My feet hurt me so last night that I could scarcely sleep a wink." Yet when Grandma was young and Grampa was in Mexico, she carried water from a windmill that was about a mile from the house. If she was crippled, we didn't know it. I thought that her hobbling along was caused by old age, because she was well over 90 when she passed on.

Old Bill

My Daddy was crippled. When I was young, he rode horseback all over the farm. He used crutches to walk, but in later years he had to use a wheelchair. As years passed, about 1947, Dad told me that he just had to get some exercise. Could I possibly build him something that he could exercise on? I built him something that he called "Old Bill". It was a bicycle-type exercising machine. You would sit on a bench seat that was the height of the seat on a wheelchair that he had to use then. It had two electric motors that had reversible switches. There were pedals like on a bicycle, except that on a bicycle the pedals were connected together. This device had two pedals which went in a circular motion like those on a bicycle, but each was independently driven by a belt, so the pedals were hardly ever in sync with each other. Each pedal was independently mounted on a swing arm that was forced mechanically to swing the pedals alternately closer together and then farther apart while the pedals went around.

Each pedal had a bracket into which the operator put his feet. He put his feet into these brackets like he would put on a pair of slippers. The brackets were pivotally mounted on the cranks of the pedals, but had extension arms that slid through an eye mounted on the front of the swing arm. This action worked your ankles up and down as the crank went round and round. A switch was mounted on the handle bar that the operator held onto while riding. The cranks were reversible by a flip of the switch.

The seat could be raised from the position where the pedals were in front of you up until you were directly above the cranks. The motor was also controlled by a reversible switch.

Dad's legs would get to hurting him so, he would get up in the night and get on "Old Bill" and ride until his legs felt better. Dad rode "Old Bill" every day, and sometimes more than once a day, until he died in 1961.

When Dad died they took "Old Bill" out of the house and put it in one of the other houses there on the farm. I felt good until I found out a family had moved into that house and set "Old Bill" out on the trash heap.

310

Original Old Bill (above) and Old Bill being made smaller (below).

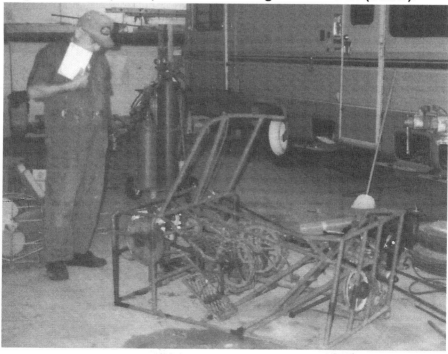

311

A dear friend that I had worked with at Sun Oil Company came to see me one day about 1993 and told me that he needed to build his grandson some kind of exercise machine. Clarence Braun and I had worked together for 21 years, and there was nothing Clarence didn't know about me. I told him, "Let's go to the farm and see if we can find Dad's old machine." We did, and I got sick when I found out it had been sitting out for 32 years. We got the machine, Clarence came to stay with me for a week in Marble Falls, and we rebuilt it. It was amazing that after all that time in the weather, we were able to salvage it. We cut it down to where Clarence thought his grandson could adapt to it with time. Boy, did I feel better knowing that "Old Bill" was off the trash heap and maybe was going to do that little fellow some good. Clarence did a real good thing for my spirits when we worked on that machine together. It is good to be with your old friends after several years of being retired.

Electric Wheelchair
Now Daddy knew that I was the dumbest farm boy that ever lived, but he wasn't the least bashful when it came to telling me what he wanted to help him get better, and expected me to do it. I tried.

Dad had rebuilt his house down on the slab in about 1946 and the garage was on the same level as the house floor. He wanted some kind of wheelchair that could be used to lift him up to the level of the truck seat so he could just slide in. That was a big order.

Fortunately I had already obtained some knowledge about electric locomotion. From my Model "T" days, I knew about electric starters, and I had a metal-cutting lathe that I had had in my YMCA room before I married. In my Model "T" days, I had learned how to rebabbitt the connecting rods in the engine. (Bad rods was one of the main reasons the junkyards were full of perfectly good Model "T"s.)

If you needed a bearing, you just cast a babbitt one. With this vast self-taught knowledge, why couldn't I build something by looking for things that I could copy? There was the scissors action jack, a device that was used to lift cars when they had a flat tire. The wheelchair seat could be attached to the top of a scissors jack. The screw device that pulled the opposite sides of the scissors together could be replaced by a pulley block system, like we used to hoist the hogs on the farm while butchering. Then the action of revolving the pulley rope around a drum like a ship's capstan (used to lift the anchor) could be used to raise and lower the seat.

I built a chair in about 1946 that had two drive wheels in the front and a crazy wheel in the back. It had a box under the seat that held batteries and the mechanical and electrical mechanism. An electric motor (an old starter) rotated two shafts in opposite directions--one shaft forward of the front wheels and the other shaft behind the front wheels. Each end of each shaft had a drum on it. So, the front wheel had a drum rotating in one direction in front of it and a drum rotating the opposite direction behind it. The wheels could be shifted forward or backward by two handles attached to the axles. If the driver pushed a handle forward the connected wheel engaged the rotating roller drum and the wheel would turn forward. If the driver pushed the other handle forward the other wheel would engage. If the driver pulled a handle back the connected wheel rotated backward.

There was an electric button on top of one handle
so when the driver put his
hand on top of the shift
lever to make the chair
move the motor would
start. If the electric motor
was running and the shift
levers were not shifted
forward or backward, the
two shafts were just turning, but the drive wheels
were not engaged.

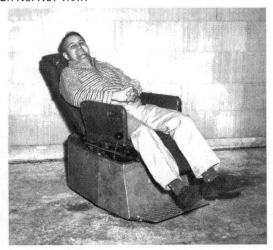

When it was time to lift the seat, the two shafts were belted to a
worm reduction that operated the lift capstan. The belts were loose
and nothing happened unless one of the belts was tightened. There
was an idler on each belt that was hooked to a piece called a
"rocking motion". If the rocking motion was rocked one way, one
belt was tight, and if it was rocked the other way, the other belt was
tight. Rocking of the idler shaft controlled the raising and lowering
of the seat.

A double solenoid was connected to the rock arm. If the driver actuated one solenoid, by passing electricity through it to run the motor
it would tighten the "up-motion" belt. The other solenoid would
actuate the "down-motion". Both solenoids were actuated by a
switch on the side of the chair arm. Up for "up", down for "down".

Once the chair was lifted to the height of the pickup seat, the right
side arm of the chair was lifted manually and laid down to bridge
the gap between the wheelchair seat and the truck seat. Once Dad
was in the pickup he would start the truck and move far enough forward so he could close the truck door. Then he was free to back up.

You can understand from reading the description of this chair that it
might need, as Tim Allen of the "Home Improvement" show might
say, "tweaking". It was nine hours from Beaumont to Derby. If Dad
called that things were not working right, we went.

314

Charcot-Marie-Tooth Disease

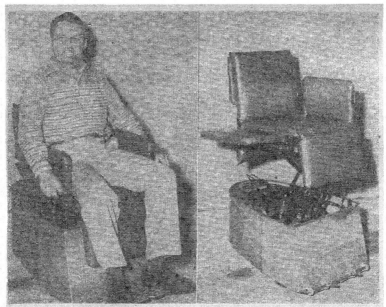

MOTHERED BY NECESSITY—John Bennett, 2461 Lucas drive, sits in the motorized wheel chair he invented and made for his invalid father, LEFT, and holds levers which control forward, reverse, turning movements. AT RIGHT, chair in raised position, showing scissors-jack mechanism underneath, arm which lowers so that user can slide across it into truck seat. Wheels on which chair moves are concealed under chair body. (Photos by Jack Hilder)

ELECTRIC WHEEL CHAIR

Beaumonter's Invention Gives New Life to Father

BY JERRY LYNAS

John Bennett simply had to invent a special electric wheel chair. There was no way out, as he saw it. So he began the task.

Three m o n t h s l a t e r—"three months of the hardest work I ever did in my life"—the chair was finished.

THE CHAIR is now giving a new life to John's father, Sidney Bennett, who operates a large farm near Derby, between San Antonio and Laredo.

John's father has had a form of muscular distrophy since he was five years old.

The elder Mr. Bennet was able to get around on crutches for years but about 10 years ago began using a conventional-type wheel chair.

In order to oversee the operation of his farm he had to get into his pickup truck. This meant continual help from his wife. The task of lifting him up to the seat proved too much for her.

JOHN BENNETT decided it was up to him to solve the problem.

He decided to build a motorized wheel chair which would lift his father to the height of the pickup truck seat.

The fact that the younger Bennett is foreman of the maintenance department at the local plant of the International Derrick and Equipment c o m p a n y somewhat simplified matters, but there were still many problems involved in designing and building the chair.

It had to be compact, narrow enough to go through doors, comfortable, have many uses, be entirely fool proof and dependable.

JOHN DECIDED a scissors-jack arrangement would be best as a means of raising and lowering the seat. He used cables to operate the jack and a car battery and car starter motor for power.

The chair has two front wheels to which power can be applied in either direction, plus a rear caster-type wheel. The elder Mr. Bennett can make the chair go forward, backward or turn it around, even in its own length.

Push buttons make the seat raise or lower.

HE RIDES in the chair out to the garage and stops beside the driver's side of the truck. He pushes a button and the chair lifts him to the level of the truck seat.

Then he lowers the arm of the chair so that it is a continuation of the seat, then slides onto the truck seat. He then raises the chair arm, so that it's clear of the truck, pulls forward and closes the truck door, then backs out and is on his way.

THE CHAIR has its own built-in battery charger. Each night the elder Mr. Bennett plugs the charger in and in the morning the battery is fresh, ready for another day's work.

As a further convenience, the chair back can be inclined and a head rest and built-in pillow put into position for television watching.

The chair is just one of a long line of inventions by Mr. Bennett. Others include a radio-operated garage door, a motorized wheelbarrow made from an oil drum and a power mower motor and a method of drilling your own water well with a pipe and water.

He's even gotten up a set of "do it yourself" plans for putting up your own television antenna.

315

Second Wheelchair

In 1956 we moved to Richardson, Texas so I could work for Sun Oil Production Research. I began to think about making Dad a better wheelchair that would not require so many trips to keep it working. I actually drew this design out and made it according to my new design. No more cut and try. This one was planned from start to finish. I had a few more years of experience on this one, and it came out perfect—well, almost perfect.

I used the same design on the electric starter running two parallel shafts that were worm driven and ran in opposite directions. On the end of each shaft was a home-built electric clutch that coupled to a large gear mounted on each of the two main drive wheels. (This came from the design of a Massey Harris farm tractor.) Engage one clutch and the drive wheel went forward, engage the other clutch and the drive wheel went backward. Four clutches: engage the two front clutches and the chair moved forward, engage the two back clutches and the chair went backward, engage a front clutch and a back clutch on the opposite side at the same time and the chair would turn in its own length.

RAISE ARM TO UNLOCK, THEN FOLD OVER

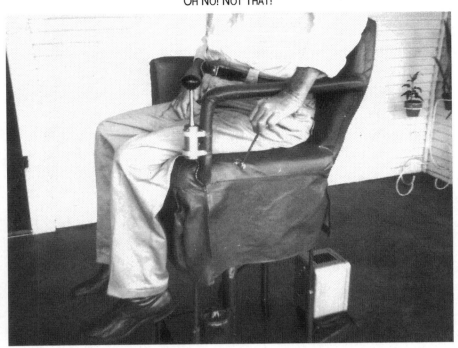

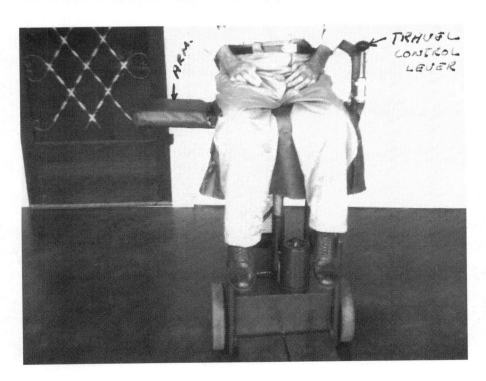

For switches, relay starter switches were used because DC current has a tendency to want to arc and burn out light switches. These heavy duty starter switches lasted the life of the chair.

The hoisting problem was much simplified. The hydraulic motor pump used to raise the top on a convertible car was used—switches, reversing valve, and all. The hoist mechanism was a simple single-acting hydraulic cylinder in the middle of the bottom of the seat, and four stabilizing cylinders were used, one on each corner of the seat.

The same kind of lay-down arm was used to bridge the gap from the wheelchair to the truck seat. This chair worked so good Dad used to chase everyone around the house in it. There was a built-in battery charger with an automatic cutoff switch to keep the battery from getting over charged. This chair required practically no maintenance. All of the gears were oil lubricated.

Rocking Bed
Now that I had Dad motorized and exercised, he had one more complaint. Dad had a lot of gas. One day I went down to see him, and

Frame for rocking bed

he said he was just about to blow up. What did I suggest? I said, "Dad, why don't we try making a rocking bed?" That idea pleased him, so I began to scout around the farm to see what I could find.

I came up with an old washing machine. I used the original motor and I modified the gear box so it could be used to rock the frame of a twin-size bed. The frame was pivoted in the middle and was supported on a main frame on the floor. The gear box was connected so that by using a crank and connecting rod, the head of the bed would go up and down a total of six inches ten times a minute. When the head of the bed went up six inches the foot went down six inches.

I put on a drawstring switch so Dad could just reach up and pull it to start or stop the motor. As he lay on that bed his stomach would move up and down by gravity, and after about 15 minutes he expelled all of his gas. He liked the rocking action so well that some nights he would rock all night.

Eating Utensils

I told you my Daddy was crippled, and my oldest brother was crippled, and he had two boys that were crippled, and they had children that were crippled. To one degree or another they couldn't use their fingers, and they had a hard time picking up a fork or a spoon to eat with. So I came up with a modified eating utensil. I took a fork and drilled four holes in the handle of the fork. I put little loops of stainless steel wire through these holes. So you could take your middle finger and stick it through one of these loops, and it would slide in there good. There were other loops that went from the left of your index finger to the right of your ring finger. You just kinda put it on like a glove. You wouldn't have to hold the fork at all, they just fit on your hand and you could just scoop up the food and eat with it. I must have made several dozen of those in my lifetime for all of my crippled relatives. They were a real handy thing to have. Actually somebody ought to have them on the market and make them available to the public.

Sid's Truck Lift

My brother, Sidney L. Bennett, Jr., was crippled, too. He was my buddy and I gave him credit for teaching me everything from how to kiss the girls to—oh, well, I can't give him credit for that. After

all, I was raised on the farm, and farm kids know everything. Like my father, Sid walked with crutches until he was middle-aged, and then had to begin using a wheelchair. Now Sid did not like the wheelchair that I built for Dad. He wanted his little light wheelchair that someone could pick up and put in his truck so he could carry it with him. But he wanted a way to be able to get from his wheelchair into his truck. He had a brand new truck. And I was living in Marble Falls at the time. I told him that I had an Airstream trailer but I didn't have a good truck to pull my trailer. I said, "Now Sid, if you'll just lend me your good truck that I could hook my Airstream trailer on and let me go up to Denver and stay a couple of weeks up there in the mountains I might be able to figure out a way to do that." "Oh No. You can't take my truck off. You've gotta do it without taking my truck off." So what could I do? I had to go to work for him.

So what I tried to do was to figure out a different way. There was some room underneath the seat of his new truck, and I thought maybe I could make a mechanism that could go under the seat. So I made a mechanism that had two electric motor-driven screws. I fixed a lift that was attached to his pickup floor at the driver's door and had a seat that would travel up and down. When it was at the bottom of its travel it would swing down and out, and when it came to rest it was at the same height as the seat of the wheelchair. Sid could slide onto the lift seat from his wheelchair. When Sid operated the correct motor he could raise the seat up to the height of the seat in the pickup truck, and it would be parallel with the ground. The second motor took care of making it level. When the lift seat was at the level of the pickup seat he could slide over onto the pickup seat. Then he would operate the second motor and swing the seat down into a vertical position so that he could close the pickup door. Then he could drive away. Eventually, when Sid died, Delma gave the lift to a company in San Antonio that rebuilt handicap equipment for automobiles.

Sid's Steering Aid
There was another job I had to work on for Sid. He had a new truck, but it was hard to steer. He said, "Johnny, I've got to have some-thing where I can steer these things." I said, "I'll see what I can do." I got into the mechanism on the steering wheel. When you turned the steering wheel it would turn just a little bit and then it would twist the shaft (a torsion bar). When it'd try to twist that shaft the part that was attached to the steering wheel would move and the other end was attached to the hydraulic valve mechanism. So you could move the top a little bit and it would operate the hydraulic valve mechanism that would work on the power steering. It was fixed so that when you turned the steering wheel a little bit it would go against a stop and it wouldn't let it twist that shaft anymore, it would turn the wheel. Well, the way I finally fixed it was that in order to make it turn easy I machined that little shaft that had to

twist every time you turned the steering wheel—I machined it where it was thinner, smaller in diameter, and could be twisted easier. So the twisting of that little shaft controlled how hard you had to turn the steering wheel in order to make the truck turn. I made it where you could take your little finger and turn the steering wheel and it would turn the wheel on the truck. He loved it. But Sid was a funny guy. The first thing I knew he said, "Johnny. You've got to fix my truck." I said, "What's the matter?" He said, "Well, I've bought a new truck." He didn't ask me anything about buying a new truck, so I had to do it all over again. I fixed two or three trucks like that for him.

Walker for Sid
When he was younger Sid used crutches. He could get around with crutches pretty good, but he needed a little more help. So I built him a special walker that was an aluminum frame that had four wheels under it. It was a U-shaped box that had armrests on the sides. He could put his arms in those rests like a crutch. When he walked he'd have his arms in those armrests and the walker would roll along on the wheels.

Trolley
When Sid was older it was very difficult for him to get on and off the commode. His bedroom was next to the bathroom, so I fastened a barn door rail to the ceiling, and it went from over the commode to over his bed. A trolley hung from the rail. On one end of the barn door rail, I mounted a modified garage door opener. The trolley that hung from the rail was moved back and forth by the garage door opener. I installed an electric-actuated cylinder that had a 12 inch stroke. The cylinder, with the aid of straps under his arms and straps around his legs, would lift him off of the commode. While he was hanging there, the door opener would move him to the bed. It worked, but was not the best that one would desire. Soon after this, in 1984 my brother passed away. I still cry every time I think about him, I loved him so.

Chapter 33
Sun Oil Company—My Play House
1956 - 1977

Sun Oil

I mentioned King Schroeder before. He happened to be the chief geologist for the southwest district of Sun Oil Company. So I fixed up a brochure of the stuff that I had done, and I gave it to King. Like a nut, I had a picture of me on the front page smoking a foot-long cigar. He took it to Philadelphia and showed it to Larry Johnson, who was the director of research for Sun Oil Company. King said, "You know, I know this guy pretty good. He wants a job and I think you ought to hire him." Larry Johnson said, "I wouldn't hire that man on a bet. He smokes, and he smokes foot-long cigars. I wouldn't hire him." (When they built the research lob there in Richardson, Texas, Larry was so against smoking that when they built the conference room all the air was fresh outside air so there'd be no smoke in it. You could not smoke in the conference room in that building.) Due to King's influence with top management I got the job anyway. Besides, I had already quit smoking.

Work Mates

Larry Johnson was head of Production Research. During the war, he was in Naval Research and had two scientists working for him that he brought with him when he came to Sun Oil. One was

Fred Mayes, a physicist, and a genius at electronics. Too bad, he eventually left our ranks and became Vice President of Research for Sun Oil. I told him that it was the greatest waste of scientific talent when he went into management. The other was Jack Jones, whom I affectionately called "Big Daddy." He had a background in optics, but he was another electronics genius. Preston Chaney, a Texas Aggie chemist and a man with a photographic memory, was a master at everything—mechanics, electronics, chemistry, clockmaking, you just name it, he knew it. Oh, besides that he was a swell guy, and for a while, my immediate boss. Fred, Jack and Preston all had masters degrees. I was the mechanical engineer, and just barely got my bachelors degree, with the minimum number of grade points.

We had Clarence Braun, who could build anything of a scientific nature, and he was a real buddy. When it was time to go back to work after lunch he would open and close 15 locker doors at the same time banging them so people within six city blocks could not sleep. He was my alarm clock that awakened me from my noon nap. We had Chuck Rhodes, who likewise was an electronic "putter-together" type guy. There was Carl Caldwell, and Dave Lewis, two of the best engineering-type machinists who could build anything you asked them to build. It was never necessary to put tolerance on drawings because if you put down a dimension, it was made exactly that size.

The above named group worked on projects that no other people in the company worked on. We came up with new ideas, worked on the ideas, and licensed other companies to use and build the items that we had invented, all with the idea of helping the oil industry, and especially Sun Oil Company. We all contributed our expertise to the projects and loved every second of it.

Larry Johnson was our overall boss. Larry's office was up in Philadelphia, at Sun Oil's home office. He came to Richardson, to our Production Research Laboratory pretty regular. Sometimes we would go to the home office, especially if it pertained to patents. Sun Oil owned its own fleet of aircraft, one of which made the trip on a regular basis.

So old Larry got to be a pretty good friend of mine. You know, I was one of these people who could not spell. King Schroeder knew that, and Preston Chaney who was the director of research at the lab knew I couldn't spell, too. One day I was in a conference with Larry and Preston, and I was trying to write something. Preston was looking over my shoulder to see what I was writing, and he'd spell the words for me as I was writing them down. I said, "Larry, I'm sorry I can't spell." Larry said the best thing to me that ever happened. He said, "John, you were not hired to spell for Sun Oil Company." They realized my handicap and really helped me out.

My brother-in-law, Wayne Melton, used to tell me that I should pay Sun Oil Company just to get to work for them because I had so much fun at it. It is true, there was never a day that I wasn't eager to go to work. It was the best company to work for there ever was. As long as the Pew family was in control, it could not be beat. I was a member of the team. Jack Pew was head of the production part of Sun Oil Company. He would come through the research laboratory at Richardson, calling every one by his name. He was the boss, but most important, he was your friend.

As can be seen by my book of bound Sun Oil Company patents, "Grindings From The Whirling Gears of John Bennett", there are 58 patents that belong to Sun, and in the back I have the seven patents that belong to Dresser Industries. At Sun Oil they even put a patent attorney, Lee Murrah, in the office next to mine to process the patents I came up with. All of these are signed over for "one dollar and other considerations". I never saw the dollar, and the "other considerations" was my salary. Now, of course, all of those patents are expired, and they're free property for anybody to use if they want to.

Once Sun hired a consultant who was a motivator to come to the research lab to talk to us. His talk was that once a person made enough money to take care of his basic needs, a raise would not make him happy very long. It was only job satisfaction that made people happy. He was right, a pat on the back from the boss, a story about you in the company newspaper, recognition by your peers, all that made you happier than money. Don't misunderstand me, money is good—but the other is better.

We did some of the most interesting projects there ever were. They were things that never had been done before and we worked at them just like we knew what we were doing. I always liked Preston's thoughts. He said, "If we knew what we were doing, we wouldn't be doing it".

The company magazine billed me as "Top Inventor in Sun's 'Dream Department'". Our group had been moved into a separate building behind the main lab. What we did was not really connected to what the people in the main building did.

One of the things that the Company did I really liked. There were a few non-geological type people at the lab and the company thought it would be nice if we all knew something about geology. They hired a professor from Arlington University to teach a class once a week to us individuals on geology. The way that he taught is what I really liked. His topic was "How to better enjoy your vacations through geology." No tests, no having to learn long names, and on top of all that, we went on some field trips and took our wives. Since we had that course we have enjoyed our vacations so much more. There should be such a course taught in college for all the students.

Pressure Gauge
Preston, Fred, Jack and I used to work together on projects. They decided one time they wanted to see if they could build a super duper pressure gauge. Y'see, if you drill an oil well and measure the bottom hole pressure of the oil well, and then you produce a certain amount of oil, and you measure the bottom hole pressure again, then you can calculate how big that reservoir is down there. So it's very important to be able to make super duper measurements. Well, there were no gauges on the market anywhere that would do that. So we decided to build one. We didn't know what we were doing, but we had more fun. Fred Mayes would come in my office and say, "Let's argue." So he would sit there and we'd argue all day long. He would propose certain ideas for that gauge, and I'd shoot them down. Then I'd propose certain ideas for that gauge, and he'd shoot mine down. The next day he'd come back again and say, "Let's argue." Well, I had convinced him and he had convinced me, and we were on the other side. So we'd argue all day again. We did that

for months. Finally we came up with a solution on how to make this super duper pressure gauge. It was a complete success. They took one of the gauges and tied it on the side of a mini-submarine and sent it down into the Puerto Rico Trench off Cuba. There's a trench there that is thousands of feet deep, one of the deepest places in the world. They sent that submarine down with the gauge recording the pressure when it went down. When it sat there for a while it could measure the tides when they changed up above. It was so accurate it was phenomenal. Well, we designed the gauge.

Sun Oil Company owned a company called Sperry Sun, which did work for all of the oil companies. Their specialty was being able to run a survey in an oil well and tell you exactly where the bottom was. You know, an oil well as it goes down, the hole kinda spirals, wanders around in a lot of different directions. Nobody ever knew exactly where the bottom of the hole was. You didn't know for sure whether you were getting oil off your land or your neighbor's land. So Sun Oil Company came up with an outfit that had a gyroscope in it and it would run a real accurate survey of where the bottom of the hole was. They did it for everybody—all of the oil companies. Sperry Sun had a real good reputation, they worked for everybody and did not reveal anything to anybody else except the ones that they were working for. So they took over marketing this pressure gauge, so that all of the oil companies could have the use of it. That's one of the projects that we worked on. I loved it, I had more fun.

We made lots of trips to south Louisiana to test instruments in wells and to experiment in the Gulf. The drilling rigs in south Louisiana back then were run by steam engines. The crew always had a coffeepot full of chickory coffee sitting on the head of the steam engine. God it was strong! We also did a lot of research on making little explosive shells that would enter a drilling well through the mudstream and explode after passing through the eye of the drill bit.

Oil Shale
When I was at Sun Oil Company I did a lot of research on different things. I've been all through the oil shale in Colorado. There is a government mine in the shale north of Rifle, Colorado. It is in the middle of a 2000 foot cliff, about 1000 feet down from the top.

There is a layer in the shale there called the "mahogany ribbon." It is about two feet thick, and probably comes from a volcanic eruption. It contains about 40 gallons of shale oil per ton of shale.

We took some of that shale to Richardson to see how to get the oil out. You do that with heat. In fact we even built a retort machine so you could retort the shale and get the oil out. I came up with the design in a dream, and drew the plan during a church service. It was a rotating kiln, a cylinder with an auger inside. It augered raw shale in one end and the spent shale came out the other end. We burned some of the oil in the middle to create the heat to release the remaining oil. It was not successful because the smoke from the burning shale went out the end of the cylinder, and we couldn't seal it.

If you ever get shale oil on your hand you can't ever get the smell out. It stinks something terrible. You can wash, you can scrub, you can use every detergent imaginable, and you can't get it off. You let one quart of that oil come out of the retort machine as smoke and you put down a smog. Several times we almost smoked the town of Richardson out, but we didn't ever let anybody know what happened. Boy, it was terrible!

At the time that I built my machine and got a patent on it there had already been 3000 patents issued on ways of taking oil out of the oil shale that is up there in Colorado and Utah. I can tell you right now that you can get the oil out of the shale, but you can't make gasoline out of it because there's not enough hydrogen in the stuff, and you've got to have hydrogen to make gasoline. You can take oil shale, and if you use natural gas and take the hydrogen out of the natural gas you can make gasoline out of it. But, if you've got all of that, why do you need the shale? So the shale is not a profitable thing. The government is wasting a lot of money on it right now. I can tell you it is not profitable.

Retort

330

Canadian Projects

We spent a lot of time working with our Canadian division. The company had decided that it wanted to explore the islands in the northern part of the Canadian territories for the prospect of finding oil. Knowledge was not available for this type operation so we were supposed to try to develop such knowledge. If we found oil, there was no known way to get the oil back to civilization. Pipelines were out of the question. There was knowledge about how to lay pipelines in the ocean, but it was difficult to lay pipelines if no ships could navigate the ice. If the line was laid, an ice storm would ridge up the ice and probably dig out the pipeline. Ships could go as far north as Resolute only three weeks out of the year, and we were looking hundreds of miles north of Resolute.

We were looking in the vicinity of King Christian Island, 200 miles

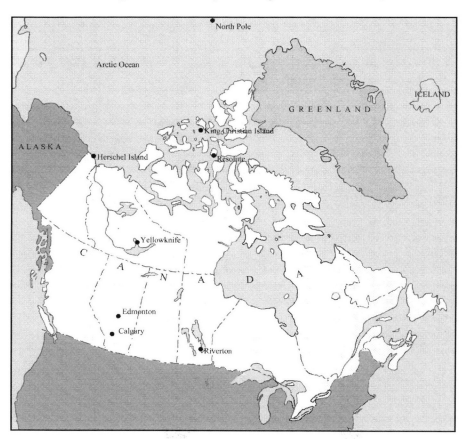

north of the Magnetic North Pole and just 700 miles from the true North Pole. We established a base camp on King Christian Island. Everything had to be flown in by airplane. The sea ice around the island was very rough. Look at the ice floating in a glass of iced tea, and then imagine the pieces of ice being 10 or 15 feet long all bunched up. It was impossible to navigate terrain like this. Everything that was brought in to base camp had to be located by survey so when it came time to retrieve it, it could be found under the snow.

Another company had drilled a well on King Christian Island. The usual practice is to drill and then set surface pipe so blow out preventers can be installed. Who would have thought that the permafrost on the island had formed a gas barrier like a cap rock, and when the permafrost was penetrated, the well would blow in before the surface pipe could be installed and the well would catch fire? The fire could be seen for 300 miles. There was no way to put out the fire until the following year when another rig was flown in, and it was used to drill into the burning well to plug it. Over six months of the year, it is totally dark.

John D at King Christian Island

Ice Chipper

It was decided that a machine should be built to try to make roads on the ice. The rough parts had to be ground down. Joe Zupanick, my boss at the time, began to investigate what could be done. We went to the Army Cold Region Research Lab in Hanover, New Hampshire to see what they knew. Seems that they had built a small ice machine that could be dumped out of an airplane on a parachute. It could be used to grade a landing strip in case of a war emergency.

We came back and I started designing. In three weeks I had designed a machine that had a drum 12 feet long and five feet in diameter. It had 300 industrial-sized ice picks on it. The drum was geared to turn 100 revolutions per minute. It was mounted on a trailer-type rig, complete with a big Jimmy (GM) diesel engine and fuel tanks. The machine was designed so it could be broken down to be loaded into a C-5 airplane. Had we built the machine in the US, Canada would have charged us a 30% fee to take it into Canada. We had the machine built in Edmonton, Canada, for $50,000. It was

John D with ice chipper

then trucked to Yellowknife where it was loaded on a C-5 Airplane and for $25,000 more flown to King Christian Island.

The machine, dubbed the "ice chipper", was pushed in front of a D7 Caterpillar tractor, gliding on steel skis. The idea was to push it across the ice grinding off all of the bumps to make a road. Everything worked just fine, and then we went to the sea ice to test it. It ground the ice so fast, it scared us to death. At 40° below zero the ice chips flowed like water. The drum was cutting through the ice so fast, every once in a while one of the skis that held the machine up, would fall in a crack between the big slabs of ice and then the drum would suddenly cut deeper. When you are out on ice that is 10 feet thick and the water below is 600 feet deep, you can visualize the drum suddenly cutting a hole right through the ice and you going right in after it while you sit on the tractor.

The funny thing was, we did all of that, and there was no known way that anybody could bring oil back from those cold regions up there. There was no way to do it. Pipelines were out. You couldn't

Ice chipper cutting through an ice ridge

bring it back in a tanker. We even bought an icebreaker from the government. It could only go to Resolute about six weeks out of the year. How in the world could you go 600 miles further north and try to bring oil out in barges? There was no way you could do it. You couldn't get a tanker up there to get it. You can't haul it out in anything. I even proposed the possibility of an atomic submarine that would pull barges underneath the ice. That was a possibility if we'd ever found the oil, but we never found oil. But, when I made that ice machine it made the possibility of a way to bring the oil back. Sun Oil had a patent on it, and that's the purpose of my doing all of this wild dreaming. They wanted me to come up with ideas so if they wanted to do it they could do it, and nobody else could tell them they couldn't do it. Sun could say, "Yes we can do it, because we have the patent."

Ice chipper making a snow cloud

We used the ice chipper one time and discarded it, but it solved one of our problems. Had we discovered oil, we could have built a large barge with a rotating ice-chipping drum floating in front of the barge. The drum would be attached to the barge with a yoke. A 5000 horsepower GE gas turbine would be installed in the drum to rotate it. As the drum rotated, it would dig its own channel for the barge to move in. With a string of barges behind the tow barge, we could move oil out of the Arctic through the ice sheet.

Ice Breaker

Another thing we got a patent on was an icebreaker ship that would use high pressure jets of sea water to cut the ice, rather than ram the ice the traditional way. It would take less horsepower to cut the ice than to break it by pushing on it in the dimension in which ice has its greatest strength.

Sea Ice

One of the problems that we worked on was to determine how strong sheet sea ice was. We didn't have any idea how thick the sea ice had to be to hold up a Hercules airplane. In other words, if you wanted to fly a planeload of drilling equipment up there, how thick did the ice have to be to hold it up? We cut some beams in the ice and weighed them and put pressure on them until they broke. It was determined that ice 48 inches thick could support a C-5 plane.

Ice Movement

One time we worked all summer long developing some instrumentation to try to find out about how the sea ice moved. So we developed this instrumentation and took it up to King Christian Island.

335

The equipment was to be powered by thermocouples heated by propane. We took the helicopter and flew our instruments out and set it on the ice. A snowstorm came along and covered our instruments up. You remember, they didn't have anything like accurate survey equipment or GPS. We surveyed from a station in England and a station in the United States. Up at the North Pole you look at the compass in the airplane and it's just going around and around and around. The North Pole is straight down under you. We went back with the propane tank and we never could find our instrumentation. There was no way of locating it.

I found out about aviation telephones, so we could take a telephone in the airplane and call a telephone on the ground. We could have the telephone on the ground turn on a strobe light. Then all we'd have to do is fly to the strobe light. Then there is another problem. You've got to have electricity to run that telephone that runs the strobe. What you do is take an auger and drill a hole down through the ice to get down to sea water. Now the sea water is 28° F. You cannot charge batteries if it is forty below zero, they won't accept a charge. But if you can get them up to 28° you can charge them up. So we made a container out of PVC pipe and put some batteries in there. Then we drilled a hole through the ice and let the container down and the batteries breathe through the cable that comes to the surface. Then I made a little wind generator. I used a propeller out of an automobile—it was a Vega, I think. It turned a little generator, and it generated electricity to charge up the batteries. If we were in the airplane and called that phone number, the batteries would turn on the strobe light and we could find it. If we'd had that before we did all that instrumentation work we would have found it. That was the last project that I worked on before I retired from Sun Oil Company, and I had a lot of fun doing that.

Satellites had put us out of business anyway. We could learn more from studying the satellite pictures than we could from our fancy equipment. Progress had made us obsolete.

One time we put out a bunch of stakes to mark places where we were going to put geophones. A polar bear came along who didn't like our stakes, and he knocked them all down—broke them off.

Chemical Reactions

One day when I was at the Magnetic North Pole, Preston Chaney was with me. I said "Preston, look at those oil barrels, they look brand new." He said, "John, do you realize that those barrels have been lying there on that ground for 40 years?" He said, "Chemical reactions double their rate of reaction every 16° of temperature rise. At 40° below zero, things just don't rust."

When my wife had to take chemotherapy for cancer, she would get sick every time she ate after taking her medicine. She would usually fix herself something hot off the stove. One day, she got sick and I remembered what Preston had told me about barrels rusting, or rather not rusting. I suggested to my wife next time she took her chemo, try to eat something cold, out of the ice box, instead of hot from the stove. She did, and she didn't get sick. Ever since this happened, we have told everyone that would listen about our discovery. Tell it to a doctor and they will tell you that they had never heard of that, but it made sense.

Great Canadian Oil Sands

Near Fort McMurray, Alberta, Sun and the Canadian government had a mine with a huge rotary bucket digger. I went through there a few times on the way to Resolute, and designed a tooth for the digger, which Sun patented.

Old Timers From Riverton

One day I was on the airplane flying from the North Pole and we stopped in Fort McMurray, Canada. A gentleman got on the plane and sat by me. My mind was wandering all around and this gentleman was telling me something and it was going in one ear and out the other. I should have been listening but my mind was wondering why it was that it took a D7 Cat and a D5 Cat together to pull one of our seismic trains. I believe I was returning home from testing the ice chipper.

When I got back to Texas after a couple of weeks, I remembered him and I wished I had paid attention to the gentleman seated next me. I called the Sun Oil trip planner, I believe it was Jackie, and told her about the incident, and I would like to talk to the gentleman. In less than 30 minutes, she had checked the plane manifest of that particular flight, found out who the man was and had him on the phone. He told me a blacksmith had made a plow to go on the front of a track-type farm tractor. During World War II, this man had hauled a lot of freight loaded on a whole train of sleds with heavy loads, all the way from Winnipeg, Manitoba, up Lake Winnipeg to Riverton, Manitoba. He had done it with a small track-type farm tractor. He knew something that we didn't know and I had to see him.

He was in Riverton when I called him and told him that I would like to come see him. He said to come on. When I got there he had the whole town turned out to meet me. To think—that a man from Texas had come all the way to Riverton to find out how to haul heavy loads on ice. When I got up there I got to see the old tractor that he used. He had built a plow on the front of that tractor that would plow the ice down to one inch above where the tread was going to be on the tractor, he had one inch of snow left right there. Now, he left as much snow as he could between the treads to where it wouldn't touch the bottom of the tractor. It was a big plow he mounted on the front of this tractor. Now as he went along that plow would take all of the snow off of the ice down to one inch above the ice. But the big secret was how he moved these big sleds. They had enormous sleds that they loaded. The secret was that they had oak runners on these sleds. And the oak runners had a little narrow band of steel right on the bottom. Kinda like when you ice skate there's a little bitty amount of the skate that touches the ice, nothing else. When they moved these heavy loads the oak would act as an insulator and wouldn't transfer the heat back and forth. These

little bands of steel were so narrow that they got hot, and when they got hot they would melt the ice and make it water-lubricated. So they would pull these tremendous loads on these little skis with these little dinky tractors.

Plow used on Lake Winnipeg

Sled used on Lake Winnipeg

These people at Riverton originally came from Iceland. It had gotten to where there were too many of them in Iceland, and they had to move to where they could fish. So they moved to Riverton, Manitoba. The way they did their fishing was so interesting. They had a thing they called a "jigger". He made a jigger and sent it to me. This jigger was a piece of board maybe a foot wide and probably ten feet long. It was turned up on the end like a ski. In the middle of this jigger there was an arm that hung and pivoted. Off this pivoting arm there was a rod that went back up that went through the ski and touched the ice. They would dig a hole through the ice and lower the jigger down. It was like a ski if you tuned it upside down and it floated up against the bottom of the ice.

Jigger

They had a rope that was tied onto this arm that hung down. When you pulled that rope that arm would push that rod up through the ski and touch the ice and it ratcheted the ski forward. So as you sat there and pulled the rope and let it loose and pulled it and let it loose it would just walk forward. So they'd drill a hole in the ice and they'd walk this thing forward 'til they got to the next hole. Then they would turn it and walk it to the next hole. What they were doing is stringing a net underneath the ice. This was the machine they used to pull the net forward underneath the ice until they came back to the original hole, which was a fair sized hole, and both ends of the net were there. Then they would hook those ends of the net to a big tractor and they seined for fish underneath the ice. That's the way they got their net underneath the ice, by using the jigger to walk around under the ice. Durndest thing you ever saw. He was quite a man, I really enjoyed that trip up there.

Our skis were made of heavy steel beams that transmitted the cold so the bottom of the ski could never get hot. No wonder that it took two Caterpillars to pull half the load that they pulled on Lake Winnipeg during the war. Engineers must learn that bigger is not always better.

Ardco Vehicles
We had a bunch of vehicles built down in Sugar Land for seismic work. They had great big, wide tires—they were about 30 inches wide. They were supposed to run across the ice. We had about eleven of them built and sent them up to Canada. They had diesel engines, but when we tried to test them out in the snow and ice, we found out that the engine was way underpowered. We had to do something about it. So an engineer from Sugar Land had bigger engines flown in from Detroit to Edmonton. He and I started putting these engines in one of the vehicles. We'd cut a part and make it fit. As soon as we

Ardco vehicle

340

did that the rest of the company built parts for the other vehicles. The people back at the research lab were having conniption fits because we were way behind schedule. We finally got them all assembled. Then we trucked them up to Yellowknife and flew them on up to King Christian Island. That was a very interesting experiment that we were doing up there. That was back at a time when none of us knew what we were doing or what the results would be.

We were trying to learn things about the ocean because we thought maybe there was oil under there. So we were doing our research there at the lab in Richardson, Texas. We did a lot of conferring with the Navy. One day one of the big shots from the Navy come down and saw what we were trying to do. He said, "Is that the best maps y'all have got?" And we said, "That's the best we've got." And they fixed us up with some good maps. And you know what? They blew us out of the water. All of the stuff that we were trying to do, the military already knew it all. They knew all about this stuff. Gosh, if we'd just had a GPS like you can carry around in your pocket, man that would have been fantastic up there. We didn't have anything like that.

McKenzie Delta
One time we were trying to learn something about the Beaufort Sea. You know the McKenzie River is a big river that runs north out of Canada. It comes out of the Great Slave Lake and runs north. When that thing freezes over in the wintertime they make it into a highway and truck freight up that river to go over to the North Slope, where they have the oil fields. The McKenzie River flows by the town of Tuktoyaktuk. You can see where they have done a lot of surveying, and have cut passages along to shoot seismic. We were trying to find out something about how the sea ice moved. We didn't know how the ice moved. You can't very well drill out on the ice if the ice is going to move, you don't know what it's going to do. So we had a guy who we sent up there and run an experiment for us. So I went up there with him. We flew up there in a de Havilland airplane. We flew out I guess ten miles north of the delta of the McKenzie River and set him up. He had an ice auger to drill holes in the ice. He had a thumping machine that was let down through the hole to the ocean floor. Every so often it would thump. We had

geophones on top of the ice. They would measure the time it took for that "thump" to get up to the geophones. If that time shifted we knew the ice had moved.

After he had been up there for a while, a week or two weeks, it was time to go get him. So I went up in the de Havilland. We looked out over the ice and could see a ridgeline where the ice had kinda broke. On one side of the ridgeline you could see a little water above the ice. On the other side you couldn't see the water, it was just ice. The problem was the guy was over there where the water was. He'd drill a hole through the ice and the water would run down through the ice back into the ocean underneath, so he had his spot kinda drained down a little bit. When it came time to pick him up we said, "You know what? We're going to have to mark those seal holes and the holes he drilled with the ice auger so we don't fly over them while we're trying to takeoff. We're going to have to stick your skis down in those holes." He had several pairs of skis. Oh! It like to broke his heart. He had some extra gasoline that he had to run his ice auger with. We said, "We can't carry this stuff out. We're going to have to pour it out, too." Oh Lord! He was an ecologist and couldn't stand that. He had to bring back every scrap of paper, and everything that he had. He was worrisome. Let me tell you about the landing. That plane had skis and wheels on it. We landed in that water and the water flew up over that airplane. I thought it was going to drown us. That's the reason we were being so careful. We had to unload everything on the first trip to fly out of there to make a return trip. We marked the holes and took off and got out of there alright, but that was an experience, I'll tell you. Those de Havilland airplanes are the toughest things there ever was in this world. That's what all of those back-country people up in Canada use to fly around with. They don't have any roads.

Hypotherm

A Dr. Weincoop invented a system to pump a cold chemical through a balloon inserted in the stomach of a person with a bleeding ulcer so that it would cause the ulcer to stop bleeding. The problem with his system was that if the chemical leaked through the balloon into the person's stomach it was hazardous. A doctor in my church, who worked at St. Paul Hospital in Dallas, told me that he was looking for someone to make a machine to do the job. I got Preston and Carl Caldwell to work on it with me. We designed a machine that would pump ice water through a rubber balloon in the patient's stomach. The balloon would be on the end of a tube inserted through the patient's nose and down into his stomach. The tube would have a second tube inside it so the water could circulate like the fluid in an oil well—in through the inner tube and out between the two tubes. We decided to use cold water so that it wouldn't cause any injury if the balloon broke. The only balloon we could find that was thin enough was a condom. The machine, called a "hypotherm", could cause a bleeding ulcer patient to need only three pints of blood instead of the usual 19. The hospital was a Catholic hospital, and the nurses were nuns. The machine was used for awhile, but its use was eventually discontinued, ostensibly because it wasn't an approved medical device, but perhaps because the nuns didn't want to buy condoms.

I retired in 1977. The company gave me a retirement party. They gave me my book of bound patents, Chuck Rhodes had made me an Aggie rocker with the rockers going 90 degrees to the conventional way. The cake, the party, the usual roast, and all my friends, it made me cry. Lee Murrah, the young man who was my patent lawyer, and who I had started calling my other son, wrote a poem for me that summed up my whole life. We had talked so much, that he knew me like a book. I cherish the poem very much. After 35 years all but one of my friends have passed on.

**Experimental rocking
ice breaker on Lake Superior**

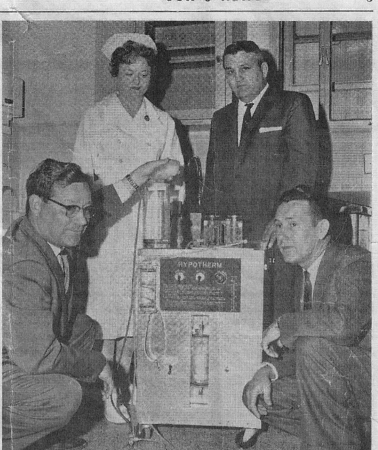

EXPLAINING mechanics of Local Gastric Hypothermia Unit to Nurse Supervisor Ruth Tollefson at St. Paul Hospital, Dallas, are (from left) P. E. Chaney, J. D. Bennett (standing) and W. E. Caldwell Jr. of Sun's Richardson Lab. Mr. Chaney holds the balloon filled with saline solution showing its size in a patient's stomach. His hand is resting on the reservoir which holds the solution that is circulated through the balloon. To the right of the reservoir is the flow control which governs the rate of circulation of the solution. Recessed in the cabinet of the machine is the float valve which regulates the volume of solution in the balloon. Directly below the reservoir is a filter which the Sun men add   the unit to catch foreign substances which   uld get into the solu   .ould a balloon break while in a patient's stomach. Solution is circulated by a pump from the reservoir through a cooling coil packed in ice in the chest to the balloon in a patient's stomach and back to the reservoir.

345

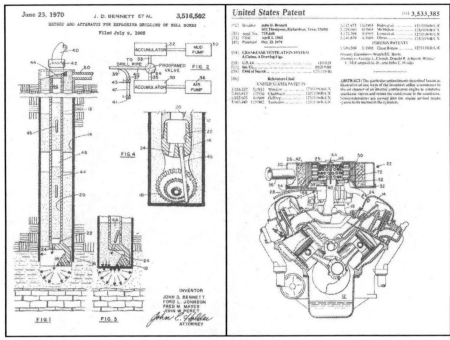

Patent drawings

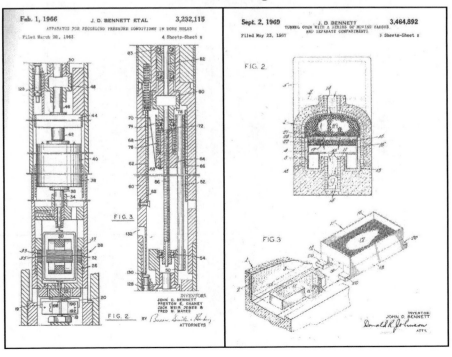

346

Chapter 34
Ballad of the Junkyard Engineer
(or an Aggie in Wonderland)

By M. L. Murrah
used by permission

I.
Come, my friends,
So you can hear
The incredible story
Of the junkyard engineer.

He was born at Derby,
A son of the land,
With a sermon in his heart
And a wrench in his hand.

Early in his life,
Even before he could cry,
He learned the art
Of how to modify.

And soon he was a terror
Wearing a hydraulic bib
And scaring the old ladies
In his motorized crib.

His ingenuity grew,
As you will see.
He built 16 cars
Or was it 25, 30, or 33?

II.
While plowing cotton,
He got a great idea—
Plow it under
and become an engineer.

The Aggies taught him slowly,
But they taught him well
How to invent
But not to spell.

His grades suffered
From the unlikely alliance
Of English composition
And *Popular Science.*

And after much doubt
He got a degree
With a major in engineering
And a minor in junkology.

III.
Those Aggie boots
He'd wanted all his life
Impressed everyone,
But his future wife.

She disliked him
From the very start,
But with a shiny new car
He won her heart.

He was very romantic
When they dated.
He read her selections
From *Mechanix Illustrated.*

Then off to war,
And it was a very big step,
Because he won World War II
Without any help.

IV.
Back at home
He took a job with Ideco,
And they were in
For more than they could know.

Work was easy,
And it was fun,
But he was too busy inventing
To get anything done.

And when he had created as much mischief
As could be done,
He left Ideco
And went to work for Sun.

So to Sun
He brought his fertile brain,
And poor Sun Oil
Was never the same.

His biggest idea
He swore was sound,
He wanted to move all Sun Oil
Underground.

He even decided the moon was positioned wrong,
But he couldn't move it.
So in a fit of Aggie inspiration
He decided to improve it.

But God didn't understand
Why it was essential
That the moon have
A Cadillac differential.

He invented voluminously,
And the Patent Office wished he hadn't.
They had to construct a new building
Just to hold his patents.

V.

Now in his middle years
He has matured a little,
And nothing has matured
More than his middle.

His constant diets
Are not very sound,
On his last one
He gained twenty pounds.

Now he's become
A T.V. star
With a windmill
And an electric car.

His famous windmill
Turns by the hour,
Generating more publicity
Than electric power.

And when the mill doesn't turn,
When the wind doesn't blow,
He tells war stories
To make it go.

His electric car
Was a minor success—
Moreso with the neighborhood kids
Than the national press.

And he'd drive it more
Than he does his Ford,
If he could only find
A longer extension cord.

He's designed more houses
Than Frank Lloyd Wright
And made more changes
Than Arabia has nights.

VI.
He's always been modest,
And if you want to know,
All you have to do
Is ask him so.

He's a good man,
And an honest one I feel,
Although he did once imply
That he co-invented the wheel.

He's a religious man,
As devout as a monk,
Why, he even loves his God
More than his junk.

Yes, some day they'll bury
This wonderful man,
With love in his heart
And a wrench in his hand.

And when he gets
To St. Peter's station
He's sure to say
"Please, just one more modification."

This poem was written by my dear friend M. L. Murrah. He knew me very well. I call him my other son.

Chapter 35
Home Life in Richardson
1956-1970

The day finally came for us to move from Beaumont. We had already been to Richardson and found a house that we could rent. I made several round trips pulling my new home-built trailer loaded with shop tools, etc. The little house with the one car garage on Apollo Road in Richardson got pretty full. We rented a moving van to move all the household items. It was January and gosh it was cold. The house that we rented was up on piers and was pretty old. Probably didn't have a bit of insulation in it. We like to have frozen, and the wind sure did blow. The weather-stripping under the north door would moan like a banshee.

We stayed in that house about two or three months and then found another house on Dorothy Drive. We had neighbors that we became very fond of. One neighbor worked for the IRS. He was a swell guy. When Billy Sol Estes of Pecos, Texas had all his trouble with the IRS, my neighbor handled the case.

Another neighbor was a traveling salesman. They became especially good

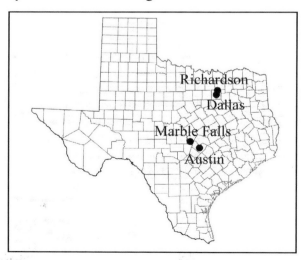

friends as they were one of the five families that help us start the Spring Valley Methodist Church in north Dallas.

Old House, New House

We rented our old house in Beaumont on a lease-purchase type arrangement. Boy, was that a mistake. Finally we had to evict the renters, and a good friend I had at IDECO wanted to buy the house. In the meantime, I had designed a house that we wanted to build on a lot that we had purchased in Richardson. A Mr. Watson arranged for loans for us and for our friend who bought the house in Beaumont. One of the conditions of the loan for our new house was that I was to manage the money. I had to pay our contractor

The shop

depending on the progress that he had made on the house. It was a good thing Mr. Watson had specified that I had to handle the money, because eventually I had to take the contract away from the contractor and arrange for finishing the house myself.

Our house in Richardson

Our house was just what we wanted because we designed it. It had a large, more than double garage, with a restroom in the garage. The garage was finished inside and heavily insulated. I had an air-conditioned workshop with an entrance into the garage, and a door into what was going to be an office for me. We had a large den with a fireplace and a living room that the contractor told Wynona that she could use to entertain her new boyfriend when I passed on. We had two baths and three bedrooms. The two bedrooms for the boys had a heavy duty sliding curtain so they could separate their rooms or make it one big room. Each boy had a built-in study desk and bookshelves. We loved our home and really used it while the boys were home.

Spring Valley Methodist Church
When we moved to Richardson we only had 6000 people in the entire town. It was a little old dinky town on the north side of

Dallas; didn't amount to anything. It was on a former interurban streetcar line. There was a little old Methodist church there that had been there forever. It was the deadest church you ever saw in your life. Nobody would do anything. There were about six of us families that got tired of that. We decided that we were going to have our own Methodist church.

We began meeting in the McCaslin's living room with different ones preaching. The group began to grow. Some of the families were friends of the District Superintendent, T. Lee Miller. So we tried to get him to help us. About that time Texas Instruments bought some land on the north side of Dallas, and on that land was an old house. They let us use that old house for nothing. We held church services in that thing until there was no more room. We filled it up. We sold watermelons at the city fair to raise money and meet people.

All of the time we were trying to get the District Superintendent to get the Bishop to let us have a church. The Bishop said, "No! You've got to go to that old church. You can't have a new Method-ist church." We didn't want to go to that old church, we wanted our own church. We finally got about 200 members. We began meeting in a school. So one day we told the District Superintendent we had to do something. Someone went and talked to Marshall Steel. He was Mr. Methodist in Dallas. What Marshall Steel at Highland Park Methodist Church said, that was the law. So Marshall Steel went to the Bishop. He said, "Now Bishop. Those people have been working for quite awhile and they've got about 200 people and they want that to be a Methodist church. You better see that they have a preacher next Sunday." We had a preacher the next Sunday. That church grew even faster.

Our church finally obtained property in the north edge of Dallas, and built a building. It was on Spring Valley Road and we called the church Spring Valley Methodist Church. The thing that was so interesting about all of that, while we were trying to get started we'd all call each other every night and say, "What did we hear from the Bishop? What did we hear from the District Superinten-dent?" Boy it was a hotbed of conversation going around. We had a visitation crew that went out every week. After they went out we'd get together and find out what they did. We'd go to the city hall and find out what people had gotten new water meters. So we'd find out who was new in town. We'd go knock on the front doors of those houses. Brand new house, there wouldn't be a stick of furniture in the living room. They were new residents who'd bought a house beyond their means and didn't have any furniture and they were just living there in a bare house. But, boy we got them coming to church.

We had church parties in our garage there in Richardson. We did all kinds of things. It was the greatest thing there ever was. That new preacher was named Jack Gibson. He was a swell guy. We really loved Brother Jack. He'd come by our house and say, "John I need some help. My engine's not running good. I think I need some new spark plugs. Would you change the spark plugs in my car?" Well at that time I had just built a new house. It was down on the creek, but they wouldn't let us pump water out of that creek. I wanted to pump water to water my lawn, so I decided to drill a water well right beside the creek. So I said, "Jack I'll work on your car. But while I'm working on your car you've got to get down in that hole and dig on my well."

The Methodist Church rotates preachers every so often, and finally Jack got transferred away. So they gave us a guy by the name of Don Benton. He was Senator Lloyd Bentsen's brother-in-law. Don Benton's wife's mother lived in McAllen. They had a private airplane, and she attended church every Sunday in Dallas. When she came she flew up with a load of poinsettias from their yard. Boy that little old church was just loaded with poinsettias when it was first started. She went to our Sunday school class, gave us all Bibles, and attended that class every Sunday.

Don loved to go flying with me in my airplane. Don knew that Wynona was a painter. He told Wynona, "I want you to paint me a picture, and I want you to paint it just like I tell you. I want you to have stormy sea and a rock cliff, and in that cliff I want a nitch with a bird that's got its nest built in that rock cliff." So Wynona painted that picture. Oh, he thought it was the greatest thing in the world.

He had it in his church office. He really did like that picture. We loved Don Benton, and he was a good pastor.

Vacations

We went on lots of vacations out west, starting when we lived in Beaumont. We went to California and Wyoming and all of the states between there and Texas. We especially spent a lot of time in Colorado. Every summer we went on a two week vacation, and we never started out with more than $300. We did a lot of camping to save money. We saw Cripple Creek, Pikes Peak, Yellowstone, Yosemite, Mesa Verde, the Grand Canyon, Zion, Bryce Canyon, the Petrified Forest, the Painted Desert, we didn't miss much.

Other Activities

Barry was in the Boy Scouts and I was a councilman. I went on lots of camping trips with the scouts. Once we went camping at Cedar Hill on Don Benton's ranch. The scouts carried our camping gear in, but when we were ready to leave, the scouts were too tired to carry anything. We loaded the gear on long poles, with each end of each pole being carried by one of the adults. I carried one end of a loaded pole on my shoulder and wound up bursting the bursa in my shoulder. It seems like I had bursitis forever.

Wayne was in the band at school. He practiced marching in the summer, and then marched at halftime at the school football games. We went to lots of football games.

Wynona started taking art lessons and continued painting for the rest of her life. She sold hundreds of oil paintings and a few watercolors, and painted tons of china.

Barry (center) was in the Scouts

Kemper's Korner

In 1959 my sister Betsy and her husband George Kemper bought a camp in Marble Falls. They were in the Air Force at the time, stationed in Bossier City, Louisiana. George would travel to Marble Falls whenever he could to work on the camp. We went down on vacation to be with the family and to help a little with the work. Relatives from south Texas would come up and we would drive down from Richardson. We spent lots of enjoyable time in Marble Falls. For a long time the main building was a shed with an

The big cabana at Kemper's Korner

Betsy leads the women at Kemper's Korner

Eating at the big cabana

enclosed room (the "bridal suite") on one end. Eventually they built a nice house on the bank of the Colorado River.

A float for a parade at the Marble Falls "Howdy Roo"

Airplanes

Dad passed away in 1961. When I got the word that he was in the hospital, I jumped in my little Renault Dauphine and headed for Derby as fast as the thing would run. It took a long time to get from Richardson to Derby; too long because I was too late. Dad had passed on and I didn't get there in time. Right then I decided there had to be a better way to travel.

One of the scientists at Sun oil had a little airplane. He started giving me flying lessons. There were troubles with him giving me instructions. He could go fly only when his wife didn't have something that he had to do. I decided that if I was going to learn how to fly, I was going to have to have my own airplane.

Scraping our money together and by borrowing on my wife's insurance, I bought an Aircoupe. It is a low wing job with a seat for two people, 75 horsepower Continental engine, twin tail rudders, and no rudder controls. All it had was a steering wheel, and my ex-navy flight instructor couldn't fly it worth a durn. He had to have all conventional controls, because he flew an airplane like he was going to land on an aircraft carrier. My $2700 airplane was too much for him.

John D's Aircoupe

I decided that he wasn't going to be able to teach me so I bought a book that taught how to fly an Aircoupe. It was simple. You didn't have to align the tail of the plane up with the runway, all you did was to head for the end of the runway, cut the power and set it down. It didn't matter if you came with your tail pointing off the runway, when it sat down, it twisted around and the steering wheel guided it right down the runway. Mr. Earnest Scott, my instructor, just couldn't take flying an Aircoupe. I loved it and learned to come in with all kinds of crosswind. Now that I had my own plane, I didn't have to get Mrs. Scott's permission to go flying, just my wife's permission.

The problem with owning an airplane was that you had to have somewhere to keep it. It needed to be available to go in a hanger if a storm came up. I kept it tied down at the Dallas Garland Airfield unless a storm came up, then the field attendant would put it in the hanger for me. The field would bill me and I would buy the attendant a carton of cigarettes for looking after my plane for me. In stormy weather, my plane was always the first in the hanger.

One day I had been to Pearsall to see Mother. When I arrived at McKinley Airfield to get my plane to come back to Dallas, the weather was perfectly clear. I hadn't been taught that when the temperature and the dew point were too close together, you were supposed to watch out. I took off and just as I cleared the ground, everything under me turned to a complete fog.

Now fog is disturbing to a man that does not have instrument rating, but you can sure learn about instruments fast. The plane had a scope-type omni detector and I had learned how to use that, so I could tell which way the omni stations were. There was fog under me and I couldn't see the ground. There was a cloud layer above me and I couldn't see up. I was in a thin layer of visibility. When I went toward Dallas the thin visible space closed down. I had to keep going straight ahead to stay in the clear. It was scary. Once I saw a hole in the fog under me and I spiraled down thinking I would find a place to land. Nothing but hilly, rocky and tree covered area was available so I climbed back up.

I kept on going, straining my eyes to try to find something that I might recognize. The first thing that I saw was Lyndon B. Johnson's

Betsy and John D with the Tri-Pacer at the Burnet Airport

private landing strip. I knew that was verboten so I kept going. The Colorado River showed up, the most beautiful sight. I had run out of fog and I was headed to Burnet Airfield. I sat down and prayed.

I knew that I couldn't carry a tune or sing, but when I was in my little Aircoupe, I would slide the canopy back and there was no one to hear me but God. I didn't care whether I could sing or not, God made me like I was and that was what He got.

No one ever flew with me in the Aircoupe except Barry. He flew a few times. I wanted something that I could take the whole family in. I traded the Aircoupe off for a Piper Tri-Pacer. It was a four place job. Why, once I even got the whole family to fly to Hot Springs, Arkansas. The kids were in the back seat sick and asleep. Wynona didn't show much enthusiasm either. I loved it.

One day I was taking my brother Sid and my brother-in-law George for a ride in my Tri-Pacer. We were flying near McKinley Field, south of Pearsall, when my plane swallowed a valve. The valve stem broke and the valve head fell off. It turned sideways and lodged in the top of the piston. Immediately George, the retired Air Force pilot said, in a calm voice, "The landing strip is 90 degrees to the left." We flew in on three cylinders and landed without incident.

Having a place to park the airplane was always the problem. The best place that I had was the Highland Park Airport. Eventually they closed the airport to build something else. I flew to Rockwall, Lake Dallas, and there must have been a few other places. I was always looking for a place that I could buy to have my own landing strip. My good friend Mac Mason lived up in the Lake Dallas area. I would fly all around there looking.

Chapter 36
The Silver Streak
1964

In about 1964 I wanted a motorhome that I could put in my garage. You know, when you live in a city having a place to put a motor-home is a big problem. I decided that if I could put one in my garage that would pass underneath the garage door I would have something pretty good. So I decided I'd build a motorhome with the most unorthodox methods you could ever imagine. You know, when you're a research piddler like I am you don't give a damn what people think about what you build. 'Course it shook my wife up when I told her what I was going to do. She said, "Oh no! Not that!" But I did it anyway.

So I got to fooling around and I found an old Chevrolet 4-door, 6-cylinder automobile, about a 1951 model, that looked pretty good. Gosh I paid $15 for it. That was lots of money. I got that thing and I took the body off. I cut the body up in pieces and set it out in the garbage. All I had left was the chassis, the wheels, axles, the radiator, and the motor.

So I began to look at that thing and wondering what I could do. You know a person stands up pretty tall, so you can't stand very high in the floor of a motorhome and not have your head be at least as high as the top of the garage door. So I decided if I could put the floor underneath the chassis instead of on top of the chassis I'd lower that thing down about six inches.

So the first thing I did is I added three feet on the front of the chassis, welded an extension on the chassis. I took the steering mechanism loose and moved it forward. Now I had a car with the steering wheel way up forward. I had to rearrange the steering arms to make things reach right. That was pretty good! In order for me to be able to extend that frame three feet I had to get the engine out of it. So I took the engine out. So I said, "Well, I'll extend four feet on the back end of this thing. That'll make it long enough for me to be able

Silver Streak under construction

to put the engine in the rear."

So now I had the car with the regular chassis, three feet on the front, four feet on the back, and I had to put the engine in it. Well, the only way to put the engine in, actually, was to turn it around backwards. So I turned it around backwards, with the radiator on the back end of the thing. It was kinda unorthodox. You know, when I did that, if you started it up the car would run backwards, and that wouldn't do. Well, the Chevrolet rear axle had the same bolt circle on the front of the axle housing and on the back. So if you took out the part of the rear end (differential) that had the bearings that held the spider gears and you put it in on the back side and turned it upside down it would make the car go forward when you ran the engine instead of going backwards. So I took it around there and put it on the back end and hooked it up, and it was pretty good. Except for one thing. That engine was so far behind the rear axle that it was tail-heavy. It really needed some more support. So there was nothing else to do but put another axle behind the existing rear axle. So the front rear axle was what drove the car and the second rear axle was just a trailing axle, and it helped hold up the rear end of the car. It worked pretty durn good. The propeller shaft was cut off to couple the engine to the differential. The radiator was mounted behind the engine and the fan blade was reshaped so it would blow air out through the radiator instead of sucking it through like it did when the engine was in front of it.

Now I had the engine way in the back and I was going to be sitting way in the front. Well, in order to make things work right I had to have a gearshift moved up further to the front. I extended the shift rods and put long shift rods that went clean back to the back so I could shift the gears in the transmission from up front. I had a pretty good setup there.

Then I decided to put a floor under it that went underneath the chassis instead of on top. That meant that I was going to have two big beams going through the living compartment of the motorhome. One of the beams was hidden in the cabinet work that was under the sink; you didn't even see that. The other one was next to the door where you got in. When you stepped into the motorhome you stepped on the floor, that wasn't but about eight inches above the ground. It was real low. But it worked alright. That beam went underneath my kitchen table and went on up to the front. I put a bench in the front that the driver sat on and another bench on the other side which the passenger sat on. I had some flaps that would raise up and bridge the gap between the driver's seat and the passenger's seat. You'd put a cushion on it, and it made a good enough spot that a person could lie down and sleep. Well, I put two benches back behind with the kitchen table between them. You could let the table down, and it would extend from one bench to the other bench, and it made another spot where somebody could sleep. So, I could sleep somebody at the front underneath the steering wheel, I could sleep somebody where the table was, and of course I had a double bed in the back which was over the engine. You could raise the bed up and there was the engine all exposed underneath it. Pretty handy way of working on it.

Well, the next thing I had to do was to get some material to make the body. So, I made ribs out of 1 x 2 wood. I framed up the body, and I had an awful lot of ribs in that thing. Even the rafters at the top were made out of 1 x 2s. I bought a bale of aircraft aluminum that had been water damaged. It was the aluminum that they used for the skin on airplanes, but it had gotten wet. The problem is when you have one piece of aluminum touching another piece of aluminum it tends to kinda corrode, or oxidize a little bit. For what I was doing it didn't hurt a thing in the world, but it sure did lower the price of that aluminum. It got it where I could afford to use the stuff. So I made the body out of it. The aluminum was held together with aluminum pop rivets.

There was a friend of mine who used to live in Colorado, and he had a trailer there that he lived in. After so long a time the trailer kinda deteriorated, but it had some good windows in it. It had windows that would swing out and you could prop them up. They had screen wire on them. He gave them to me. I had windows in the very back of the motorhome and windows on each side of the bed in the sleeping compartment, and I had two windows up where the table was, and I had a window over the kitchen sink, and windows on the driver's side and the passenger's side up front. They were all nice windows. So it made a pretty doggone handy gadget.

For a gasoline tank I used a 55 gallon barrel that was mounted back in the back underneath the bed. It would hold a lot of gasoline. I even put a toilet and a shower in there. I built an air conditioner out of an old window unit. You know, that thing, when I finally got it fixed right, would run like a scared coyote. I could get 60, 65 miles an hour out of that thing. The reason being, it was so low there wasn't much frontal area to it. It would really travel. It had all of the conveniences of home, including air conditioning, shower, stove, refrigerator, and dinette table.

The engine used to have a fiber gear on the camshaft that raised the valves up and down. Evidently that thing had been replaced at one time. Those fiber gears had two marks on them, that were supposed to straddle a mark on the crankshaft of the engine. When you put the gear on, if you didn't make it straddle the mark on the crankshaft your valving wasn't in order. The distributor was turned off of the camshaft. Even though the distributor was not set exactly right you could set the camshaft to where it would work the distributor and the points would fire right. Well, that's the way it was when I built it. After I ran it a while it got extremely hot. I thought, "Well, that's because the engine's in the back and the radiator's in the back." But anyway, I thought I could put up with it. It didn't get so hot that it was really disturbing.

First Trip

We decided that we wanted to go to Kerrville so Wynona could paint. Wynona and her friend Janis were going to sleep in the motorhome on the bed, and Barry and I would sleep outside the motorhome on cots. Wynona and Janis were going to go to a camp at Bridgeport to pick up Barry, while I drove the motorhome to Kerrville. When I was approaching Johnson City, all of a sudden that motorhome quit running. It just conked out on me. I thought, "Oh my gosh, what was I going to do?"

Well, we had loaded Barry's motorcycle in the motorhome. So I had to find out what was wrong, and I found out that that fiber gear had stripped. I guess it had lived too long, and it was time to die. So I took the radiator off the back end of the motorhome so I could get to the engine. I took the cover off the engine and saw what had happened. I took the gear off and got on the motorcycle and rode down to Johnson City where I found an auto parts place. Now Johnson City is a pretty small place. Would you believe it, they had one of those gears. So I took the gear back up there and put it on. I said, "I've got to be really careful how it put it on, because I've got to line that gear up right." Well, I put it all back together and got ready to start it up, and it wouldn't start. I checked the timing, and the timing was off. So I had to retime the thing. After I retimed it, it ran like a million dollars. When I bought the engine the gears had been installed wrong. I'm telling you it didn't make any difference how fast I went, it didn't get hot. It was a going Jessie.

Well, Wynona was embarrassed to death about that motorhome. She did not like that motorhome at all. One day I drove into a filling station to put some gasoline in it. Some guy just couldn't believe what he was seeing. He got so enthusiastic about it he just opened the door and went in it. Boy, Wynona could have shot him. I'm telling you that was the wrong thing for him to do. That made her hate it that much more. She just hated that motorhome. I loved it! Anyway, I kept the motorhome up in Denton, and we rode around in it quite a bit. Eventually I traded it to my nephew for a trailer.

Barry (left) and Wynona in the door of the Silver Streak

Chapter 37
Corinth
1970-1977

Remember I was looking for a place to keep my airplane. Finally, I found a place that I could buy. It was at Corinth, Texas, just south of Denton. It had a fairly flat field with sandy soil, and half of a hill with oak trees and cedar elms.

This property that I bought was part of

the Jones farm that had been divided among its heirs. Every time one of the heirs wanted to sell their piece of their land, I would buy it. I finally got all that was available (19 acres). I even had to go to Huntsville State Penitentiary to get one owner's signature. When you go in that place and the big iron doors slam behind you, it makes you want to be a good boy. I guess that is the reason I am such a good boy now.

I now had a piece of land that was 1100 feet north and south and 1300 feet east and west. The flight book said the landing strip for a Piper Tri-Pacer should be 1600 feet if you were fully loaded. I could make it with only 1300 feet with just me easy. Most of the time the wind was from the south so I landed that direction. I had two perpendicular runways, with power lines across three of the four runway ends. Every time I'd land Wynona would come out and say, "That's not a helicopter you're flying."

My brother-in-law, George Kemper, was selling mobile homes in Marble Falls. We bought one from him and he delivered it to our property in Corinth. We sold our house in Richardson, the best place we ever had, and moved into a mobile home. If ever a wife had a right to say, "Oh no, Not that," it was when I moved her out of her fine home and into a mobile home just so her husband could have an airplane hangar on their own land. What price love? I did promise her that we would build a big home in Corinth and move "Boney," as we called my mother-in-law, into the house with us.

The House
I designed a 4000 square foot Spanish hacienda. Wynona and I would discuss what each room of the house would look like. When we decided, we would draw the room in a notebook and both of us would sign the page. Then we built the house on the side of our hill. The house was almost a square, 72 by 76 feet, and had an enclosed courtyard with three trees in it. It had a 20 by 20 foot room on the southwest corner that included a bath and a closet. This was Boney's room, and the first part livable. The next part was a 16 by 32 foot den area that had a four foot overhanging roof in the court yard. On the southeast corner was a 20 by 20 foot studio for my love, the accomplished artist. On the east side of the house was a section that was 16 by 32 feet. This section of the house included the kitchen and the utility room which held the deep freeze, washer, dryer, water softener, and a toilet behind the door.

Leading out of this utility-kitchen area were steps that went down into a 24 by 24 foot garage that had a double wide garage door on the east side and another double wide garage door on the west side that opened into the courtyard. Above the garage was a 20 by 24 foot bedroom with steps leading up that were located next to the steps that led down into the garage. Upstairs was a 4 by 24 foot balcony over the garage.

In the 20 by 24 foot area was also a bathroom and large closet. We had an elevator from the bedroom down to the garage. Stairs went down from the northwest corner of the bedroom, down into the courtyard inside the wall that was built along the north side of the courtyard.

The west side of the courtyard was the section for the boys. Wayne and Barry both came home from the Navy in 1970. Wayne had a bedroom and an office in his section. The bath was between Wayne's room and a room that was for Barry. Barry decided that he wanted to be on his own so he moved out and lived with his friend who had a motorcycle, too. Wayne stayed with the old folks and really helped me with the house. There was a greenhouse section between Barry's room and Boney's room. That totally enclosed the courtyard.

The courtyard

Accessories
The airplane hangar was out back. It was a pole barn that was about five feet longer than the wingspan of my Tri-Pacer and about three feet deeper than the length of the plane. It had a folding door the length of the long side. Wayne decided that we needed a pit in which we could get to work on our cars. So we dug a pit, essentially

The barn (hangar) without the airplane

under one of the wings of my airplane. You would drive your car over the pit and under my airplane wing and stand down under the car to work on it. It had lights built in the walls. We loved the pit.

Eventually we built a shed on the end of the hangar to cover a travel trailer and Wayne's old Willys, and added a blacksmith shop on the back. Between the hangar and the house was a small tin building for Barry's motorcycle.

Boney, our emergency banker, lent us $600 to buy an 8N Ford tractor. We used that to work on the house and the landing strip. Wayne used it to do everything out in the field. I thought for a while he was going to give up working on his Masters Degree in Industrial Arts and turn into a farmer. His uncles, Sid and Harry, the world's greatest peanut farmers, would have been proud of him.

Construction
The house was a very typical John Bennett construction. It used 3000 feet of two inch oil well tubing, 10,000 feet of 3/4 inch sucker rod, another 10,000 feet of concrete reinforcing steel, besides the steel that was used in the concrete. Four foot deep post holes were dug where the walls were. They were four feet apart. Two inch pipe was set in the post holes that were longer than they had to be to make the roof support. They were concreted in place. A string was stretched along the top of the posts so they could be cut off with a torch at the correct height.

Working on the house at night after a days work at Sun Oil

Wall under construction

A-shaped welded steel trusses were used to stretch from wall to wall over the rooms, so there was a two foot overhang on the posts that were 20 feet apart. On those sections that had posts 16 feet

Applying stucco

Finished house

apart, there was a 6 foot overhang that made covered roof porches in the courtyard area.

Horizontal bars were welded from post to post to form the walls. This made a very strong all welded structure, even with cross bracing. Stucco lath was tied to the horizontal bars. The walls were stuccoed both inside and out to make the surfaces. It was so rough, we effectively called it "meskin" style. Vermiculite insulation was

placed in the hollow spaces that were formed between the stucco wire lath.

On the roof there was a horizontal sucker rod welded every 12 inches from one span to the next span. This made the structure to which galvanized tin was tied with galvanized twist wire. The twist was underneath.

The windows were double paned, but there were a total of 48 openings in the house, something that would become very important during the 1973 energy crisis. The doors were made of heavy wood. The ceilings were suspended, covered with sheet rock on the bottom and a fabricated beam that crossed the ceiling every four feet.

This structure was John Bennett construction from start to finish with Wayne's hidden tidbits such as the day he was stuccoing the kitchen wall and, unknown to anyone until later, he had put the outline of the state of Texas in the texture which could plainly be seen after he finally showed it to us. Wayne made a colored pane window of the state seal with dates engraved in the stucco below the window. His willing baloney is what kept me going. I had to put a board in front of my waist and a board behind my back with a belt around both to squeeze me in like a sandwich to keep my back in operation. That house wore me out. I got so tired, I quit flying, the last year logging only six hours, so I sold my plane to my "other son", Lee Murrah and his uncle-in-law.

City Government

Corinth was a small town with a volunteer government, except that the city secretary received a nominal salary. We would attend city council meetings, held around the mayor's kitchen table. I was the chairman of the zoning board. The town installed a water and sewer system, and for a while Wayne was the volunteer water meter reader-bill mailer-check depositer. He also made a land map of the city.

Energy Crisis

In October of 1973 several Arab nations attacked Israel in the Yom Kippur War. OPEC started an oil embargo in order to encourage the US to cease supporting Israel. Gasoline became quite expensive and rare in the US. Suddenly all of those windows caused our propane bill to skyrocket. We were heating the house with propane, and burning an awful lot of it. Wayne was attending North Texas State University, which was four or five miles to the north in Denton. One day I asked Wayne to check the library and see if he could find anything on solar energy. Well, he came home with many books about solar energy. It seemed like they were doing solar energy all over the world. Everywhere except in the United States.

So, I started studying his books and decided I was going to start playing with solar energy and see what I could do. Well, the first thing was, we had a big roof that went east and west on the south side of the square. On that roof we decided to start experimenting with hot water. You know in the summertime you look at a black automobile and the roof gets so hot you can't touch that automobile because it'll burn you up. But at night time that automobile will radiate its heat away to the space above and it'll get so cold that the car will get soaking wet with condensate. The cold surface condenses the moisture out of the air and makes the car wet. You can take advantage of this to collect heat in the daytime or cold at nighttime.

First Roof (Asphaltum)

We decided to build a solar collector on the south-facing roof that would collect hot water. The house originally had a red tropical-looking "waterproof" tile roof. But that roof leaked, so we had re-placed it with galvanized sheet iron. So we painted the roof black

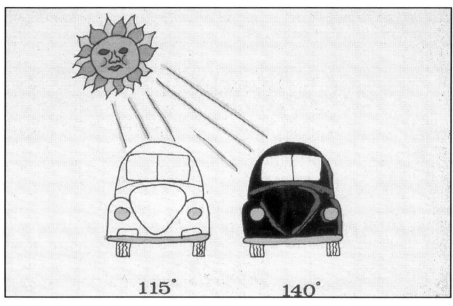

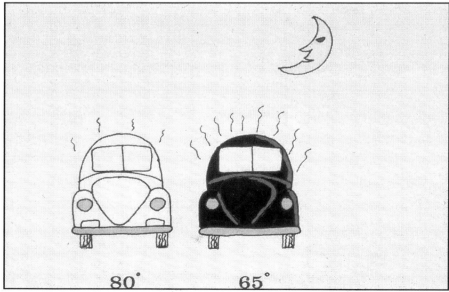

with asphaltum. We put a PVC header at the top of the ridge that had a whole bunch of little holes in it. We drilled a hole in the header so that a little stream of water would come out for every corrugation in the corrugated iron roof. It would let a little trickle of water run down the corrugated iron roof, a stream in each valley. Down at the bottom of the roof we had a gutter that would collect the water. Behind the house we installed a 2000 gallon insulated water tank. The water from the roof would run from the gutter by pipe into the water tank.

We had a plastic cover over the top of the iron roof. A sheet of clear plastic was stapled to 1 x 2 wooden spacers, which held it above the sheet iron. Ultraviolet light from the sun would shine through the plastic and strike the black roof. Then it would change its wave-length and not be able to reflect back through the plastic. It would heat up the roof and the airspace between the roof and the plastic. Even in the winter the water got almost to the boiling point. At the bottom of the roof there was a hole in the valley of each corrugation a few inches up from the edge of the sheet iron. The gutter was completely under the sheet iron, rather than under the end of it in the position of a normal gutter, so the tank wouldn't fill up with

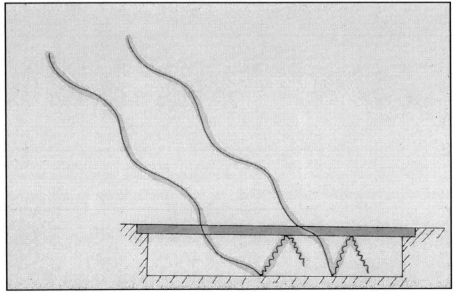

Ultraviolet light changes its wave length when it strikes the roof.

cold rainwater. Rainwater ran over the top of the plastic cover and ran onto the ground. The problem was that our heated water didn't wet the asphaltum and it wouldn't stay in the bottom of the valleys as it ran down the roof. It would snake around like a river in flat country, with lots of bends. Sometimes it would go completely around the drain hole and run off the end of the sheet iron and run onto the ground. The water we had heated was being wasted on the ground.

The plastic deteriorated in the UV light, but by the spring we had saved enough money on propane that previous winter to pay for the solar collecting roof.

Second Roof (PVC pipes)

So we decided to put the water in PVC pipes the next year. You know, I didn't have an unlimited amount of money. That house was built from my salary, and I paid for it as I went. I knew all along that the best thing would have been to have black steel pipe on the roof instead of PVC. Well, we put the PVC pipe on top of the roof and had it fixed up where we'd circulate water though that PVC pipe. Then we put up a sheet of plastic again. Once again that air-

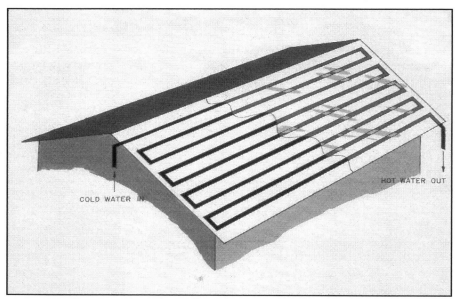

COLD WATER IN

HOT WATER OUT

The second roof

space underneath the plastic got extremely hot. Well, we would run water through the black plastic pipe and then it went over into the water tank.

In the house we had a radiator out of an old automobile, which was mounted under the return air for the air conditioner. The idea was that we would circulate the hot water through that radiator. Then as the air conditioner ran and circulated air through the house, the radiator would give up its heat to the air going through it and help heat the house.

Well, we had a lot of problems. Once again the plastic deteriorated in the UV light in the springtime, but enough remained on the roof the next summer that the pipes melted. You know, when they make PVC pipe they put a material made out of white lime in the pipe to keep the ultraviolet from deteriorating it. But it doesn't keep it from melting when it gets too hot.

One time the radiator hose came loose in the house and dang if we didn't nearly empty the 2000 gallons of water into the house. But once again, we saved enough on propane in the winter to pay for the system.

Third Roof (Hot air)
After doing all of that experimenting we decided maybe it would be better if we used hot air instead of hot water. So we modified the roof again the next year. We put on second corrugated iron roof on top of the existing one. The top of the ridges of the bottom roof contacted the bottom of the ridges of the top roof, so that there was an airspace between the two iron roofs. On the ridge of the roof we put a duct made out of mortar that extended the length of the roof. We had openings in the side of the duct so we could admit air into the duct from the hot roof. At one place we put a hole underneath that duct so we could collect the air from the duct and take it into the house.

We painted the roof black with latex paint, which is soluble in water. The only problem was we painted the roof late in the afternoon. Now I told you before, a black object will radiate its heat away to the universe above at night and get cold. When it gets cold it condenses the water out of the air. If you just painted the roof with black latex paint you'd condense so much water out of the air that the water would wash the black latex paint off. That's what happened to us. We were learning as we went.

We would suck air into the bottom of the roof between the two layers and it would go into the duct at the top and we'd suck the air into the house. That did pretty good and there wasn't much to get messed up about that.

Windmill

Not only did we do that experimenting with the solar energy, we were doing something else at the same time. I was fascinated by these old Dutch windmills. I decided to try to get some heat from the wind. I had already embedded a wire in the bedroom walls in such a way that the walls would get warm if you ran electricity through them. This is a common practice that they do nowadays.

Well, we built this big windmill tower. I started out by enclosing the 2000 gallon water tank with concrete blocks. Above the tank was a room that was probably seven feet high. It was our little research room in this round tower and contained electrical instruments. Above that was another floor which contained our electric generator. This floor had tin walls that tapered like an inverted cone. Above the generator room was a small cylindrical space that housed the support for the windmill blade.

Now this windmill that I built up there was a very peculiar windmill. I wanted a gear system to speed up the speed that the windmill turned so that I could get enough speed to turn the generator to get electricity. So what I used was a car differential. I welded the spur gears inside the differential and removed the axle out of the housing from one side of the rear end. The differential was mounted in the top of the tower so that the drive shaft hung down vertically. The other axle stuck out and the windmill blade was mounted on that axle on the hub of the wheel. Now that windmill blade had six arms. It was 16 feet in diameter, and had six sails on it. When the wind would blow the sails would make it turn. The first set of sails were like a three-sided diaper. One side was fixed to the wooden arm and the sail came back to a point. At the end of that point was a

The sails are tattered, but you can see the tail wheel in his photo.

spring that was attached to the next arm. When the wind would blow it would push the sail back and stretch the spring. The harder the wind blew the more pitch the sail had, so that would govern the maximum speed at which the windmill would turn. A strong wind would change the pitch so that more wind was dumped and the blades wouldn't turn too fast. And that kept it from running away.

That axle pointed a little above horizontal because wind rolls near the ground. Higher wind is faster than lower wind, and a tilted blade is perpendicular to the wind. The differential and windmill blades pivoted on some kind of bearing that is a trade secret. (Translation: I can't remember how I did it.) The drive shaft had a housing that became the pivotal point about which the blades would rotate with a change of direction of the wind. The drive shaft went down into the tower, to another differential fixed like the first one. The drive shaft of the upper differential turned the axle of the lower differential. The drive shaft of the lower differential had a big pulley which drove a V-belt to run the generator. The generator was really a five horsepower DC electric motor. Turning the electric motor made it act as a generator. The first differential stepped up the speed, and the second differential stepped up the speed some more, and the large pulley turning a smaller pulley stepped up the speed again. So you had a pretty good increase in speed of rotation.

Now you had to have the windmill face into the wind to do any good. So I copied the tail wheel from old English windmills. I got the gear rings off the flywheels of two automobiles. I opened them

Economy Tests: Three '75s from Detroit

Mechanix ILLUSTRATED

THE HOW-TO-DO MAGAZINE

MARCH 1975 ONLY 60¢

Tom McCahill Buys a Used Car!
We Visit the Mars Lander
The RV Scene for '75
12 Ways to Beat Inflation

In Color:
New Workhorses
For Your Lawn

HEATING A HOUSE WITH WIND POWER

HOW-TO:
Build a T-Bar
Dual Work Center
Lathe Cuts Without a Lathe
How to Make
See-Thru Furniture
The ABCs of Framing

up and welded them together to make a great big bull gear that was fairly round. I mounted that gear on the top of the tower. On the back end of the windmill behind the axle for the blades I built a steering mechanism to steer the windmill blades into the wind. I built a smaller windmill wheel about three feet in diameter. It had six blades and was mounted on the shaft of a little worm gear. The bigger gear had a shaft that went down, and on the bottom it had the gear off of an electric starter. When the little windmill at the top turned, it would drive the little spur gear at the bottom. The worm gear mechanism was mounted on a pivot arm and the spur gear was held in contact with the big bull gear by a spring. The little windmill blade was mounted at 90 degrees to the big windmill blade. So when the wind blew from the side it would hit the little blade on the back of the windmill and when it spun it would steer the big wheel into the wind. When the big blade faced the wind the little blade would stop turning. It would constantly seek the direction of the wind when the wind would shift. It worked like a charm. When a blue norther blew in the windmill would be facing south. The little wheel would start turning like crazy and in about five minutes it would steer the windmill around to the north. That windmill was really a showcase. It was later put on the cover of the *Mechanix Illustrated* magazine, and written up in *Science and Mechanics* magazine. It was put in the 1976 edition of the Nature/Science Annual published by Time Life Books. It caused a lot of attention.

At a later time we decided to do some more experimenting with the windmill. At one time we had six rectangular sails. On another occasion we decided to see if we could make the windmill turn faster. So we made some new blades—three of them made with a polyurethane core coated with fiberglass. The shape was similar to an airplane propeller.

All of this was fixed up so that we could generate electricity to heat the wires in my mother-in-law's bedroom. We never did really gather too much heat from the system, but we had a lot of fun experimenting with it.

Concrete Solar Collectors

At one time we decided to make some solar collectors out of concrete. You know a good mechanical engineer never does things exactly like other people. They've got to do them the way they think they can do them and the way they can afford to do them. So I made a couple of solar collectors out of concrete. I built a form to cast concrete panels and put Styrofoam strips inside the concrete. It had a section on top that could be painted black and would hold

Concrete solar collectors after one was broken by a freeze. Each of the rectangles was covered by a pane of glass.

Wind generator for charging car batteries

glass panels to make the concrete hot. We wanted to be able to run water through that thing. We dissolved the Styrofoam strips with gasoline, creating channels inside where we could circulate water. The energy crisis eventually went away, and we didn't do too much more with it.

Electric Car

In between, while all of this was going on, we had another project. Y'see I lived about 35 miles from work. I could visualize not being able to drive to work because gasoline was getting so short. So I decided to see if I could make an electric car. I built a car using a Renault Dauphine. The Dauphine had the engine in the back. It had a little differential there. I had gotten ahold of a great big electric motor that was used to screw the landing gear down on a World War II bomber. It was a big thing. It would run just great on 24 volts. So I took the engine out of the Renault and I mounted this electric motor so it bolted up to the faceplate where the engine had been. So if you ran the electric motor it would drive the wheels. 'Course I wanted to get rid of all the extra weight of the automobile, and I got rid of that. I built the frame up to where I could put a bunch of 12 volt automobile batteries in there. We'd charge up those batteries and we'd run that little electric car all around the area. Had a lot of fun with it. We'd run it up and down my runway. You know if you're going to have an electric car you gotta have a source of electricity. So I visualized that maybe I ought to make a big wind generator. So I had a great big windmill blade that I mounted on top of a highline post and hooked it up to a generator. When the wind would blow that big windmill blade would spin the generator and generate electricity and I'd use that to charge up the batteries on my electric car. Well, we just about had that all hooked up and in working order, when the energy crisis went away.

Publicity

One day while the crisis was still going my wife called me at work and said, "John, you'd better come home. There's a man here from CBS and his name is David Dick." He had his crew out there. So I drove home, and there was David Dick out in my yard lying underneath a tree looking up at the sails on my windmill. He said that that was the prettiest sight he'd ever seen in his life. He really liked that. Where was his cameraman? He was up inside the windmill tower trying to take pictures of all my gearworks. Anyway, to make a long story short, David Dick took pictures of all the stuff that I was doing.

Wayne was taking industrial arts classes at North Texas State University, and we had a few lessons in my living room for some of the boys in his classes. Then the Denton paper got ahold of the story. They wrote an article about it. When that happened *The Houston Post* wrote a story about it. Then nearly every newspaper in the country read *The Houston Post* article. There was a man who worked with me at the research lab in Richardson. He was a PhD, and I was just a mechanical engineer with a BS degree from A&M. Not very smart, just barely got out. This doctor was from Canada. He was working on some of the projects I was working on. When the energy shortage happened he decided he better go back to Canada. So he went back to Canada and became the minister of energy. They told the David Dick story on *60 Minutes* and on a CBS energy program. After that came out this gentleman called down to the research lab. He said, "My God! Bennett's all over the television and newspapers in Canada!"

One night about 10 o'clock we heard a knock on the door. We went to the door to see what it was. There were three women. They said, "We would love to see your house. We're for Arkansas, and our husbands told us when we went through Corinth to be sure and stop and look at this house." We said, "It's ten o'clock at night!" They said, "That's alright, we've got our flashlights." So they went out and looked at the house, just as happy as larks. Then my wife told me, "If you make one more talk and I have to clean this house up one more time I'm going to divorce you. I'm tired of cleaning this house up for people to come and look at it!" That poor woman. I drove my wife crazy with all of my piddling around. I didn't have any better sense. That's where the phrase came from "Oh no! Not that!"

Chapter 38
Marble Falls
1977

I retired from Sun Oil on April 13, 1977, my 59th birthday. Sun paid me supplemental Social Security until I was 62. It helped greatly as my pension was not enough to get alarmed about, having worked for Sun Oil only 21 years. I had five years and three months with Uncle Sam, and 10 years with IDECO.

We decided to move to Marble Falls, in Central Texas, to be near my sister, Betsy, and her family. Betsy and George had bought a camp in Marble Falls in 1959, and named it Kemper's Korner. Through the years they built it up by adding cabanas, pads for trailers, docks, a boat ramp, and other things. They built a nice A-frame house on the bank of the Colorado River. We spent many enjoyable vacations in Marble Falls helping with the camp and enjoying being with our family.

Marble Falls House
By the time I retired we had already acquired 10 acres near Marble Falls and had a septic system put in. I had designed the house while working for Sun.

We had a well drilled 315 feet deep through solid rock. It only had three feet of casing at the top. Using a mirror to shine a sun spot down the well you could see that it had the most perfect rock wall. The well never produced over 3½ gallons per minute, which wouldn't even run a good hose.

I had traded my old motorhome I built, which Wynona hated, to my nephew John Kemper for a trailer frame that once had a mobile home built on it. I rebuilt it so I would have a trailer on which I could move my Ford tractor and accessories from Denton to Marble Falls.

We had a concrete slab poured for a steel barn 24 by 24 feet. I had fabricated the trusses in Corinth and moved them on the trailer. John Kemper was still working for a company learning how to make tilt-up slabs in Austin.

I went to Dallas to buy siding and the roof material. We were loading the long pieces of sheet iron onto the trailer, with me holding one end and a helper the other. The iron was so long that one of the pieces buckled in the middle and it pulled out of the other man's hands. When he dropped it it fell on one of the trailer tires. That made the other end come at me like a buzz saw. It was vibrating after hitting that tire and going sideways. It sliced my leg open, and about 10 minutes later I was on the way to the hospital, where 60 stitches were placed in my right thigh just above the knee. Having been through much combat in World War II, I knew that I had to grab my leg and hold it tightly pushed together. Very little blood was lost.

Before long I had the trailer load of sheet metal moved to Marble Falls. My leg wasn't bothering me too much, so I put up the framework for the barn. I got ahold of a young man named Luis Rodriguez to help build the barn. He put the sheet metal on my framework.

Building the House
John Kemper became my building contractor and Luis his assistant. We had previously bought an Airstream trailer and we moved it to the location to serve as a dining hall and office during construction.

I built a hoist on the trailer that I got from John. I built a tower on the back of the trailer. Then I got a winch that had been on the front of a World War II truck. I mounted it on the front of the trailer and powered it with an electric motor from a World War II bomber. I took the batteries from the electric car I built in Corinth and used them to run the electric motor. We had a hitch on the front of my 8N Ford tractor and used it to push around the trailer with the hoist on it. We used it to stand up the precast wall sections we had made

John Kemper standing up a wall panel

Standing up a wall panel

for the walls of the house. The heaviest of those wall sections weighed 8000 pounds.

The house was essentially a rectangle with an office and garage added onto the back. It had a broad porch across the south side and sat on a high hill overlooking Marble Falls and miles of the Colorado River valley. The walls were precast concrete with Styrofoam panels attached on the inside and pieces of limestone on the outside. The north, west, and east walls had an interior concrete wall and an exterior concrete wall with a four

Top view of wall showing four foot space filled with rocks

foot thick void in between. The void was filled with rocks about the size of a baked potato. The rocks sat on concrete panels with slats to allow air to circulate through a duct below the rocks. Above the rocks was an air space that acted like another duct. Air could circulate through the ducts and also through the rocks.

The roof was made of steel beams a foot thick with sheet metal on top and another layer of sheet metal on the bottom. This created

394

Wynona with a section of the outside wall

"ducts" between the beams running from the lower end of the roof to a horizontal duct at the top. Fans could circulate air through the roof and through the ducts above and below the rocks in the walls, and also through the rocks.

The roof would get hot in the daytime and cold at night, making the air inside the roof "ducts" either hot or cold. In theory in the day-time in the winter fans would pull hot air through the roof, and push it through the ducts above the rocks, down through the rocks, and through a vent into the house. It would warm the rocks and the house at the same time. At night the roof would be left out of the cycle and the air would circulate through the rocks (picking up heat from the rocks) and through the house. In the summer cold air would be collected from the roof at night and circulated through the rocks and into the house, cooling the house. In the daytime the roof would be left out of the cycle and cold air would circulate through the rocks and the house, keeping the house cool. I say this was "in theory" because we weren't actually able to use the system that way. When we put the rocks in the walls they were dirty. The circulating air would bring dust into the house and Wy would have headaches. So we had to use the system like a cave. It averaged the

395

Adding beams to support the upper roof

The house in Marble Falls

temperatures of day and night, and made the house easier to air condition with a conventional air conditioner.

The house that I built was a solar home with walls four feet thick. The floors and walls of the house weighed over a million pounds. The house was very successful. The utility bills were very low. If I do say so myself, the only real money I ever made was from the real estate, homes, etc., that I had built.

Other Things
Betsy and George had moved to Derby to take care of my mother. There could never have been a better son-in-law than George had been to my mother. He left his home in Marble Falls, moved to Derby, down on the farm, and then became the best oil field supply salesman in the Austin Chalk oil field out of Dilley, Texas. Wynona and I moved into Betsy and George's house in Marble Falls as we built our house. All this started on July 4, 1977. We stayed in their house for one year, and then we moved into our new unfinished house.

When we moved to Marble Falls, we put our dear Boney, Wynona's mother, into a nursing home. It was the hardest thing that we ever had to do. Wayne Melton, her son, came down to help share the grief when we told her that she was going to the nursing home until her room was finished in our new house. She took the flu and died seven months later on February 13, 1978. Reverend Zeke Zirkle braved an ice storm to come to Corsicana for the funeral and then went to Long Prairie Cemetery where her husband Andrew Melton was buried. While we were gone to Boney's funeral, John Kemper supervised the pouring of the slab on our house. They did a pretty good job, considering the terrible weather.

On September 11, 1978, Wynona had her first mastectomy. It had to come out all right because she had such terrific prayer support. She was a real trooper. The same year she joined the Art Guild. Wynona had her second mastectomy on February 4, 1980. Complete knee replacement, broken hip, a gold mine in tooth repair, cataract eye surgery but with every one, she got more valuable and more indispensable.

Our youngest son, Barry, the motorcycle kid, found himself a delightful girl, Debra "Deb" Duff. We just love her. Barry and Deb live in Arvada. Barry's company makes blood-handling equipment. Barry designs machinery that automatically makes and assembles and tests the blood-handling equipment. He is good at it and designs equipment that is beyond my best imagination. Deb is in Human Resources in a different company.

When Betsy and George moved back to Marble Falls, they brought Mother back with them. The house had a separate apartment downstairs and mother lived there.

In 1981 there was a flood on the Colorado River that flooded the downstairs part of Betsy and George's house and Mother had to be hauled upstairs. Mother passed away in Burnet on March 28, 1983. She was buried next to Pop in the Bennett plot in Pearsall along with my grandmother and grandfather Bennett, and some uncles and aunts. Wynona and I will be buried in the same plot.

I designed some granite processing machinery for my brother-in-law, George Kemper. It was very successful, and Lee Murrah (my former patent attorney) wrote up a royalty agreement for George and me. It made me good money. In all, I built George a coring machine for granite, a vase-turning machine that made vases used with monuments for cemeteries, and the machine used to polish the vases.

We decided that we would like to have a place in Derby, so we acquired a city block in the town of Derby and I built a large barn. Later we built a nice little apartment in the barn. When the barn was closed, it was just a barn and nobody knew that a nice little air conditioned apartment was inside. This is very important because "Wet Backs" coming up from Mexico would break in every house out in the country looking for food.

My brother Sidney died on February 13, 1984. He was the reason that we wanted a place that we could visit in Derby. We all loved Sid very much and I still want to cry every time that I think of him.

Oil

In 1990 there was a new oil boom in Derby. Derby sits over the Austin Chalk, and oil companies had started drilling horizontal wells there. We had part interest in a well about 400 feet from the barn, and every day I could look out the door and watch the progress. We didn't make much money, but it was fun.

On October 28, 1991, Wynona and I celebrated our 50th anniversary at the most out-of-the-way place imaginable: Catarina, Texas. Now, you can't get there from anywhere. Go south about 50 miles down highway 35 from Dilley, Texas, and west about 50 miles and you are out in the land of nowhere. About the time I was born shysters were trying to sell no-good land to the people from the north that didn't know any better. They found this no-good dry land and built a real nice hotel to take the suckers to. There was a railroad that went by this location. A town was laid out and people brought in by train to this nice hotel and were given the slick sales talk. Finally the hotel closed because it was on the road to nowhere.

Former Governor Dolph Briscoe bought all the land around the town. In fact Briscoe was the largest land owner in Texas. All this sorry land only grows deer, cactus, rattlesnakes, and oil wells. When the Austin Chalk oil play was on in south Texas, the little hotel opened up again. That is where we had our 50th anniversary dinner.

36th Division Tour
We made a little money from the oil well and I divided it between Wynona, Wayne, Barry, and me. With part of mine Barry and I took a trip to Italy with the 36th Division Association tour. We visited all the old battlefields. We met the commanding general of the German army that opposed us at Casino. He was a fine Christian man. We all loved him. He prayed some of the nicest prayers that I had ever heard over the dead soldiers on both sides.

Vacations
While we were in Corinth and Marble Falls we continued to take vacations around the US. We traveled to Boston, Miami, San Diego, and Seattle (all on separate trips, some of them more than once.) We traveled first in a diesel Volkswagen Rabbit, then in a motorhome. In 1984, we bought our first motorhome, a used Travco. In 1986, we bought our second motorhome. It was a brand new Pace Arrow, 31 feet in length, with twin beds in the back, pull down bed in front, couch that made a bed, stove, oven, refrigerator, microwave, pop-up toaster, the works. We loved it. We went 57,000 miles to San Diego, Vancouver, the Great Lakes, Nova Scotia, and lots of places in between.

On one memorable trip we rode the train through the Copper

Canyon in Mexico. We caught the train in Ojinaga, across the border from Presidio, Texas. We rode it through the Chihuahua Desert and the Copper Canyon, finally arriving on the Pacific coast of Mexico at Topolobampo. While we were crossing the desert, about to go up into the mountains, the train stopped and the crew got off. We were in the car behind the engine, and when the train stopped I went to see what was going on. They were trying to replace a brake hose that connected the cars, but they had only one wrench to break a fitting loose. (The engine has to supply air pressure through the hose to release the brakes.) I looked around and found a place on the engine where they could wedge the hose, and that allowed them to use their wrench on the other side of the fitting. They fixed the hose and we went on our way.

Eggheads

Lee Murrah had moved to Cedar Rapids, Iowa to work for Rockwell International. While working for them he became involved with the University of Iowa. He promoted what was called "Invent Iowa." There was a chief engineer of the John Deere tractor company, who had made a lot of money with John Deere. The gentleman gave the University of Iowa a large grant to try to find out what made prolific inventors the way they were.

Lee told them about me, so I was one of the 34 inventors that they invited to come to the university to be interviewed. All of these inventors had lots of patents. I had 65 at the time. The interesting thing was that we all fit into the same mold.

Some of the things they found out were that most of the inventors interviewed could not spell.[4] Most had gone to a one room school in the early stages of their education. Most were introverts. Most were very poor in reading and made poor scholars. Most were very religious. Most worked alone. Anyway, the similarities went on and on.

The university decided that people like me could no longer pass the entrance exams to enter college. The enrollment system needs to be

---

4 *The Iowa Inventor's Project, A Study of Mechanical Inventiveness*, by the University of Iowa College of Education, 1987.

changed so innovators could be exposed to learning.

The chief engineer of John Deere Company said that what every engineering department needed was one innovator and five PhDs to work on the ideas the innovator had come up with.

The university ran what they called a "brain scan" in which the thought characteristics of each individual were plotted on a circle and divided like a pie into four sections. Not all people had equal pieces of pie but my scan was all screwed up. I was way egg-shaped. One section of the pie was academic, one was innovation, a third section was leadership, and I can't remember the fourth section. The first and fourth sections were very small. "Innovation" was way larger than the other three sections with "leadership" coming in second. They came to the conclusion that you cannot create an egghead by education—it is hereditary.

The university invited me to come back to Iowa again because they had looked at kids' science projects and wanted us to talk to them. The kids had been called to the university based only on the science pro-jects and it had absolutely nothing to do with their academic grades. It was a very interesting experience and made me feel very good.

36th Division Tour Again

Time moved on and in 1991, Wynona and I took another 36th Division tour, but this time it was to France, Germany and Austria. We visited all the old spots again. The same German general met us again, but this time we voted him a member of the 36th Division As-sociation. I felt better after seeing that all of the things I shot up had been rebuilt.

Wayne finally found a girl that he wanted to marry, Allison Lewis. Now we have two good daughters, and a grand dog. Wayne's wife's father is a retired vice president of Texaco. Oil runs in our blood.

We sold the remaining property that we had in Corinth. We sold our barn in Derby to my second cousin Randall Roberts and his wife Guiche.

It was a sad day on October 3, 1996, when our beloved brother-in-law George Kemper passed away. Then Betsy was on an extended trip when on June 23, 1997 a terrible flood went into her house to the top of the ceiling of the downstairs apartment. Lucky for her the city decided that they wanted her house to add to the city park system, so they bought it for a real fair price. Now sister has a wonderful new house on top of the most beautiful view in Marble Falls, high above the river.

Nothing but trouble hit us in 1997. I had three heart attacks, Wynona had a complete knee replacement and a broken hip.

We finally sold our house for $295,000 and moved into a rented condo. No grass to mow, no taxes, and a lot of sleep.

In 1998, Wynona, Wayne, Allison, Barry, Deb (our tour director) and I took a 10 day trip to England. We had a wonderful time. Wy even climbed the stairs in Admiral Nelson's sailing ship—Wayne pushing and Barry pulling and me grunting.

Now Wynona has financed a trip for her dentist and his family of four to Alaska. I had cataract surgery on the left eye that is now perfect. I am reading ads that talk about making old men young again.

We had been scouting out Ridgemont Village before Wynona's accident. We had measured the place all up. We knew exactly what we wanted to do. I could open the blinds in my bathroom and look right into my sister's garage. So we knew this is where we wanted to live, 'cause it's right up here by Betsy. But Wy died May 23' 2006, a few days after a fall in Walmart. I moved in in June. I stayed with Betsy a few days 'cause I couldn't go back to my condo, I just couldn't live there. So I made a sign and I sold my condo almost immediately.

Chapter 39
By The Grace of God

Friday, January 31, 1997, about 5:00 PM is when I was hurting so that I told the Lord to go ahead and take me. I didn't think that I could stand pain like that much longer.

All the signs had been there but I had not recognized them. I was in trouble with my heart. I couldn't possibly have been having trouble with my heart, I thought. I had been too healthy, there was never anything wrong with me

We were going to be in our new Church building on January 21st. It was nowhere near complete and the opening could not be postponed, as our Bishop was to be there to dedicate the building. On Friday and Saturday, there were a bunch of the church congregation that spent the day over at the church trying to help get everything in order. I must have moved a million chairs and a whole bunch of tables into the new classrooms, etc.

That Sunday, I ushered and felt pretty good. Anxiety was running high. Monday, I went to the Emmaus meeting at the Baptist Church. Tuesday, I went to the doctor because I knew that I was having indigestion problems. He gave me an EKG and said that he thought that it looked pretty good. He did give me some nitroglycerin tablets and some medicine to stop the flow of acid to the stomach. The doctor thought that I had indigestion problems, too.

By Friday, I was hurting pretty bad. Pain in the chest and arms, and it even extended about a foot beyond the ends of my fingers. The doctor phoned in another prescription for pain. Wynona went to the drug store and got the medicine. By the time she got back, I was crying and hurting something fierce. I took one of the real strong pain pills about 4:30 PM. By 4:45, the pain was so severe, Wynona called the doctor again. He said to take another pill and head for the hospital at Burnet. The doctor called the hospital and had them all ready for me when I got there.

When I got to the hospital emergency room, there was a young doctor in charge. I had heard so many reports on TV about how they were working the new doctors such long hours, I ask the young man if he was dry behind the ears yet, and he assured me that he had handled cases like this before. I told him to get with it.

The doctor told me that he wanted to give me a new drug that had a risk with it and that one out of a hundred developed a stroke from it, but he thought that it was the best possible course. The medicine was given intravenously. It was to dissolve any clots that might have formed and was causing the blockage of blood to the heart muscles. It worked like a charm and all the chest pain went away.

Wynona called Wayne and Barry, and they kept the phone lines hot. Everybody was calling everybody.

I was taken to St. David's Hospital in Austin in the ambulance. Before I left, a cardiologist had to be found to handle my case at St. David's. The doctor that was chosen was Dr. Roach. He was excellent.

They told me to keep my glasses on so that I could watch the monitor when they took me into the operating room. I was assured that I would be awake and could see the show.

I was awake and could hear them talking and I thought that they were just getting ready when I heard them say that they were through. I missed the whole show. I told them they would have to do it over because I had missed it.

The doctor told me that I had done fine but I had a significant bit of damage to the left ventricle of the heart. I had an 80% blockage of the artery that ran down the front wall of the heart and he got that down to about 30% with the balloon. The artery wasn't big enough to put one of those stents in it, but he thought it would be OK like it was.

The doctor told me that he would give me a movie of the angioplasty, as I had missed the whole program.

We came home Thursday, February 6th. My sister Betsy Kemper was a real trooper. She stayed with Wynona the whole time. The first two nights they stayed in a motel near the hospital. Wayne and Allison came up from Sugar Land and stayed there too. Then Wynona, Betsy, Wayne and Allison stayed in a condominium on 6th street that belonged to Betsy's son and his wife, John and Belinda Kemper.

The thing that is important about having heart attacks is the attention that you get. When your kinfolks and friends start coming in to see you, the phone begins to ring, with people checking on you, you begin to realize how important everyone is to you and you didn't even have to die for all that to happen. It gives you a new outlook on life and makes you realize that the only thing in life that matters is your family and friends. You really appreciate it when Butch and Jan drive over from College Station or Harry and Jo Annelle drive up from Pearsall. Life really is worth living.

You might rock along, not paying the correct attention to what is happening, but when the Lord wants to get your attention, He sure knows how to get it. It is only by His GRACE that I am here feeling just as good as can be, and even losing that middle that I have carried all these years.

More Heart Attacks
I had another heart attack on March 7, 1997, and this time they gave me a stent. Later I got two more stents. I was still taking nitroglycerine in 2001 when I had yet another heart attack on September 20th. They couldn't give me any more stents, so I had a triple bypass operation instead. Soon after the operation I started having more heart pains. I started doing some reading and found out about oral chelation. Chelation is a Greek word meaning "grab ahold of" and oral means you take it by mouth. Oral chelation is a pill like a multiple vitamin that has one important ingredient added: EDTA. EDTA is what the federal government makes baby food manufacturers put into baby food to protect babies from any heavy metal that might get into the food from farming or manufacturing. Oral chelation

grabs ahold of heavy metals in your body and you expel them when you urinate. But it does something else too. When you order oral chelation they instruct you to pee in a bottle and set it aside before you take any pills. Then after taking them for a week you pee in another bottle. You hold the two bottles up to the light and compare them. The second bottle of urine is cloudy. The cloudy stuff is plaque that the oral chelation has removed from your arteries.

Oral chelation also includes a second bottle of pills containing minerals. This is to replace any important minerals that have been removed from your body by the chelation.

I have been taking oral chelation for over ten years and haven't had any more heart trouble. The ordinary doctor doesn't know anything about it. You need to learn about it yourself. Google "oral chelation" to find out.

Doctors spent almost a million dollars on my heart, but now I'm doing fine with oral chelation costing me $106 for a three month supply.

Chapter 40
Who is Going to Tell Me, "O No, Not That!"?

I lost my guiding light of 64½ years on May 23, 2006 when my sweetie passed on to be with her Lord and Savior. She did her best to keep me in line. Now it is up to my children, and my sweet daughters-in-law. They do their best but I am a Bennett and Bennetts are notorious for being Hard-Headed.

Many people do not know that I work on the theory that "Nothing is going to happen to me until the Lord is ready." He has brought me through 95 years unscratched. During the war I decided that there was nothing the Germans could do to me until the Lord was ready. He still has me by the hand. I don't understand why my kids think that I am a traffic hazard when I know Who is guiding me. The number of wrecks I have had proves that. Close wrecks; now the Lord uses them to make other people realize they had better get right with their Maker too. I might scare a few, but those are usually the ones riding with me. Just cowards, that is all!

My sweetie had a serious fall in Walmart on the afternoon of May 18, 2006 about 6:45 PM. We had been on our usual afternoon outing to Walmart when we stopped to visit with friends. After talking to them, I was picking up some strawberries off the counter to put in my cart and accidentally touched the box next to mine when the lid flew open letting some berries go to the floor. I stooped down to pick them up. When I looked for Wynona, who had been standing right behind me, I turned and saw her in a puddle of blood and on the floor. People who saw it said that she had taken three steps backwards and fell over hitting the back of her head.

407

I was dumbfounded but the good people of Walmart rushed up and took charge of the situation. The assistant manager called the EMS and notified my kinfolks. The EMS did a superb job and air lifted her to Brackenridge Hospital in Austin.

Without my good friend Liz Murrah, who was with me all the way, I could never have made it. My niece Betsy Jane Kemper has had experience with hospice and she was right by my side coaching me while Wynona was passing. I will be forever grateful to her for her experiences in such occasions. She passed on May 23rd at 11:18 PM.

Wynona was interred in the Pearsall Cemetery on Saturday, May 27th at 10 AM. Reverend Stan Troy held a wonderful service for which I will forever be grateful. The Pearsall United Methodist Church had refreshments after the service. Wynona and I consider Pearsall United Methodist our home church. They came through with flying colors. Sunday, May 28th we had a memorial service for Wynona at the First United Methodist Church of Marble Falls, Texas. We have been members of the church since 1977. Dr. Ralph Mann and Rev. Mike Morris held the service. Cindy Lester, our friend of many years, sang. Sharon Dare furnished the music.

I can't believe that she is not here telling me, "Oh no! Not that!" All I have now is an empty heart and lot of wonderful memories, and I am thanking God that He let me have her so long. It seems very short.

Chapter 41
Epilogue

John D Bennett went to be with his Lord on April 14, 2014 after a few weeks of declining health. He always said that nothing would happen to him until the Lord was ready. He celebrated his 96th birthday the day before his death, and announced that he was ready to go. On the 14th he was visiting with his "third son," Lee Murrah, when he died suddenly, after a chain of events that only the Lord could have arranged.

John D was a unique individual. He must have looked at every new thing with an eye to improving it. He invented continuously. On the day he died he presented his son with a drawing of a new tissue box holder he wanted him to build.

He tirelessly explored alternative medicine, and subscribed to every alternative medicine newsletter known to man, always having just found the magic potion that would extend his life to 120. This resulted in his being on a new diet every week. John D truly wanted to help people and was always promoting the latest cure he had read about.

He posted a list on his doorframe to remind him of things he needed to remember when he left his room: glasses, sunglasses, hearing aids, zipped up fly, walking cane, and phone. He tried to get the Methodist District Superintendent to send out a suggestion to all Methodists in the district to make such a list, which would also remind them to pray and to take a check to church.

John D loved to tell stories of his life, and was really excited when the first edition of *Oh No! Not That!* was published.

He was sharp and active until his death. He never lost interest in new inventions, as attested by his room full of mechanical and electrical gadgets. He was always looking things up on the internet, though not always without operator trouble. He is certainly missed.

Wayne and Barry Bennett

From a poster from John D's retirement party: the Pearly Gates complete with Cadillac differentials. Sign says,"J D Bennett Auto Gate Opener, Pat Pending."

Appendix A

Top inventor in Sun's 'Dream Department'

John Bennett holds more patents than anyone else in Sun's NAE&P group. He has a windmill in his yard, uses the sun to heat his home and takes an inventive approach to everything from Arctic drilling to baking cakes

by Beverly M. Dotter

JOHN BENNETT LIKES TO TELL ABOUT the workshop he had when he was growing up on the family farm in the small Texas town of Derby. How he spent a lot of time in there, tinkering, building things. Best of all, trying out the ideas that even then were swirling around in his head.

It presented a problem for John's parents. "They had trouble getting me out of there," he recalls. "But the shop's light switch was in the house. So, when it got to be too late, they simply doused the lights. And there was nothing to do but go in."

He laughs a little self-consciously when he tells the story. Maybe because he realizes that it's all still true. That the grown up, 56-year-old John Bennett is still like that—caught up in his own world of ideas and trying them out.

And he says that "people are always trying to straighten me out." Translated: they're still trying to get him out of his world into theirs. And sometimes, when he has no choice, he reluctantly consents.

John Bennett has a 1939 degree from
continued

411

Texas A&M University that says he's a mechanical engineer. Sun Oil Company's North American Exploration and Production group has employed him for the past 18 years as a production research scientist in its Richardson, Texas, research lab.

But if the academic world handed out diplomas and the corporate world handed out job titles that precisely described a man's profession, for John Bennett they would both read "inventor."

He has his own word for it. "What I really am is a 'piddler'," he says.

John Bennett holds more patents, individually or jointly, than any other person in the NAE&P group—53 at last count.

Currently, he's working in the Arctic operations group, whose job it is to support Sun's Canadian Arctic operations.

"It's a whole new world up there and conventional solutions to problems don't

Three Arctic trips have given Mr. Bennett a feel for unusual problems Sun faces there. In his search for new answers, he doesn't always stick just to "official" projects

always work," he says. "We try to come up with new answers."

But the true inventor doesn't always wait for the questions to be asked.

"I try to figure out what the company is going to need so when it gets ready to do something, the know-how will be there."

And a man whose brain ticks out ideas with the regularity of a clock ticking out

the seconds sometimes finds it difficult to stick just to the "official" projects. Tucked away in nooks and crannies of Mr. Bennett's office are rough sketches and half-completed mockups for those projects, which, he says, "don't have a project number."

Joe Zupanick, head of the Arctic Operations group and Mr. Bennett's boss, says it's sometimes a problem channelling all that energy. "But John Bennett has proven his worth to Sun Oil Company, so most of the time we let him do the thing he does best—invent."

Mr. Bennett is proud of his 53 patents, but the Bennett personality is liberally laced with modesty.

"It isn't the number of patents that counts," he says. "It's coming up with the one you need when you need it. If you can do that, all you need is one."

Boiler and battery box are part of propane generator for the Arctic developed by Mr. Bennett (left) and built by machinist Carl Caldwell. Many Bennett ideas become reality in Mr. Caldwell's skilled hands.

Bennett method for fighting Arctic cold: Into boot goes a pad, rubberized to act like a bellows when stepped on. Rubber hose, attached to propane heater, runs from boot to glove. "Bellows" sucks in heat, sends it up hose.

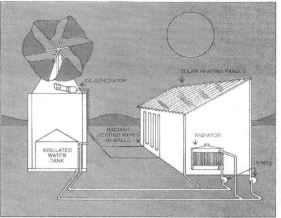

Using Instrument Panel Mr. Bennett can check wind generator voltage, air temperature in solar panels and water temperature in tank. Franklin Stove is Bennett version of a living room fireplace. It also heats water in built-in boiler for yet another source of heat.

In the two main parts of Mr. Bennett's heating system, the windmill powers a generator which furnishes electricity to radiant heating wires in the walls of one room of the house. Water from 2,000 gallon insulated tank beneath windmill is pumped to roof peaks where

it is solar heated as it runs down the roof and flows by gravity back to the tank. Solar heating system incorporates features of worldwide research. One good source of data was a group of papers on a 1960 United Nations conference on additional sources of energy.

He says that people look at inventions in the wrong way—insisting that "everybody invents in some way or another. Baking a cake is an invention."

That's nice. But unless you've ever invented anything, it's hard to believe.

Finally you find yourself asking the question you had resolved not to ask. "How does an inventor invent?"

That question would stymie lesser men but John Bennett doesn't even pause. He's answered it before and besides, after "piddling," the thing Mr. Bennett does best is talk.

He tells you that everybody has a talent. You just have to recognize it and develop it. In his case, that means being curious, observant and having an open mind.

But to him the most important part of the process is what he calls his nature theory.

"All you have to do is look at nature. You can hardly find an invention of any kind that's not in nature. Why, the whole Bell System is right up and down your

spinal column. And nature has already eliminated the things that won't work."

He recognized his talent early. "I knew what I wanted to do from the time I was five years old," he says. "Turn my ideas into inventions that would work."

And from the workshop on the farm in Derby flowed the first Bennett inventions.

At age 10, he built his first Model T from old parts. As a teenager he designed a new motorized unit for the farm's thrasher, utilizing the drive-shaft-universal joint principle. It's commonly used on farm equipment today but back then it had industry representatives visiting the Bennett farm to see what he had come up with.

So he's gotten used to being the center of a certain amount of attention. But recently his fame has been spreading—beyond Sun Oil Company, Beyond Texas, even.

Part of the reason is a windmill.

If you know John Bennett, it doesn't

seem a bit unusual to drive up to the Bennett home in Corinth, about 30 miles north of Dallas, and see an English-style windmill, white sails billowing in the breeze, standing only a few feet from the house.

The Spanish-style house was entirely designed and built by Mr. and Mrs. Bennett and their sons Wayne, 27, and Barry, 23.

And when Mr. Bennett got around to the problem of how to heat the 6,000 square foot structure, he took his own advice. He anticipated a problem—the energy shortage—and he went back to nature—the sun and the wind.

The windmill is part of a three part heating system he built into the house.

First is a propane unit, set at 68 degrees and thermostatically controlled to heat the entire house. But it's basically just a back-up system.

The windmill power operates a generator that sends heat to sets of radiant wires embedded in the plaster walls of one wing of the house.

The 2,000 gallon water tank beneath
continued

413

the windmill is part of a solar heating system that helps warm the rest of the house via the roof.

Only when the sun doesn't shine or the wind doesn't blow does the conventional propane system take over.

"My ideas aren't really new," he says. "People have been using the sun for heat for a long time in parts of the world. I just did some research and adopted what was already known. And I wasn't looking for the ultimate way. It had to be something I could afford."

He estimates that he spent about $1,000 on the system. He doesn't have any figures on how much money the system has saved in heating bills. But this heating season he used only 800 gallons of propane, compared with 2,800 the year before.

But you get the impression that the purpose of it all wasn't to save money, and only partly to counteract any effects of the energy shortage. Because John Bennett says he has more fun making things than buying them. There's nothing he enjoys more than seeing something tangible evolve from one of his ideas. And what could be

After more than 30 years of marriage to a non-stop idea man and confirmed do-it-yourselfer, Mrs. Bennett has gotten rather used to it all. Sometimes it even has special advantages

more fun or more tangible than a windmill in your own backyard.

Mr. Bennett's 19 acres of land give him a lot of backyard to have fun in. More than enough room for his airplane, a hangar, two landing strips, numerous pieces of farm equipment, a huge garage and the 24 by 72 foot workshop he plans to add to the house. The workshop will feature metal and woodworking areas, a photography lab and an electronics shop.

The Bennetts have been working on the house for about three years. To a visitor it's beautiful, comfortable and finished. But, as with all his inventions, Mr. Bennett has all sorts of ideas for ways of making it better.

If you've barely managed to avoid an in-

feriority complex after a day with John Bennett and his inventions, the rest of the Bennett clan will push you over the edge.

As Wynona Bennett, John's wife, takes you on a tour of the boys' rooms, you see evidence of their penchant for making things—sculpture, furniture, drawings and plans for future projects. It's not surprising considering that they once had the nicest toys of any kids on the block. Their electric car, motorized merry-go-round and customized gym set (all built by Mr. Bennett, of course) made the Bennett lawn more crowded than the neighborhood playground.

Mrs. Bennett is an accomplished artist whose oils and watercolors adorn nearly every wall of the house. She's talented enough to have sold over 100 of her paintings.

How does she feel about having a roof that does more than bounce rain, the strangers that pop in unannounced to see the windmill, the TV and newspaper reporters asking questions?

The people she treats with warmth and hospitality. The solar roof, like many of Mr. Bennett's inventions, she treats with good humor.

Mrs. Bennett has even learned to graciously accept the fact that wherever Mr. Bennett goes there's a job waiting.

"Last summer we took a train trip through Mexico," she says. "When the train broke down, guess who figured out how to fix it? But it has its advantages. We got pretty special treatment the rest of the trip."

She admits she doesn't always understand the technical aspects of her husband's inventions. But after more than 30 years of marriage to a non-stop idea man, she's gotten rather used to it.

"John invents 24 hours a day," she says. "Never stops. He even gets up in the middle of the night to write down an idea or make a sketch. I guess he must dream them."

Well, John Bennett did submit a report to Sun management once outlining a new idea—for an atomic-powered underwater tanker—and he signed it "John Bennett: The Dream Department."

That only partially explains John Bennett. There's a great deal more to both the man and his inventions than just dreaming of course.

But the air in John Bennett's rarefied world can leave you breathless. So you're willing to accept that because it is as good —or at least as easy-to-understand—an explanation as any. ◆

Mrs. Bennett takes her turn working in the flower and vegetable gardens but most of her time is spent at her easel. An accomplished artist, she's good enough to have sold over 100 of her oils and watercolors. She also does ceramics and paints designs on china plates.

Top Inventor in Sun's "Dream Department" from *Our Sun* magazine, Summer 1974. Used by permission.

Photo Credits

P. 209: *USS Joseph T. Dickman*, US National Archives photo 26-G -12-14-43(4)

Pp. 312-315: Photos by Jack Hilder in the *Beaumont Journal*, circa 1946

P. 321: Photo by Scott Bennett, compliments of Sharon Bennett

Pp. 409-412: Article from *Our Sun* magazine, Summer 1974 edition, used by permission

All other photos from family archives

Index

Made in the USA
Lexington, KY
16 December 2019

58573697R00240